The Red Orchestra

The
Red Orchestra

V. E. TARRANT

John Wiley & Sons, Inc.

NEW YORK   CHICHESTER   BRISBANE
TORONTO   SINGAPORE

Library of Congress Cataloging in Publication Data available
on request from John Wiley & Sons, Inc.

ISBN 0-471-13439-2

Edited and designed by Roger Chesneau/DAG Publications
Ltd.

Printed and bound in Great Britain.

10 9 8 7 6 5 4 3 2 1

To my wife Val – a little saint on 'The Way'

Contents

Maps

Preface

This is the story of a loosely connected group of Soviet spy *apparats* (networks) which operated in Nazi Germany, Nazi-occupied France, Belgium and Holland and neutral Switzerland during the Second World War and which were collectively known as *Die Rote Kapelle* – the Red Orchestra.

The Red Orchestra was not only one of the strangest spy *apparats* in the history of espionage, it was also one of the most effective, playing a vital part in the eventual destruction of the vile scourge of Nazism. Its agents and informers included Russians, Polish Jews, Frenchmen, Belgians, Dutchmen, Hungarians, Swiss, Germans and Englishmen. Although the Red Orchestra was a GRU (*Glavno Razvedyvatelno Upravlenie*, or Soviet Military Intelligence) *apparat*, its members included people from diverse political persuasions, ranging from committed Communists to right-wing conservatives, and from many different social classes, from aristocrats right across the spectrum to the proletariat. They included amongst their ranks professional GRU agents, businessmen, publishers, factory workers, civil servants, writers, artists, students, prostitutes, ordinary soldiers, a fortune teller and a group of high-ranking, strategically placed German officers who provided the Red agents with the day-to-day decisions and planning made by Hitler and the German High Command relating to the course of the war on the Russian Front. This diverse collection of men and women, who in normal circumstances would have had very little in common, were united by a single common denominator – a hatred of Nazism.

The German counter-intelligence agencies became aware of the existence of the Red Orchestra shortly after Hitler launched his invasion of the Soviet Union in June 1941, and thus began a hunt for the Red agents by the *Abwehr* (Military Intelligence) and the *Gestapo* (Secret State Police) which lasted for over two years. During this time, by dint of slow, painstaking detective work, lucky breaks, the application of 'intensified interrogation' (the euphemism for torture) and betrayal, the German sleuths slowly prised open the Red Orchestra. But by the time the investigation had been brought to a successful conclusion the German forces on the Eastern Front had been defeated, thanks in the main to the information sent to Moscow by the Red Orchestra.

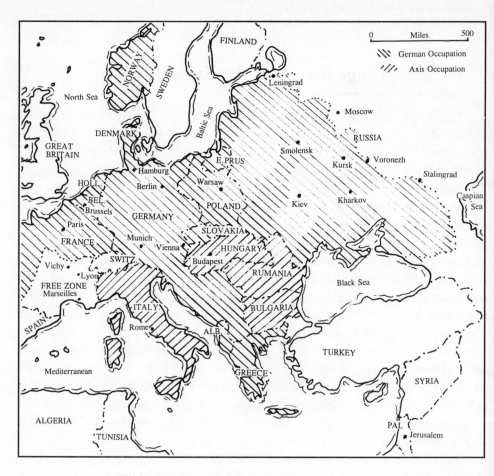

Occupied countries

ACKNOWLEDGEMENTS

I wish to thank the following publishers for permission to quote from the copyright material indicated: Century Publishing, from Costello and Tsarev's *Deadly Illusions*; Oxford University Press, from David Dallin's *Soviet Espionage*; Libraire Artheme Fayard, Paris, from Gilles Perrault's *L'Orchestre Rouge*; Hodder & Stoughton, from Read and Fisher's *Operation Lucy*; and Albin Michel, Paris, from Leopold Trepper's *Le Grand Jeu*.

1. Strange Bleeps in the Ether

At 3.15 in the morning of Sunday 22 June 1941 a gigantic radial lightning flash, followed a split second later by a deep thunderous roar, rippled along the German–Russian frontier as thousands of heavy-calibre guns simultaneously belched forth fire and steel. This massive bombardment heralded an onslaught by more than three million German troops, who poured over the Bug and Niemen rivers to invade the Soviet Union. Four days later, at 3.58 a.m. on Thursday 26 June, while Hitler's panzers were smashing through the forward Russian defences, a German long-range radio monitoring station sited at Kranz on the Baltic coast of East Prussia intercepted a Morse code message being tapped out on the key of a clandestine short-wave radio transmitter. The operator who intercepted this message had tuned in to the frequency employed by partisans of the Norwegian Resistance, who made nightly contact with London, usually relaying a short message consisting of no more than ten to a dozen cipher groups. But the call-sign the operator intercepted on the morning of 26 June was entirely different from those used by the Norwegians: 'KLK from PTX . . . KLK from PTX . . . KLK from PTX. 2606.03.3032 wds. No. 14 qbv.' This strange call-sign was followed by a message composed of thirty-two five-figure cipher groups, ending with the Morse signature 'AR 503.85. KLK from PTX.'[1]

During the course of the next four nights the Kranz station intercepted further messages from the PTX pianist (as an enemy radio operator was termed in German counter-espionage parlance), and when the nature of these messages was reported to Lieutenant-Colonel Hans Kopp, commanding officer of the *Funkabwehr* (Signals Security), whose headquarters was situated on the Matthäikirchplatz in central Berlin, he ordered the radio monitoring stations in Germany and Nazi-occupied Europe to pay special attention to the PTX transmissions: 'Essential discover PTX schedule. Night frequency 10,363 kilocycles. Day frequency unknown. Priority 1a'.[2]

As the PTX transmitter had burst into life only a few days after the invasion of the Soviet Union, Kopp was apprehensive that the recipient of the PTX messages might well be housed in Moscow and that the enciphered messages were the result of information gleaned by a Soviet spy ring at work somewhere in the Reich or the occupied territories. During the course of the next two months the monitoring stations intercepted some 250 messages tapped out on the key of the PTX transmitter, but attempts to discover the location of the clandestine set by taking cross-bearings on the source of the signals produced inconclusive results: all that the radio experts could suggest was that PTX was operating from somewhere in an area covering southern Holland, Belgium and north-eastern France. As it was essential to locate the city or town in which the pianist was holed up before a hunt by German counter-espionage agents could be mounted, such an imprecise report was as good as useless: they may as well have suggested the North Pole!

In the meantime, however, a far more disturbing report landed on Kopp's desk. Early in July the monitoring stations at Kranz and Breslau, while searching the air waves for further PTX transmissions, intercepted messages from a second transmitter which was employing the same five-figure cipher as the PTX pianist. In addition, it was noted that the schedules and frequencies employed by this second pianist were closely related to the *modus operandi* of PTX, which strongly suggested that the two pianists belonged to the same espionage *apparat*. Moreover, attempts by the monitoring stations to pin-point the location of this second transmitter by cross-bearings had produced far more positive and alarming results: it was housed somewhere within a radius of less than five miles from *Funkabwehr* headquarters in the very heart of Hitler's capital! To make matters worse, the *Funkabwehr* codes and cipher evaluation analysts had come to the conclusion that the cipher employed by both pianists was of Russian origin, which presented Kopp with the unpalatable certainty that a Soviet spy ring was at work in Germany.

Kopp reacted to this discovery as though he had received a violent electric shock, for on the eve of the invasion of Russia the counter-espionage agencies in the Reich has assured Hitler that Germany had been swept clean of Communists and Soviet underground agents. Indeed, the campaign to smash the German Communist Party – in its day, the most powerful in Europe – along with the Communist espionage and informer organizations of the Comintern (Communist International) had commenced immediately after the Nazis seized power in January 1933. During the next eight years thousands of German Communists vanished behind the barbed wire of the concentration camps, while the *Gestapo* (Secret State Police), SD (SS Security Service) and *Abwehr* (Military Intelligence) methodically tracked down and liquidated the Comintern underground of saboteurs, informers and agents operating in the Nazi state.

This violent campaign to rid Germany of 'reds' had obviously not been thorough enough, as evinced by the sudden appearance of the Berlin pianist. Goaded into action, Kopp dispatched three radio monitoring squads on to the streets of Berlin at the beginning of September to hunt down the enemy pianist, who had already relayed over 500 messages through the ether to Moscow. Theoretically, the location of a transmitter was a relatively easy matter. Three monitoring squads, each equipped with a direction-finder set (a receiver with a rotatable loop aerial) posted themselves at three different positions some miles from each other and each took a bearing on the clandestine transmitter when the pianist began tapping out his messages. The bearings were obtained by slowly turning the loop aerials until they reached a position where the enemy transmitter's signal sounded loudest in the direction-finder receivers. The resulting data were then reported back to the squads' commander, who drew the three reported lines of bearing across a street map commencing from the known positions of the three squads. The point at which the three lines intersected would then reveal the position of the transmitter on the street plan. That was the theory, but in practice the process of detection proved to be far more difficult.

When Kopp's monitoring squads began their hunt, disguised in post office mechanics' uniforms and employing post office maintenance vans and canvas street shelters to hide their bulky direction-finder sets, they found their task beset with problems. Unlike the PTX pianist who transmitted practically every night, the Berlin pianist functioned capriciously, alternating bouts of feverish activity with spells of silence which sometimes lasted for days at a time. To compound this difficulty the monitoring squads also had to cope with the pianist's campaign of subterfuge. To throw the hounds off the scent he constantly changed his call-sign and transmitted on a variety of wavelengths. For example, on one particular night he put out his call-sign on 43 metres, received his acknowledgement from Moscow on 39 metres and then switched to 49 metres to transmit his message. He also introduced an additional stratagem by putting out a fresh call-sign when he switched from 43 to 49 metres, to give the impression that another transmitter had joined in.

To complicate matters still further, it soon became apparent from the bearings taken by the three squads that the pianist was transmitting from three different places. Nevertheless, by 21 October 1941 the detection squads had managed to narrow down the search to three approximate locations, each being less than two miles from *Funkabwehr* headquarters: one was near the Bayrische Platz to the south-west of *Funkabwehr* HQ, the second was to the eastward near the Moritzplatz and the third was due north in the area of the Invalidenpark.[3]

By this stage Kopp was confident that a few more days of short-range direction finding would pin-point the actual tenement blocks used by the pianist, and a raid launched when he was actually tapping out his messages would bag the elusive quarry. During the night of 22 October the three squads searched the air waves in vain for the tap of the pianist's key. Frustratingly, it seemed, the pianist had lapsed into one of his periodic bouts of silence. Night after night the three squads continued to search the air waves without success until, more than a week later, it dawned on Kopp that the pianist, by some ocular means, had discovered or been warned that the hounds were closing in for the kill.

Left with no alternative, Kopp withdrew his monitors and ordered the long-range stations to pay special attention to the Berlin area so that the *Funkabwehr* would be alerted should the wary pianist began transmitting again – if he ever did. In the meantime Kopp had to admit defeat: the trail had gone cold.

2. The *Abwehr* Takes Up the Hunt

Shortly after the Berlin pianist lapsed into silence, the long-range monitoring stations reported a marked increase in the output of the PTX transmitter, which was now working for up to five hours at a stretch every night. Kopp drew the obvious conclusion that the PTX pianist was relaying the silenced Berlin pianist's messages in addition to his own workload. By this time the long-range stations had established through further cross-bearings that PTX was operating in Belgium, most probably in the coastal area between Ghent and Bruges. As the *Funkabwehr* had no detection squads on hand in Belgium, Kopp turned for help to the *Abwehr*, whose headquarters was situated in two old but rather grand, turn-of-the-century town houses on the Tirpitzufer – literally just around the corner from Kopp's HQ on the Matthäikirchplatz.

The *Abwehr*, under the command of Admiral Wilhelm Canaris, was divided into three main sections. Section I dealt with intelligence-gathering and espionage, mainly abroad, Section II was concerned with sabotage and commando-like operations and Section III was responsible for counter-sabotage, national security and counter-espionage. It was to the counter-espionage branch of Section III – Group IIIF, under the command of Colonel Rohleder – that Hans Kopp appealed for help in tracking down PTX.

Rohleder's network of counter-espionage agents, which was spread wide over practically every city and major town in occupied Europe, had the largest staff of all the German secret service agencies and was, in 1941, even more efficacious than the anti-spy sections of the *Gestapo* and the SD.[4] In response to Kopp's request for help, Rohleder contacted his senior Group IIIF agent in the Ghent/Bruges area over the 'Adolf circuit', the direct scrambled telephone net linking *Abwehr* HQ in Berlin with all its agencies both in the Reich and the occupied territories.

The agent entrusted with the hunt for PTX was 48-year-old Captain Harry Piepe, 'a short, stumpy figure with a huge nose, a massive neck, giant ears and a stentorian voice'.[5] Born in Uelzen in 1893, a small town some fifty miles to the south-east of Hamburg in the province of Lower Saxony, Piepe had served as a lieutenant in a cavalry regiment during the First World War and as a commander of an anti-tank company in a panzer division after being recalled to the colours on the outbreak of the Second World War.[6] On his return to civilian life in 1919 Piepe had entered the legal profession, rising to the rank of Senior State Attorney in the State Prosecutor's Office. He worked in the assessor courts, which involved the interrogation of suspects, and it was his experience as an interrogator in conjunction with his fluency in French and English that brought him to the attention of the *Abwehr*'s recruiting officers. Ordered to report to the *Abwehr* office in Hamburg at the end of 1940, Piepe was curtly told that he would henceforth be serving in Group IIIF for the duration of the war, and without being given or offered any training was precipitately dispatched to Ghent with nothing more than a bundle of *Abwehr* technical literature to instruct him in the esoteric art of spy-catching.

This amateur sleuth began his battle with Moscow's trained professionals by attempting to infiltrate Belgian Communist circles. Drawing on the services of a network of Belgian informers which was run by two Flemings who had worked for the German secret service in the First World War, Piepe dispatched his agents into taverns which were known haunts of the Communist fraternity. Logically, it seemed to Piepe, this is where trails leading to the troublesome pianist would be found. In fact he was searching where no one with any knowledge of Russian conspiratorial methods would have looked, because Soviet agents were forbidden to risk drawing attention to themselves by consorting with local Communist Party members – as Piepe would eventually discover after wasting much valuable time. Not surprisingly, then, the informers drew a blank, with nothing to show for the time they had spent eavesdropping in the taverns of Bruges and Ghent apart from a substantial claim for expenses. According to their reports, the local Communists were frightened and passive and had suspended all activities so as not to attract the unwelcome attentions of the *Gestapo*.

In the meantime the continuing systematic search by the long-range direction-finders to pin-point PTX had produced more positive results. On 17 November 1941 Kopp informed Rohleder that further cross-bearings indicated that the clandestine transmitter was operating from Brussels. In turn the Group IIIF chief ordered Piepe to quit his office in Ghent and carry the hunt to the Belgian capital. Rather than move into the Brussels *Abwehr* headquarters on the Rue de la Loi, Piepe decided to go under cover by posing as a businessman. To this end he rented a comfortable apartment on the prestigious Boulevard Brand Witlock and set up a bogus company under the cover name of Riepert Imports and Exports with an office situated above a tailor's shop at 192 Rue Royale in the city centre. To this office his informers could come and go, posing as company employees without arousing suspicion.

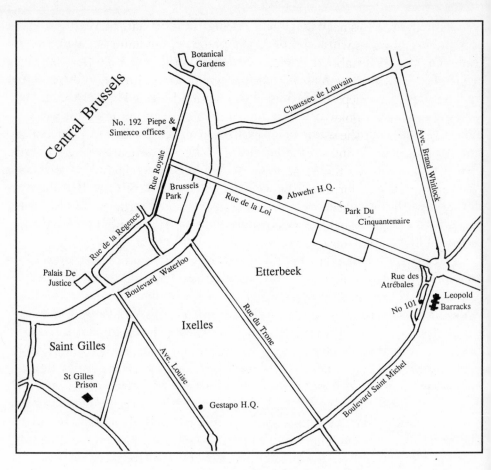

Brussels

On the same floor as Piepe's office, and adjacent to it, was the office of another business enterprise called Simexco. The wall dividing the two offices was so thin that Piepe could hear his neighbours moving around, and to exercise caution he made enquiries regarding the nature and credentials of Simexco through the senior German commissariat officer in Brussels. It transpired that the firm was owned by a Uruguayan businessman called Vincent Sierra and managed by a Belgian called Nazarin Drailly, both of whom were known personally to the German commissariat officers as the firm did a considerable amount of business with the German paramilitary Todt Organization , which supervised all works of construction and fortification for the German armed forces. The commissariat was able to put Piepe's mind at rest by declaring that the firm's personnel were supporters of the German cause who frequently treated the officers of the commissariat to business lunches and other entertainments. From then on Piepe felt confident enough to ignore the close proximity of his neighbours other than doffing his hat and exchanging the normal pleasantries whenever he passed them on the stairs leading from the street to his office above the tailor's shop. Accepting the commissariat's reassurances was something that Piepe would learn bitterly to regret.

From his office Piepe once more naïvely dispatched his Flemish informers to eavesdrop in the smoky, seedy haunts of the local Communists, with equally negative results. But he was at a loss to think of anywhere else to search in a city which sprawled over 60 square miles and was home to nearly a million souls. To find one man in this human jungle seemed a hopeless task, but on 30 November Piepe's fortunes changed with the arrival of Captain Hubertus Freyer of the *Funkabwehr*, who had been sent from Berlin with a squad of experienced short-range monitoring operators equipped with the very latest radio-detection gadgetry.

Freyer's team arrived in Brussels with three radio detection-finder (RDF) vans, fresh from the factory of the Loewe-Opta-Radio Company. Although these vans represented the very latest technology in radio-monitoring, the first attempt to take bearings on the PTX transmitter, carried out during the night of 1/2 December 1941, was an unmitigated disaster. Because the nature of the vans' duties was made conspicuous by the 3ft diameter revolving loop aerials attached to their roofs, they took their first bearings from the outskirts of the city. But when they reported the data obtained back to Freyer, who had set up a reception centre in the courtyard of the Leopold Barracks, he was puzzled to find that the three lines of bearing drawn on his Brussels street plan did not intersect at any point. The reason became apparent when, on the following morning, Freyer ordered the van crews to take test bearings on a German radio station in the city whose co-ordinates on the street plan could be accurately determined in advance. This test disclosed that the RDF vans' sensitive detection equipment was out of true by several degrees. The problem was easily overcome by making allowances for the various deflections when new bearings were taken on the following night. But this did not end Freyer's difficulties.

During the course of the next five nights it was discovered that there was not one but three pianists operating three separate clandestine transmitters in Brussels, all – at different times – using exactly the same call-signs and the same wavelengths. One set was tracked down to the Etterbeek district to the south-east of the city centre, the second was in the suburb of Ukkel due south of the city centre while the third was to the north-east in the Laeken district.[7] Despite this complication Freyer was confident that, given time, his *Funkabwehr* team would eventually pin-point all three hide-outs, allowing Piepe to bag all three pianists simultaneously.

Piepe, however, decided on a more expeditious course of action. It was discovered that the set in Etterbeek was working far more assiduously than the other two. Deducing that this must be the master set of the three, the amateur spy-catcher made the naïve assumption that if he homed in on the Etterbeek pianist he would be able to wring a confession out of him that would betray the location of the others. This impetuosity was engendered to a large extent by irate calls over the 'Adolf circuit' from Colonel Rohleder in Berlin demanding that Piepe silence the clandestine transmitters without further delay.

3. Omens in the East

Rohleder's impatient demands to silence the trilogy of transmitters in Brussels was generated by the turn of events on the Eastern Front. The German plan to defeat the Soviet Union centred on the need to destroy the bulk of the Red Army to the west of the Dvina and Dnieper rivers in huge, encircling, 'cauldron' battles designed to prevent the mass of the enemy forces from withdrawing deep into the vast Russian interior. This was to be achieved in a lightning campaign which was to be concluded by the autumn of 1941, before the onset of the harsh Russian winter and before the Russians had time and opportunity to mobilize their vast reserves of manpower.

Although the German forces made spectacular advances during the summer and autumn months they failed to prevent the withdrawal of the Red Army over the Dvina and Dnieper and by the second week of November, having suffered over 700,000 casualties, they had been drawn some 600 miles into the Russian interior. Moreover, the war of decisive manoeuvre, on which Hitler had banked all, had degenerated into the nightmare of a slogging match of pure attrition. The great depth and speed of the German advance had been impressive – 900,000 square miles of western Russia had been overrun – but the conquest of territory was not the yardstick of success: despite having suffered horrific casualties numbered in millions, the Russians were still able to field over four million men in the front line.

To add to the Germans' discomfiture, Russia's great and perennial ally 'General Winter' began to curl his cruel and merciless fingers around the throat of the invader. The climatic friend of the Russians descended on the battle front with more than average severity and the temperatures fell far below the seasonal norm. Throughout November and December 1941 daytime temperatures rarely rose much above $-25°C$, falling to as low as $-40°C$ at night. At the start of the campaign Hitler declared that the issue of winter clothing was totally unnecessary as Russia would be finished long before the cold weather set in. This arrogant boast condemned the German troops to shiver and freeze in the murderous temperatures, clad in nothing more than their thin denim summer uniforms. They were exhausted by the hundreds of miles of marching and bitter fighting and weakened by dysentery and an inadequate scale of rations, and 'General Winter' was able to reap a rich harvest of misery and death amongst the insufficiently clad, half-starved invaders.

Although the German forces were slowly freezing and bleeding to death, Hitler clung to the conviction that the Red Army was at the end of its tether and that a final lunge would be sufficient to capture Moscow and salvage the situation. As a result, on 15 November there began what became known as the 'Flucht Nach Vorn' ('The Flight Forward'). Moscow lay only fifty miles from the German front line, but to the frozen, exhausted, wretched German troops it was fifty miles too far. Clawing their way forward into the face of fanatical Soviet resistance, through blinding blizzards and temperatures that dropped as low as −56°C, the advancing troops came to a halt twenty miles short of Moscow seventeen days later. The extremes of cold, the infinite horizons of the hostile terrain and the toughness and indomitable tenacity of the Russian soldiers had ground Hitler's war machine to a standstill: but it was not to stand still for long. On the morning of Friday 5 December Stalin unleashed a massive counter-offensive on the Moscow front, forcing the Germans into a headlong retreat that threatened to degenerate into a rout.[8]

The shock of this sudden reverse caused Rohleder to question whether the indecipherable messages relayed to Moscow by the enemy pianists had been responsible for the débâcle. By the beginning of December 1941 the long-range monitoring stations had intercepted well over a thousand messages, which made Rohleder wonder where all this information was coming from and to what extent the agents and informers of the enemy spy network had penetrated the ministries of the Reich. For all he knew German strategic and tactical planning on the Eastern Front might have been hopelessly compromised. The only way to end this potentially deadly situation was to deprive Moscow of the Reich's military secrets by silencing the enemy pianists as quickly as possible.

4. The Atrébates Raid

The quickest method of homing in on the Etterbeek pianist was for the RDF vans to patrol the warren of streets in the heavily built-up area. However, rather than risk alerting the pianist, Freyer decided to employ another technical innovation that his team had brought with them from Berlin. This was a transistorized short-range direction-finder which was housed in an unobtrusive suitcase into which the aerial was built. From the case an ultra-fine connecting wire led to a miniature microphone which fitted into the operator's ear like a conventional hearing-aid. With no engine noise, and no vans with their tell-tale revolving aerials on their roofs to give warning of the approach of the *Funkabwehr*, the enemy was unlikely to guess that an innocent-looking pedestrian carrying a suitcase was in fact a member of the German security forces.[9]

Carrying the 'suitcase' detector, a sergeant from the *Funkabwehr* team, dressed in civilian clothes, took nightly walks in the cobbled streets of Etterbeek. By 10 December he had narrowed the search down to the bottom end of a 'narrow seedy-looking street with hardly any stores – the Rue des Atrébates'.[10] Backing on to the houses on this end of the street was a tenement that had been requisitioned by the Todt Organization to house its paramilitary employees. Piepe commandeered the top flat in this tenement for a few days, from where the *Funkabwehr* sergeant was able to take further bearings with a more powerful radio-detector set on the nightly PTX transmissions. By 12 December he had narrowed the search down further to three adjoining houses, numbers 99, 101 and 103.

Acquiring ten members of the *Abwehr* Secret Field Police from *Abwehr* headquarters on the Rue de la Loi and twenty-five German garrison troops from the Leopold Barracks on the Boulevard Saint Michel (where Freyer had set up his reception centre and which, ironically, was only two streets away from the Rue des Atrébates), Piepe planned a raid on the suspect houses which was timed to take place at 2.00 a.m. on 14 December. His plan was simple: to raid all three houses simultaneously with the field police while the troops, with heavy woollen socks pulled over their jackboots to muffle any noise, sealed off both ends of the street. Piepe took up position with the *Funkabwehr* sergeant in the tenement backing on to the Rue des Atrébates and at zero hour, when the sergeant confirmed that PTX was transmitting, he gave the signal for the raid to commence.

Quietly opening the front doors of the three houses with specially prepared keys, the field police charged in. With pistols drawn Piepe and two field policemen dashed into number 99, startling the wits out of the Flemish family living there. A rapid search of the house made it apparent that this was not the target. When Piepe rushed back out on to the street he collided with a policeman who ran out of number 101 shouting, 'In here! It's in here!' At that moment a man bolted out of number 101, hotly pursued by a policeman.

Knowing that the fugitive was unwittingly running straight into the arms of the garrison troops, Piepe hurried into number 101. On the ground floor he found a woman in a nightdress sitting up in bed, sobbing and shaking with fear. 'She was a beautiful girl of about twenty-five or so,' Piepe recalled, 'but Jewish, typically Jewish.'[11] On the second floor he discovered another woman, 'tall, very attractive, between twenty-five and twenty-eight, very Jewish',[12] who had thrown a pile of enciphered messages into the fireplace when she heard the sound of the policemen running up the stairs. One of the policemen had pulled the papers out of the fire grate and stamped out the flames before the material could be consumed. In another room on the second floor was the transmitter, still warm from use. It was on a table and beside it lay a sheaf of papers with endless columns of figures written on them.

The fugitive who had bolted out of the house was brought back to number 101 by the garrison troops. He had tried to hide in the basement of a building on the opposite side of the street and had put up a fight when the troops apprehended him: he was bruised and bleeding when he was dragged in front of Piepe. This was obviously the pianist. He was a well-built man, with square, chiselled features and dark, slashed-back hair. He protested that he was a neutral South American and his identity card, made out in the name of Carlos Alamo, a Uruguayan citizen born in Montevideo on 12 April 1913, seemed to bear this out. However, his cover story was compromised by the fact that he spoke French with a heavy and obvious Slav accent. Anyway, Piepe enquired, what was a Uruguayan citizen doing operating a clandestine radio transmitter in German-occupied Brussels? The tall woman on the second floor also protested her innocence of any wrongdoing, producing an identity card made out in the name of Anna Verlinden, a French national. When Piepe pointed out that for a French woman she spoke very poor French, she lapsed into a defiant, tight-lipped silence.

The distraught woman who had been in bed on the ground floor proved to be far more co-operative. She was the only one to give her real name – Rita Arnould – and she wailed to Piepe that she was glad that it was all over and that her boyfriend had made her join the Atrébates cell against her will.[13] Piepe calmed her down by assuring her that he was not a *Gestapo* man but an *Abwehr* officer and that he would make things easy for her if she told him everything she knew. He ordered one of his men to fetch a couple of bottles of wine so that he and Rita could have a little drink together.[14]

The road which had led Rita Arnould to the Rue des Atrébates was tortuous. Born in Frankfurt of Jewish parents, she became a Communist activist at the urging of her boyfriend Isidor Springer, a Jew and fellow student whom she had met at Frankfurt University while studying philosophy. When Hitler seized power in 1933 she and Isidor fled to Brussels, being doubly marked in the eyes of the *Gestapo* as both Jews and Communists. She had intended to continue her studies in the Belgian capital, but shortly after her arrival she escaped her impecunious condition by marrying Monsieur Arnould, a comfortably off Dutch textile salesman more than twice her age who had settled in the city. Turning her back on Isidor, her studies and her political activities, Rita settled down to a life of mundane domesticity until fate intervened. Her husband died suddenly, shortly after the Germans invaded Belgium in May 1940, leaving her unprovided for. As a German Jewess and a fugitive from the *Gestapo* she was in a precarious situation and she sought out Isidor for help. By this time Springer had become a successful diamond merchant and had married a Belgian woman called Flore (*née* Velaerts) – a perfect cover for his work as a Soviet agent, having been recruited into the GRU during 1939. Despite his marital status, Springer installed Rita in 101 Rue des Atrébates as his mistress, where she earned her keep by working as a housekeeper and a courier for the agents using the aliases Carlos Alamo and Anna Verlinden. (Rita could not help Piepe as to their real identities.)

Having told Piepe how she came to be in the Rue des Atrébates, she tried to convince him of her sincerity by telling him to check the walls of the room occupied by the Verlinden woman on the second floor. Acting on this cryptic information Piepe ordered the field police to make a thorough search of the room. One of them tapped the wall behind Verlinden's bed and it sounded hollow. She was sitting on the bed, and when Piepe told her to get up she refused to do so. She was pulled to her feet by the policemen and thrust aside, the bed was pulled away and a hidden door in the wall was discovered which led into a small room dimly lit by a red bulb. Inside was a forger's workshop, containing all the equipment needed to produce counterfeit documents. There were shelves laden with bottles containing inks, chemicals and crystals and drawers full of blank passports, official forms and official rubber stamps. Amongst all this paraphernalia Piepe discovered passport-size photographs of two men.

When Piepe showed the photographs to Rita she was able to enlighten him that they were of the *'Grand Chef'* ('Big Chief'), the leader of the network, whom she had only met once, and the *'Petit Chef'* ('Little Chief'), the former man's deputy, who was a frequent visitor to the Rue des Atrébates. Although she professed to know nothing of the whereabouts of the *Grand Chef*, she did know that the *Petit Chef* and his mistress, a tall, blonde woman, lived somewhere on the Avenue Slegers, a side street off the Boulevard Brand Witlock where Piepe had rented an apartment. It came as quite a surprise to learn that he was a near neighbour to the deputy leader of the spy network he was hunting! As for 'The Cobbler' (*Abwehr* jargon for a forger) who worked in the hidden workshop, Rita could only say that she was sure he was a Polish Jew, a short man of swarthy complexion who wore thick, pebble-lens glasses and operated under the alias 'Adash'. She had no idea where he lived. Neither did she know Isidor Springer's current address, but she was able to tell Piepe that he regularly visited the Brussels *Bourse* (Stock Exchange) and a 'cut-out', a man called Dow who managed a fur shop on the Rue Royale (only a hundred yards up the street from Piepe's bogus company office), where Rita collected messages 'dropped' by agents and conveyed them back to the Rue des Atrébates. She also betrayed the whereabouts of her cousin, Yvonne Kuenstlunger, whom Springer had also recruited as a courier. After packing off Carlos Alamo and Anna Verlinden to the Saint Gilles prison in Brussels, Piepe made arrangements for Rita to be installed in a hotel under the guard of a field policeman. As an experienced interrogator he knew that he would elicit far more information from her by winning her confidence – appearing as a confidant rather than an accuser.

Dawn was breaking when Piepe finally withdrew from the Rue des Atrébates, leaving two field policemen and an interpreter in the house to apprehend anyone who called during the course of the day. The first caller claimed to be the owner of the house who had come to collect the rent. The veracity of this claim was quickly established by a telephone call to the Brussels Housing Department and the man was allowed to leave. At 11.30 a.m. an unshaven, scruffy looking man carrying a basket full of dead rabbits rang the doorbell. Ordered into the house by the policemen, he produced an identity card made out in the name of Albert Desmets, a Norwegian born in Orschies on 12 October 1903. He explained that he was a street vendor who frequently sold his wares to the lady of the house. This seemed a reasonable explanation, but the police were suspicious and when they searched him they found several enciphered messages in his pockets. Clapped in handcuffs, Desmets was dispatched to the Saint Gilles. Half an hour later a tall, thick-set man appeared and in a domineering tone inquired whether anyone knew what time the garage across the street opened. When he was ordered to step inside and show his papers, he produced an identity card in the name of Jean Gilbert along with a special pass issued by the president of the Todt Organization in Paris who had commissioned the bearer to look for materials required for German construction projects. Uncertain of their ground, the police decided to ring *Abwehr* headquarters, who ordered them to release the man immediately, little suspecting that they had let the *Grand Chef* – the head of Soviet espionage in Western Europe – slip through their fingers.

5. Piepe's Pyrrhic Victory

On the morning after the Atrébates raid Piepe reported to Lieutenant-Colonel Dischler, head of the *Abwehr* office in Brussels. Delighted at the success of the raid, Dischler immediately began drafting a report on the case for Colonel Rohleder in Berlin. But what code-name could they give to the 'orchestra' (*Abwehr* jargon for an enemy spy ring)? Dischler suggested 'Russian Orchestra', but Piepe had a better idea – *'Die Rote Kapelle'* ('The Red Orchestra'). A name had been found for the greatest espionage enterprise of the Second World War.[15]

The most important clue that Rita Arnould had divulged was that the *Petit Chef* and his mistress lived somewhere on the Avenue Slegers. Dischler dispatched an *Abwehr* agent, armed with the photograph discovered in 'The Cobbler''s workshop, to question people who lived on the avenue and he quickly discovered the *Petit Chef*'s address. As darkness was falling that evening (14 December) a fleet of black Mercedes, full of *Abwehr* agents and field police headed by Piepe, swept into the Avenue Slegers. They were too late: the birds had already flown.

When questioned, neighbours reported that the couple had left the house only a few hours earlier in a car loaded with suitcases. They also divulged that the gentleman of the house was a Uruguayan businessman. If Piepe had been quicker on the uptake he would have investigated the possibility that this South American and the owner of Simexco, the company whose office adjoined his own bogus establishment in the Rue Royale, might be one and the same person. But it did not occur to him, and the chance to short-circuit the investigation was lost.

The *Petit Chef*'s residence was of palatial proportions, containing twenty-one luxuriously furnished rooms. In the master bedroom was a large fitted ward-robe which contained fifty suits of the finest quality. But amongst all these trappings of wealth not a single incriminating clue was found, nor anything that revealed the identities of the fugitive occupants.

Having so narrowly missed capturing the deputy chief of the Red Orchestra, Piepe turned his attentions to Isidor Springer. On 16 December he sent one of his Flemish informers to the fur shop in the Rue Royale which was managed by the 'cut-out' man called Dow. The informer told Dow that he had an urgent message from the *Grand Chef* for Springer and asked him to arrange a meeting. Dow asked him to return in forty-eight hours. This clumsy ruse had predictable results: when the informer returned to the shop on 18 December he found that Dow had disappeared.[16] Piepe was more discriminating in dealing with the courier Yvonne Kuenstlunger. Rather than approach her or intimidate her in any way, he had her every move shadowed by *Abwehr* agents in the hope that she would lead them to Springer and other links in the Red Orchestra network. However, he met with no success.[17]

The only other avenue which might lead to Springer was Rita's information that Isidor often did business in the Brussels *Bourse*. Piepe followed up this lead himself, again without success: Springer had also disappeared into the shadows without trace. However, while making enquiries he was tipped off that if he was interested in Springer he should keep an eye on the woman in charge of the *Bourse*'s typing pool. He had her placed under surveillance and discovered that she was interpolating cryptic messages in the *Bourse*'s official correspondence and that these messages were being relayed to a woman working in the Paris

Bourse, who Piepe deduced must be acting as a 'letter box' for the Soviet agents. She too was placed under surveillance.

Apart from this slender lead, Piepe was unable to make any inroads into the Soviet *apparat*, for interrogations of the three agents incarcerated in the Saint Gilles prison (Alamo, Verlinden and Desmets) proved totally unproductive: all three remained tight-lipped. As a result of Piepe's inexperience the Atrébates raid had been a wasted effort. A more astute investigator would have put all three transmitters in Brussels out of action simultaneously instead of giving the other two pianists time to go to ground. Despite Rohleder's exhortations to silence PTX as quickly as possible, Piepe should have stood his ground and, rather than pounce on the bait, exercised patience. Having identified 101 Rue des Atrébates as one of the Orchestra's haunts, he should have set up an observation post in one of the houses on the opposite side of the street so that *Abwehr* agents could observe, photograph and tail everyone who called there. This would eventually have led to the centre of the enemy web. As it was, the trail had gone cold again.

Fortunately, a new lead came from an unexpected direction. Shortly after the Atrébates raid *Abwehr* agents arrested five men involved in resistance work on the Franco-Belgian frontier. None of these – Marcel Vranckx, Louis Bourgain, Reginald Goldmaer, Emil Carlos and a man called Boulangier – had anything at all to do with the Red Orchestra; but when the *Abwehr* discovered that Vranckx and Goldmaer had served in the International Brigades during the Spanish Civil War (which implied Communist connections) they made Piepe aware of the case. He immediately jumped to the conclusion that this group of militants must belong to the Red Orchestra, and he sent a report to this effect to Rohleder in Berlin.[18] Although Piepe was on the wrong track, this turn of events served as a catalyst to change the whole complexion of the investigation.

6. The 'Gentlemen' of the *Gestapo*

Early in January 1942 Piepe was summoned to Berlin, where he learned that Hitler had ordered that henceforth the *Gestapo* was to take a hand in the *Abwehr*'s endeavours to liquidate the Red Orchestra. There was nothing unusual in the *Gestapo* and *Abwehr* working in tandem, as some authors have suggested,[19] particularly where Communist espionage was concerned. In an *Abwehr/Gestapo* agreement of December 1936 it was decided that the former could participate in the latter's interrogations of Communist suspects, or interrogate their prisoners and inspect their interrogation files, and vice versa, and this became normal procedure.[20] To assist Piepe, *SS-Gruppenführer* (Lieutenant-General) and *Reichskriminaldirektor* (Police Director) Heinrich Müller, the head of the *Gestapo*, selected an experienced officer from the counter-espionage section of the Secret State Police, 41-year-old *Kriminalkommissar* (Criminal Commissioner) and *SS-Hauptsturmführer* (Captain) Karl Giering.

The son of a magistrate, Giering was born in 1900 in the small town of Pechlüge, near Schwerin in the state of Mecklenburg. He was conscripted into the army in 1918, shortly before the armistice, after which he served briefly in the Lüttwitz Free Corps before transferring to the *Reichswehr* (Regular Army) in 1920. Discharged three years later on account of poor health, he found employment as a night watchman with Osram, the electric light bulb company. In 1925, when his health had improved, he started a new career in the Berlin Criminal Police, transferring to the Political Police during the turbulent years of the Weimar Republic before joining the *Gestapo* in 1933. By the time war broke out in 1939 he had earned the reputation of being one of the sternest guardians of the Nazi regime, and one of the ablest police officers in Germany. He played a leading role in the investigation into the attempt to assassinate Hitler with a bomb in the Munich Bürgerbräukeller on 7 November 1939 (which resulted in the arrest of a German watchmaker six days after the assassination attempt), thereby earning the good will of the *Führer*.[21] A very tall, thin, cadaverous-looking man, Giering spoke with a gravelly, husky voice, the result of a cancerous growth gnawing at his throat which he 'treated' by imbibing prodigious quantities of coffee liberally laced with brandy. He entered the investigation determined to destroy the Red Orchestra before the tumour in his throat destroyed him.[22]

When the *Gestapo* master-investigator studied Piepe's report he disputed the *Abwehr* sleuth's premise that, because two of the five militants apprehended after the Atrébates raid had served in the International Brigades, a connection with the Red Orchestra could be inferred. However, a photograph of the pianist calling himself Carlos Alamo, who had been captured in the Atrébates raid, caused Giering to recall that GRU agents he had interrogated two years previously, after the break-up of a network operating in Czechoslovakia, had referred to a Soviet airman called Mikael Makarov, with whom they had trained in the GRU training centre in Moscow. Referring once more to the files on the Czech case, he found that the description of Makarov seemed uncannily like that of Alamo, and, working on this hunch, he ordered the prisoner to be flown to Berlin from the Saint Gilles prison.[23]

An astute professional with vast experience in the anti-Communist struggle, Giering was not devoid of psychological awareness, and rather than have the prisoner tortured in the *Gestapo* cellars he decided to employ more subtle methods. In his office in the *Gestapo* headquarters in the Prinz-Albrecht-Strasse,

Giering had a series of 'friendly chats' with Alamo over a bottle of brandy during which the prisoner admitted that he was in fact the Russian agent Mikael Makarov although he refused to reveal anything else of consequence.

Having sent Makarov back to the Saint Gilles, Giering arrived in Brussels at the end of January 1942 in company with his right-hand man, *Kriminalobersekretär* Wilhelm Berg, a short, rather plump man who provided a comic contrast to the spindly Giering and whom Piepe referred to in his deposition as an unscrupulous butcher. Having installed himself in the *Gestapo* offices at 453 Avenue Louise, Giering subjected Makarov and the agents calling themselves Albert Desmets and Anna Verlinden to a different style of questioning, which the *Gestapo* referred to as 'intensified interrogation' − i.e. torture. On separate occasions all three prisoners were driven from the Saint Gilles to the *Gestapo* offices, where specially selected masters in the art of 'intensified interrogation' subjected them to vicious beatings and immersion in baths of freezing water to the point of drowning. Giering's main line of questioning centred on the need to elicit information of the courier lines that he hoped would lead him to the centre of the *Grand Chef*'s widespread web and to the key to the PTX cipher so that the intercepted messages could be decoded by the *Funkabwehr* cryptanalysts, revealing the nature of the information being relayed through the ether to Moscow and the extent of the Soviet penetration.

Makarov revealed nothing. He was in fact a native of Kasan who had served as an officer in the ground staff of the Red Air Force, experiencing combat with the International Brigades in Spain before being recruited by the GRU as a radio operator. He arrived in Belgium to join the *Grand Chef*'s network, posing as Carlos Alamo, in April 1939, bringing with him a short-wave transmitter hidden in a suitcase. As a cover he managed a branch of the rainwear firm Le Roi du Caoutchouc (The Raincoat King) in Ostend, one of four companies which served as a cover for the Red Orchestra. When the Germans invaded the Low Countries in 1940 the shop in Ostend was destroyed by a German bomb, and on the *Grand Chef*'s orders he moved into a villa on the Avenue Longchamp (renamed Avenue Winston Churchill after the war) in the Ukkel district of Brussels. There he remained until the middle of November 1941, when he moved to the Rue des Atrébates − just four weeks before Piepe launched his raid.

Makarov's place in the villa on the Avenue Longchamp was filled by the agent calling himself Albert Desmets. He was in fact David Kamy, a Palestinian Jew and a veteran of the International Brigades, who had married a Frenchwoman and settled in the Fifth *Arrondissement* in Paris, where he was talent-spotted by the GRU during the late 1930s. Before being recruited into the Red Orchestra he had worked in the technical department of the French Communist Party (under the cover name 'Camille'), specializing in radio work and, as an amateur chemist, in the production of invisible ink and microfilm, 'a field in which he achieved perfection.'[24]

Kamy was one of the three pianists that the *Funkabwehr* RDF vans had detected (transmitting in the Ukkel district), but he revealed none of this under torture and the Germans never realized that they had captured another of the Brussels pianists. However, Kamy did not remain entirely silent during the 'intensified interrogations'. He fed the *Gestapo* a ruse 'revealing' that he was Second Lieutenant Anton Danilov, a Russian who had been seconded to the Soviet Embassy in Paris immediately after completing his GRU training and that he had been responsible for liaison between General Susloparov, the Soviet Military Attaché in the Paris Embassy, and the GRU agents working in Belgium. The *Gestapo* believed this to be a true confession, as attested to in their report on the Red Orchestra.[25] Heinz Höhne was also taken in by Kamy's disinformation, identifying him in his book *Codeword: Direktor* as Danilov.[26]

Despite the brutality she was subjected to, the cipher expert arrested in the Atrébates raid, operating under the alias Anna Verlinden, refused to reveal the key to the PTX cipher. All the *Gestapo* managed to drag out of her was her real name, Sophie Poznanska, and that the she was a Polish Jewess who had been born in Kalisz, a small town in western Poland some 150 miles south-west of Warsaw. Little is known about this shadowy figure, who also operated under the code-name 'Juzefa', save that as a young woman she had been a Communist militant who had fled to Palestine to escape arrest by the Polish police during a purge by the fascist Pilsudski regime. During her time in Palestine she joined a Communist cell which was run by the man who was destined to become the *Grand Chef* of the Red Orchestra; but exactly when she joined the Orchestra in Belgium is unrecorded. Sophie, whom Piepe described as a 'tall, very attractive woman',[27] finally cheated the *Gestapo* by taking her own life in the Saint Gilles prison on 29 September 1942.

Unable to break the conspiracy of silence, Giering transferred Makarov and Kamy to the Breendonk *SS-Auffanglager* (Reception Centre) during June 1942. Breendonk was a fort that had been built in 1906 beside the main Brussels to Antwerp road. It was requisitioned by the SS on 29 August 1940 and placed under the command of *SS-Sturmbannführer* (Major) Schmitt. An SS guard greeted new arrivals with the spine-chilling statement, 'This is hell, and I am the devil!' He was not exaggerating, for starvation rations, beatings and torture constituted the prisoners' daily lot. Some of the unfortunates who experienced Breendonk were on transit to concentration camps, while others were incarcerated there for the purpose of protracted interrogations. For this reason one of the fort's arsenals had been equipped as a torture chamber, reached by way of a long, narrow corridor. Hanging by their hands from a pulley block, the prisoners endured medieval tortures, including thumbscrews, head vices, red-hot iron bars and wooden wedges.[28] However, despite being subjected to constant brutality, Makarov and Kamy obstinately refused to talk and the trail leading to the Red Orchestra stopped short for the men of the *Gestapo*.

7. The Search for 'The Cobbler'

By the spring of 1942 the only clue provided by Rita Arnould that Piepe had not followed up concerned the forger 'Adash' who had worked in the hidden room in the Rue des Atrébates. Her description did not give Piepe much to go on, but in dealing with a 'cobbler' he was at least on familiar ground: he had brought several forgers to justice during his legal career. Working on the premise that it takes years for a forger to master his craft, and that there was every likelihood that he must have attracted the attention of the police at some stage in his career, Piepe made enquiries at the Brussels Police Headquarters. His hunch paid off because in the police files was the record of a Polish Jew called Abraham Raichmann, who had been suspected of manufacturing counterfeit banknotes before the war. The description in the record tallied with that given by Rita: 'Adash' and Raichmann were obviously one and the same. But how was Piepe to find Raichmann, who would have gone to earth after the Atrébates raid?

Shortly after he commenced this line of enquiry, Piepe chanced to discuss his search for the 'cobbler' with Lieutenant Bödiker of the counter-espionage branch of the *Abwehr* office in Brussels. This gave Piepe a lucky break. To provide his Belgian informers with cover stories, Bödiker was purchasing forged identity cards from a Belgian police inspector called Mathieu, who acted as a middleman between a forger and his clients. Piepe arranged a meeting with Mathieu, whom he described as 'a tall, broad-shouldered specimen, as Aryan as they come',[29] and learned that he had long been in the pay of the *Abwehr* and was one of Bödiker's most important informers as he had deliberately courted contacts with certain resistance groups, through which he had made the acquaintance of the very 'cobbler' Piepe was searching for – Abraham Raichmann.[30]

Raichmann's past was obscure. The *Gestapo* considered that, in addition to his connections with the Red Orchestra, this 'tough and devilishly clever Polish Jew'[31] was one of the leaders of a ring of gangsters, with no political motives, specializing in forgery and smuggling. It is believed that this master-forger learned his trade under the tutelage of the legendary *Pass-Apparat* set up in Berlin by the Comintern in the mid-1920s. This was a full-scale 'factory' specializing in the production of false papers ('shoes' in *Abwehr* jargon) for use by the Comintern underground in Germany and Western Europe. Reputedly some 170 people worked in the *Pass-Apparat*, which was equipped with machinery for printing and engraving and for photographic processing. From 1927 to 1932 the *Pass-Apparat* produced some 450 collections of documents each year. Each collection consisted of a passport and a 'legend' – false identities backed by elaborate biographical details and bogus documents to confirm the identity of the passport bearer, such as birth certificate and employment record. In addition each passport was endorsed with visas and frontier stamps: the police paid less attention to a well-used passport because it implied that the traveller had already been checked and found to be bona fide.[32]

After the break up of the *Pass-Apparat* by the *Gestapo* in 1933 Raichmann fled to Belgium, where he set up a thriving covert business selling forged papers and passports to Jewish immigrants driven out of Germany, local Communists and the criminal underworld. To augment his stocks he bribed employees of various Latin American consulates to provide him with blank passports and certificates of naturalization. Betrayed to the Belgium police in 1939 by another 'cobbler' vying for trade, Raichmann was arrested but acquitted at his trial for lack of corroborative evidence. It was while he was in prison awaiting trial that he was recruited by the GRU, who had learned of Raichmann's reputation as the most talented 'cobbler' in Europe. The Red agents not only employed the best lawyers to assure his acquittal but also provided for his family, who were left without resources during his incarceration.[33] Despite promising to cease his 'private' activities after being recruited into the Red Orchestra, Raichmann continued to provide 'shoes' for disparate groups of the resistance and the criminal underworld. This eventually proved to be his undoing, because he did not realize that Inspector Mathieu was purchasing his forged identity cards, at 1,000 francs a card, for the *Abwehr*.

Rather than arrest Raichmann, Piepe decided to place 'the terribly short and dark, loathsome Jewish criminal'[34] and his contacts under surveillance in order to learn more about the scope of the Red Orchestra as a whole.[35] This paid off, for, during May 1942, Raichmann asked Mathieu if he would hide a suitcase which had become 'too hot' for him to handle. The Inspector offered to conceal it in his garage. Raichmann looked the place over and agreed. The very next day Mathieu informed Bödiker, who in turn notified Piepe. When he examined the suitcase Piepe found that it contained a short-wave radio transmitter. Experts were called in who carefully dismantled the radio set and photographed every part of it. When these were compared with photographs of the set that had been captured in the Rue des Atrébates it was found that both sets clearly originated from the same source.[36] When the examination was complete the transmitter was returned to its hiding place in Mathieu's garage, which was then placed under *Abwehr* surveillance. Piepe was confident that eventually a pianist from the Red Orchestra would call to collect it. In addition Piepe placed 'The Cobbler' under even stricter, round-the-clock surveillance, although he seemed to be leading a comparatively dull existence with his mistress Malvina Gruber (*née* Hofstadyerova), a plump, matronly Czech.[37]

8. The Laeken Raid

During February 1942 the Berlin pianist, after nearly five months of silence, came to life again. However, he only transmitted sporadically and was on the air for such short periods – and always from different locations – that the *Funkabwehr* were unable to pin him down. During March the long-range radio monitoring stations also intercepted messages, enciphered in the by now familiar Soviet five-figure groups, which, cross-bearings indicated, were being transmitted from somewhere in Holland. To cap it all, in mid-June the Kranz monitoring station reported that one of the Brussels transmitters had burst into life again.

Once more a *Funkabwehr* tracking team under Captain Hubertus Freyer was dispatched to the Belgian capital from Berlin. The RDF vans spent the first few nights taking the usual preliminary bearings from the outskirts of the city, and they very quickly discovered that the clandestine transmitter was operating in the Laeken district – one of the three locations detected in the lead-up to the Atrébates raid. Their task was made easier because the pianist was working his set all night long on practically every night of the week. Piepe recorded:

> I must confess I could never understand the Russians' attitude. Were they really so overworked? After all, an underemployed pianist is more use than a pianist locked up in jail. Was it that they simply were not aware of the advanced RDF techniques we were employing? I cannot conceive of any other possible explanation: not unless they were cold-bloodedly sacrificing radio operators.[38]

The very same *Funkabwehr* sergeant who had taken to the streets of Etterbeek with his 'suitcase' short-range detector back in December now took to those of Laeken. But this time his task was not so easy. An electric railway ran through the district, and the overhead lines caused so much interference that the sergeant was unable to home in on the transmitter. Only the powerful equipment of an RDF van could overcome this problem, but to send a *Funkabwehr* van on to the streets of Laeken would alert the pianist that the hounds were closing in. In an attempt to guard against this risk one of the RDF vans was camouflaged to look like a commercial vehicle, but this subterfuge was not devoid of complications, as Piepe explained:

On the other hand there was a risk that we ourselves might be stopped and questioned by the Belgian police, and that was something I wanted to avoid at all costs. I certainly did not want reports leaking out that a mysterious vehicle was roaming the streets at night, and that the police were not interfering with it and so on.[39]

But that is exactly what happened, as Piepe recalls:

On the very first night we bumped into a police patrol. We were all wearing civilian clothes, of course, and carried 'genuine false credentials' which we had obtained through Mathieu [forged by Raichmann!]. The police examined our identity cards and asked what we were doing outdoors at that hour. I intimated that it was something connected with the black market. I did my best to talk them out of it, but they insisted on examining the inside of the van. I could not allow that: they would have seen our apparatus. I tapped my driver on the shoulder and he drove off at full tilt, scattering the policemen. We managed to shake them off, but the hunt was over for the night. The second night also ended in farce! There was a *Luftwaffe* barracks in the area and we drove past it so often that the sentries became suspicious and they pounced on us! We were taken to the guard house, and we had to show our papers and explain ourselves and telephone my superiors for confirmation. I was furious.[40]

Luckily for Piepe the pianist remained unaware of the patrolling *Funkabwehr* van, and he continued to transmit his messages to Moscow throughout the hours of darkness. Finally, during the night of 29 June 1942, the exact house was pin-pointed – 'a tall tenement near a railway with a lumber yard on one side and a shop on the other'.[41]

At 3.00 a.m. the following night – 'a clear, moonlit night'[42] – Piepe launched a raid with ten *Abwehr* Secret Field Policemen, backed up by fifteen airmen from the nearby *Luftwaffe* barracks who sealed off both ends of the street. They discovered the short-wave transmitter in the attic of the tenement, but the pianist, alerted by the sound of the police searching the rooms below, escaped through a skylight in the roof. When Piepe stuck his head through the skylight he was shot at by the pianist, who was crouching behind a chimney. This caused the airmen on the street below to begin shooting with their rifles. Galloping down the stairs, Piepe rushed out on to the street shouting to the airmen to stop shooting as he wanted to capture the pianist alive. Looking up, Piepe could clearly see the man silhouetted in the bright moonlight as he jumped from roof to roof, firing at the Germans with a pistol in between leaps. When he reached the last roof in the block he smashed a skylight and disappeared into the attic of the building. The field police raced into the house and searched every room, finally discovering the fugitive hiding under an overturned bathtub in the cellar. He put up a fight but was beaten into submission by the police, who dragged the bleeding, half-conscious man into a car, which delivered him to *Abwehr* headquarters on the Rue de la Loi. There he was interrogated by Piepe, who recalled that

He was a short, thick-set, hard-featured man, about forty years of age, terribly working class. He did not make much of an impression on me. His first question was whether I was *Abwehr* or *Gestapo*, and he was visibly relieved when I reassured him that I was not a *Gestapo* man. He spoke in French, but badly and with a heavy accent. He asked me to fasten his hands in front of him, instead of keeping them handcuffed behind his back. I refused, telling him that that was an old trick and that he was just looking for a chance to jump me. He insisted that he had no such intention, but I was not convinced. As a gesture, however, I laid my gun on the desk and told him he had nothing to fear. He complained of the beating he had received, but I pointed out that it was his own fault: he should have surrendered without a fight. Eventually he calmed down and we started talking in German. He told me that his name was Johann Wenzel and that he had been born in Danzig in 1902. But he added that he was not the kind of man who made bargains and that he would not betray any of his associates. He was true to his word and, realizing that, apart from his identity, I would not get another word out of him, I packed him off to the Saint Gilles Prison.[43]

On the morning following the raid Piepe arrived back at his apartment on the Avenue Brand Witlock and, despite being tired after a sleepless night, began glancing through a pile of documents that had been found alongside Wenzel's transmitter. The majority of the documents contained long messages in five-figure cipher groups, but as Piepe thumbed through them he came across two messages in 'clear', all written in German. These two messages revealed for the first time just how deeply the Red Orchestra had penetrated the vitals of the Third Reich.

One of the messages addressed to Moscow gave highly detailed statistics about German tank and aircraft production, and of losses suffered on the Eastern Front. But it was the second message written in 'clear' that riveted Piepe's attention. It gave the fullest possible data concerning German strategic planning, the order of battle and the operational intentions for 'Case Blue', the German summer offensive designed to capture the Russian oilfields in the Caucasus which had commenced only two days previously.

Horrified, Piepe jumped into his old Chevrolet and sped to *Abwehr* HQ to report his find to Colonel Habs-Karl von Servaes, who had relieved Dischler as head of the Rue de la Loi office earlier in the year. So serious was the matter that, in addition to reporting the nature of the captured messages to *Abwehr* HQ in Berlin over the 'Adolf circuit' scrambled telephone link, Servaes ordered Piepe to deliver the Wenzel messages to Berlin in person. As all the flights to Berlin were full, Piepe decided to drive the 400 miles to the German capital in his Chevrolet.

The offices of the Berlin *Abwehr* HQ were installed in a block of converted four-storey, sandstone town houses at 72–76 Tirpitzufer, on the north side of the tree-lined Landwehr Canal. When Piepe arrived at the main entrance in the evening of 1 July the officer in charge of the guard asked him to open his briefcase so that he could check the contents before allowing him into the building. Piepe recalled:

> I refused, and when he insisted I drew my Luger pistol, pointed it at him and said, 'If you try to take this briefcase from me, I'll shoot.' This caused quite a stir, as can be imagined.[44]

He was finally rescued by Colonel Rohleder, the head of Group IIIF, and when Piepe showed his chief the Wenzel messages Rohleder immediately informed Major-General von Bentivegni, head of *Abwehr* Section III (of which Group IIIF was a sub-section), who in turn reported the matter to Admiral Canaris, the chief of the *Abwehr*. After reading the message relating to 'Case Blue' Canaris whisked Piepe off to the War Ministry on the Bendlerstrasse to report his discovery to Field Marshal Keitel, Chief of the German High Command. Keitel was thunderstruck, for the contents of Wenzel's messages implied that someone in the highest echelons of the armed forces was supplying the Red Orchestra with extremely sensitive information. The question was – who?

9. Wenzel's Double Game

While Piepe was attending Berlin in person, Giering got in touch with *Gestapo* HQ on the Prinz-Albrecht-Strasse via teleprinter, enquiring if the *Gestapo* Registry had a file on Johann Wenzel. The answer was affirmative: Wenzel had been a prize candidate on the *Gestapo*'s black list for years. A German national born in Danzig, Wenzel was brought up in the East Prussian town of Niedau near Königsberg and had become a Communist militant at an early age. A close friend of Ernst Thälmann,[45] the leader of the German Communists, Wenzel had been recruited by the GRU late in 1934 and under the cover name 'Hermann' had run a group of industrial informers in the Ruhr, providing Moscow with details of German armaments, particularly tanks and artillery. When the *Gestapo* began arresting members of the group in 1935 Wenzel slipped over the frontier into Poland to escape capture and made his way to Moscow. There he attended the GRU training centre, showing such brilliance in espionage and radio work that he earned the nickname *Le Professeur*.

Infiltrated into Belgium in 1936, Wenzel set up a small intelligence *apparat* called 'Group Hermann', which specialized in collecting information on the armaments industries of the western European powers. This group was absorbed into the *Grand Chef*'s circuit late in 1938, and Wenzel was employed in training the *apparat*'s pianists. *Le Professeur* was one of the three pianists detected by Freyer's *Funkabwehr* team (transmitting from the Laeken district) during the lead-up to the Atrébates raid, after which he went to earth, maintaining radio silence until the beginning of June 1942, when the amount of information accumulating for dispatch to Moscow had become to prodigious that the *Grand Chef* decided to reactivate 'Hermann''s transmitter – with disastrous results.

When Giering received the Prinz-Albrecht-Strasse's reply to his enquiry about Wenzel, he immediately transferred the luckless pianist from the Saint Gilles prison to the Breendonk *SS-Auffanglager*, where the masters of 'intensified interrogation' set to work. When Piepe saw him again some eight weeks later he did not recognize the broken wreck of a man who, unable to endure any more brutality, had agreed to work for the Germans. We cannot imagine the agony suffered in the torture chamber of Breendonk that caused Wenzel to crack:

> Where the *Gestapo* began, there humanity ended – and with it logic. A hundred and fifty pounds of flesh bleeding under the torturer's lash is no longer quite human; it is not quite animal; it is something in the process of becoming either a hero or a traitor. The final metamorphosis is unpredictable, often surprising, occasionally incomprehensible. It is not for us to judge: the right to judge belongs only to those who were once forced to step into the cage where Giering's men stood waiting with their implements.[46]

Wenzel's treachery took the form of agreeing to take part in a *Funkspiel* (radio 'play-back') with Moscow. Radio 'play-back' was a standard stratagem employed by all counter-espionage agencies during the war. By 'turning' an enemy pianist not only was it possible to gain a better insight into the enemy's espionage activities, it also provided the opportunity to confuse the other side by passing disinformation over the air waves.

Wenzel's 'play-back' was organized initially by *Kriminalkommissar* Thomas Ampletzer, a *Gestapo* expert in *Funkspiel* who was flown to Brussels from the Prinz-Albrecht-Strasse for the purpose.[47] By the beginning of September, after recovering from the worst effects of his torture sessions, Wenzel made contact with Moscow on his transmitter, opening up a channel of communication for the *Gestapo* to the man who, for the German counter-espionage sleuths, was the most mysterious being imaginable – the Director of the GRU, General Ivan Terenchevich Peresypkin.

As every pianist had an individual Morse 'signature' – his personal touch and rhythm on the Morse key which was as recognizable to a trained ear as handwriting to a graphologist – Wenzel had to make the transmissions to the GRU 'Centre' in person. After a two-month break in transmissions the 'Centre', situated in Kropotkin Square in Moscow, was naturally suspicious when Wenzel suddenly made contact again. As a result the first two *Gestapo-*

composed messages that 'Hermann' transmitted had a dual purpose: to allay the Russians' suspicion, and to set a trap to capture the *Grand Chef*:

> Hermann to Director. Urgent. The usual liaisons with the Grand Chef are under surveillance. Request instructions for meeting with the Grand Chef. Very important I meet with the Grand Chef. Hermann.[48]

A few nights later the ploy was repeated:

> Hermann to Director. Very Urgent. According to what we have learned from German sources, our cipher system may have been compromised. I have not yet been advised of a meeting with the Grand Chef. My contact with Centre can now function regularly. German surveillance has ceased. How am I to arrange my liaisons with Grand Chef. Request immediate reply. Hermann.[49]

According to Trepper, this ploy failed because Wenzel included an alarm signal in the text of the messages which warned the 'Centre' that the message had been composed by the Germans: Red Orchestra pianists never referred to the *Grand Chef* in their messages.[50] But Trepper's assertions that Wenzel was never really 'turned' and that his alleged treachery 'was a crude *Gestapo* manoeuvre designed to discredit a veteran militant and a friend of Ernst Thälmann'[51] were in themselves pieces of disinformation designed to protect Wenzel's reputation. For Trepper's contention is at variance with Wenzel's part in the 'play-back' game, which led to the arrest of a number of Soviet agents and couriers.

In mid-September 1942 a message from the 'Centre' ordered 'Hermann' to instruct an agent to make a rendezvous with a courier at 4.41 p.m. on 17 September at the Potsdamer *U-Bahn* (underground) station in Berlin.[52] That Wenzel was fully complicit in passing this instruction along one of the courier lines linking Brussels with the Reich capital is confirmed by the fact that the *Gestapo* were present on the Potsdamer station when the agent made contact with the courier. The agent in question proved to be *Dr* Hans Heinrich Kummerow, a telecommunications engineer who had run a group of informers which had been providing Moscow with secrets of the German armaments industry since 1932.[53] Amongst the papers which Kummerow handed over to the courier were highly secret drawings of the FX 1400 radio-guided bomb, which was under development at an experimental establishment at Nauen, twenty-five miles north-west of Berlin. The directors of the base were astounded that Kummerow had learned of the existence of the bomb, let alone obtained copies of the highly secret plans; they therefore suspected that Kummerow must have a 'source' inside the establishment. But, despite, an exhaustive investigation, this person, or persons, was never discovered.[54]

Apart from arresting Kummerow's wife, Ingeborg, who had typed her husband's memoranda for Moscow on a specially prepared typewriter which produced a curious blurred effect, the *Gestapo* were also put on the trail of Klara Nemitz, a courier who was acting as a go-between for several Communist resistance groups in the Reich connected with the Red Orchestra. By placing Klara Nemitz under surveillance the *Gestapo* rounded up Wilhelm Guddorf and his mistress Eva-Maria Buch in Berlin on 10 October, who were printing and distributing anti-Nazi leaflets and tracts along with the bi-monthly underground Communist paper *Die Innere Front* (The Home Front), the main organ of Soviet propaganda in Germany. Klara also unwittingly led the *Gestapo* to Bernhard Bastlein, a Comintern functionary operating a resistance group in Hamburg. Bastlein and his agents, along with Wilhelm Fellendorf and Erna Eifler (two German GRU agents who had been trained in Moscow and had parachuted into East Prussia during the night of 16/17 May 1942), were all swept up by the *Gestapo* during mid-October.

From Hamburg the *Gestapo* picked up fresh trails which led back to Berlin – to the radio and photographic business run by Emil and Opa Hübner and their son Max, who turned out false passports from a forgery workshop in the back of their shop. Their business premises was also the principal 'safe house' in Berlin for Soviet secret agents parachuted into the Reich, where they were provided with false passports, money and essential documents. The Hübners were assisted in this work by their married daughter Frieda, her husband Stanislaus Wesolek and their sons Johannes and Walter. All seven were arrested by the *Gestapo* between 18 and 20 October.[55]

Mainly on account of these round-ups Wenzel gained the confidence of the *Gestapo* to the extent that they installed him, under police guard, in a small apartment at 68 Rue de l'Aurore in the Ixelles district of Brussels, not far from the Saint Gilles prison. A former member of the *Gestapo* recalls that

Wenzel's love for his work became a real passion. We treated him reasonably well, and he had a certain amount of freedom, and his relations with the German officers supervising him improved as time went on.[56]

Gaining the *Gestapo*'s confidence paid off, for on one cold morning early in January 1943, when Wenzel's guard turned his back on the prisoner to light a stove, Wenzel pounced on him and knocked him out. Locking the unconscious guard in the apartment, Wenzel dashed down the stairs and out on to the street and quickly disappeared amongst the crowds. Eventually he crossed the border into the Netherlands, where he hid for the remainder of the war.

10. Martyrdom in Breendonk

Not all of the Red Orchestra's transmitters were detected by the long-range radio monitoring stations. Between February and the end of June 1942 a pianist in Paris tapped out over 600 lengthy messages on his Morse key, none of which was intercepted by the Germans. However, during the first week of July the pianist's luck ran out. A radio direction-finder unit of the *Ordnungspolizei* (the regular uniformed German police), under the command of Major Schneider, had set up a post on a farm near Garches to the west of Paris. This unit was engaged in tracking down the short-wave transmitters of the French Resistance, and at the beginning of July Schneider's RDF vans detected a transmitter operating in the suburb of Maisons-Laffitte to the north-west of Paris. When Schneider reported this find to *Kriminalrat* Beumelburg, the head of the *Gestapo* in occupied France, he immediately assigned a squad of secret policemen to the case, under the command of *Kriminalkommissar* Heinrich Reiser.

During the night of 9/10 July 1942 Reiser and his men, packed into two black Mercedes, followed one of Schneider's RDF vans as it patrolled the streets of Maisons-Laffitte. Suddenly the van halted half way along the Grand Avenue. One of the *Ordnungspolizei* jumped out and pointed to two houses on either side of the street. Reiser's men leapt out of their cars and, with revolvers drawn, charged up to the two houses. Reiser forced his way into the house on the left-hand side of the street, terrifying the sleeping occupants but quickly realizing that this was not the target when one of his men on the opposite side of the street yelled 'We've got them!'[57]

The *Gestapo* had overpowered a dark-haired man who had been working his set in the attic of the house. They had also captured a woman who had attempted to escape through the back garden; she was carrying a sheaf of papers which turned out to be a pile of enciphered messages. Handcuffed, the couple were roughly bundled into the Mercedes and driven to the *Gestapo* offices in the Rue de Saussaies (the past and present location of the French *Sûreté*). Both refused to talk, despite being badly beaten up and tortured by submersion in baths of ice-cold water. However, when the *Gestapo* held a gun to the man's head and threatened to blow his brains out unless the woman talked, she revealed that they were Hersch and Myra Sokol.[58]

Hersch was born in Bialystock in 1908. His well-to-do Jewish parents paid for him to study medicine in the Universities of Geneva and Brussels. Shortly before graduating at Brussels he met and eventually married Myra, a Jewish girl born in the Vilna ghetto, who capped an outstanding academic career by obtaining a doctorate in Social Science at Brussels University. Because they were aliens, Hersch was unable to set up a medical practice in Belgium and

Myra could find no suitable openings. He was reduced to earning a living as a travelling salesman in medical supplies, while she became a secretary to a Socialist member of parliament. During 1935 they both joined the Belgian Communist Party, and although their activities were chiefly cultural (lecturing on Marxism) they were expelled from Belgium in 1938 because Belgian law prohibited political activities by aliens. They took refuge in France, and when war was declared Hersch enlisted in the Foreign Legion. He was demobilized after the signing of the armistice.

German-occupied France was no place for two Jewish Communists who were out of work and bereft of funds, and so, in the summer of 1940, they applied for repatriation to Russia at the Soviet Embassy in Paris. Advised by a minor official at the embassy that technicians would have a better chance of being repatriated than a physician and a PhD in social science, Hersch described their occupations as radio repairmen on the application form. With this false declaration they signed their own death warrants, for when General Susloparov, the Soviet Military Attaché in the Paris Embassy, learned that two radio technicians were seeking repatriation he made them a proposition: if they joined the *Grand Chef*'s *apparat* as pianists they would be provided with false papers, accommodation and money. Accepting the offer, the Sokols were set up in a house in Maisons-Laffitte, where they were trained in their clandestine role by an agent operating under the code-name 'Duval'. They did not start transmitting until February 1942, the messages being delivered, already enciphered into the five-figure grouping, by Vera Ackermann, one of the Red Orchestra's cipher experts.

At first Reiser and his men did not realize that Hersch and Myra were GRU agents, because the short-wave transmitter they were using did not have sufficient wattage to broadcast all the way to Moscow. The *Gestapo* were unaware that the Sokols transmitted their messages to the Soviet Embassy in London, which then re-broadcast them to the 'Centre' in Moscow.[59] This led the Germans to conclude that the Sokols were working for the French Resistance, but when the enciphered messages captured with the couple were sent to the cryptanalysts on the Matthäikirchplatz they quickly identified the Sokols' cipher as being identical to that employed by the Red Orchestra. When Giering was informed he had Hersch and Myra transferred from the Fresnes prison in Paris to the Breendonk *Auffanglager*.

The suffering endured by the Sokols in this hell on earth are recorded by Madame Betty Depelsenaire, a Brussels lawyer who was imprisoned in Breendonk from September to December 1942:

They tried every technique of police brutality to make Myra talk. After subjecting her to long days of waiting with her hands handcuffed behind her back, they played the scene of intimidation in the presence of several SS officers to urge Myra one last time to become 'reasonable'. After that several confrontations took place, accompanied by violent slaps. Then the torture began.

The examiner seized Myra as if she were a wild animal, placed his hand over her mouth, and dragged her by the hair. A dark, narrow corridor, whose walls were like the walls of a cave, led to the torture chamber. The room had no windows, and fresh air never reached it. An odour of burned flesh and mildew rose into the nostrils and turned the stomach. The fittings consisted of a table, a footstool, a heavy rope attached to the ceiling by means of a pulley and a telephone communicating directly with the *Gestapo* office in Brussels. The examiner ordered Myra to kneel and bend over a footstool. The whip fell, once, twice. The police realized they would have to be rougher on her. The commandant of the camp, two SS men and police dogs were there to complete the scene. They unfastened the handcuffs, and Myra was made to hold her arms out in front of her. Chains were attached to the handcuffs, tightened a notch, and attached to the rope so that Myra could be hoisted up in little jerks until the tips of her toes were just touching the floor. The blows from the whip rained onto her hanging body. But the whip was not stout enough. They used a club, and finally a heavy cudgel. Myra screamed – it helped – but she did not talk. The enraged examiner, the sweat running down his forehead, decided to raise the rope so that Myra would swing in space. The full weight of her body fell on her wrists, and the edges of the steel handcuffs cut into the flesh. Since Myra did not remain motionless, the weapon had less purchase, and an SS man, at a sign from the examiner, seized her body to keep her trunk in a vertical line; in this way the blows were more effective. Myra lost consciousness. When she came to, she saw that her hands had turned blue. She lifted her face to her enemies again. Their anger was not long in coming. The whole process was repeated. Again she lost consciousness, and the torturer gave up for the day.[60]

Myra was then placed in the 'tortured prisoners' hut. Hersch was already there, having suffered a similar experience. The hut was divided into a number of cells, but the partitions ended about eighteen inches from the ceiling, and although Myra and Hersch were separated by the whole length of the hut they were able to communicate by shouting. If a guard heard them, a beating inevitably followed. Each cell had a drop bench for the prisoner to sleep on, but they were forbidden to sit down during the day, which exhausted the Sokols' remaining strength.[61]

They endured this treatment for four months, but the only secret they betrayed was that the *Grand Chef* used the alias 'Gilbert'. By the time Hersch was dragged into the torture chamber for the last time he weighed only eighty-one pounds; and this spectre of a man died suspended from the ceiling by his wrists while being belaboured with whips and truncheons, his legs being savaged by the commandant's alsatian dog. His remains were interred in an unmarked grave in the former army firing range just outside Brussels – the place where nurse Edith Cavell was shot by the Germans during the First World War. In April 1943 Myra was transferred to a concentration camp in Germany, where she died of starvation, further brutality and the effects of the torture sessions.

11. The Russian Adviser

The *Abwehr* shadowed Abraham Raichmann, 'The Cobbler', for more than two months without result. Then, suddenly, at the end of July 1942, Mathieu, the Belgian Police Inspector, reported to Lieutenant Bödiker, at the *Abwehr* office on the Rue de la Loi, that Raichmann had approached him requesting a blank police identity card for a friend. Bödiker instructed Mathieu to promise the card to Raichmann but first to demand a passport photograph of his friend, using the argument that he could get the card stamped by the relevant authorities if he had such a photograph.[62] A few days later Raichmann not only handed over the photograph but gratuitously informed Mathieu that his friend was the head of a group of Communist agents with whom he, Raichmann, was working.[63]

When Bödiker reported this turn of events to Piepe and Giering they decided to play for a grand slam and set a trap for Raichmann's 'friend'. Mathieu was ordered to persuade Raichmann to send his friend to pick up his card in person, and a meeting was arranged for midday on Thursday 30 July, at the bridge overhanging the Brussels Botanical Gardens, situated at the northern end of the Rue Royale. Piepe recalls that, on the day in question, he

> . . . turned up at the rendezvous along with two car loads of the *Geheime Feldpolizei* [Secret Field Police]. When Mathieu was joined in the middle of the bridge by a tall, lanky, fair-haired man, we stepped in and arrested him just as he was handed the identity card by the Inspector. He made no attempt to escape – not that he had a chance – but he was very indignant! I have listened to some protestations of innocence in my time, but nothing to rival his. We were committing an unspeakable outrage. He was a loyal subject of Finland, whose soldiers were fighting side by side with the Germans against the Russians. He demanded to be allowed to call the Finnish consulate. To calm him down I told him that if he really was a Finn he had nothing to worry about.[64]

The suspect was driven to the *Abwehr* HQ, where he was interrogated by Piepe and Giering. He was carrying papers showing that he was a Finnish student, Eric Jernstroem, from Vasa, who was studying chemistry at the Brussels Polytechnic. He denied vehemently that he was working for the Russians and insisted that Piepe telephone the Finnish Consul-General in Brussels to confirm his story. To Piepe's chagrin the Finnish Consulate confirmed Jernstroem's statement, and a search of his apartment yielded no suspicious clues. 'His disguise was perfect in every detail, down to the last button on his underwear,'[65] except that the alleged Finn could not speak Finnish. When an interpreter was called in he confirmed that Jernstroem could not produce a single fluent sentence in the language. Neither could he explain why he had asked Raichmann to provide him with a false identity card. All pretence ended when Giering had Johann Wenzel brought to the *Abwehr* offices from Breendonk. When confronted with the suspect Wenzel informed the Germans that the alleged Finn was in fact 'Bordo', who had taken over as the head of the Red Orchestra in Belgium after the flight of the *Petit Chef* following the Atrébates raid.[66] Wenzel's statement left 'Bordo' with no alternative but to play the German game. Faced with the choice of torture and eventual execution or remaining unharmed if he collaborated, 'Bordo' opted for the latter.[67]

'Bordo', alias Jernstroem, was in fact a Ukrainian called Konstantin Yefremov, a Soviet Army captain who, after his recruitment into the GRU, had been infiltrated into Belgium via Finland and the United States in 1939. According to Trepper, his achievements in intelligence-gathering were unimpressive:

> It was an amateurish performance bordering on caricature, which consisted of collecting gossip and snippets of information picked up in nightclubs frequented by officers of the German armed forces. Information gained in nightclubs could be useful, but only when it was carefully checked out. Yefremov, however, with the help of snatches of unconfirmed information, would compose long 'syntheses' for the 'Centre' based largely on his own imagination.[68]

For a few days Yefremov tried to temper his statements with caution, and he set the Germans off on false trails. But within a short time a curious change took place, as sometimes happens with arrested spies, and Yefremov went beyond the role of betrayer to the point of actually identifying himself as part of the German counter-espionage *apparat*:

> He saw himself in the role of adviser, showing the clumsy Germans the right way to do things. 'You are wrong,' he would say, 'you must do it another way.'[69]

For their part Piepe and Giering listened, almost enthralled by their new assistant as he led them ever deeper into the Soviet espionage network.[70] To begin with, he betrayed Wenzel's mistress, Germaine Schneider, who operated under the code-names 'Schmetterling' (Butterfly) and 'Odette'. She was promptly arrested by the *Gestapo*, but she insisted that her relationship with *'Le Professeur'* was entirely sentimental and that she knew nothing about his espionage activities. Giering believed her and let her go, whence she quickly disappeared. Only later did the master-detective learn that Germaine was deeply involved with the Red Orchestra. 'Schmetterling' was thirty-nine years old and married to a Swiss national, Franz Schneider, who played a very limited part in his wife's covert activities. She had lived in Brussels since 1920 and for twenty years had worked for the Comintern as a courier and 'cut-out', in addition to allowing militants to use her apartment as a 'safe house'. She was recruited into the Red Orchestra after the outbreak of war, serving as a courier between Belgium and Germany. Indeed, most of the secret information gathered in Berlin had been conveyed to Brussels by this vital cog which Giering had foolishly let slip through his fingers.[71]

Piepe and Giering also questioned Yefremov about the Red Orchestra's radio links with Moscow, learning that the Belgian network had only two short-wave transmitters left. One of these was hidden in Mathieu's garage (it was Yefremov who had instructed Raichmann to find a hiding place for this set), while the other was in the possession of a pianist in Ostend. Yefremov betrayed the location of the latter, and on the strength of this information the Germans arrested Augustin Sesee on 28 August 1942. He was packed off to Breendonk, where he was 'invited' into the torture chamber. Despite being brutally treated, Sesee, like the Sokols, remained steadfast.[72]

After the arrest of Sesee, Yefremov assured the Germans that the Belgian network had no other pianists or transmitters to call on, which, Piepe recalled, 'came as a tremendous relief'.[73] This was only the beginning of Yefremov's treachery, for his subsequent disclosures were to deal fatal blows to the Red Orchestra.

12. The Demise of 'Hilda'

The detection of a Soviet pianist operating somewhere in the Netherlands by the long-range radio monitoring stations during March 1942 was the Germans' first indication that the Red Orchestra's tentacles extended into Holland. Further evidence of the existence of a Dutch circuit was obtained during July. On a moonless night that month the GRU agent William Kruyt, equipped with a short-wave transmitter, was parachuted into Belgium. Kruyt, who was sixty-three, was a Dutch ex-Protestant minister who had converted to Communism. He fled to Russia when the Germans invaded the Low Countries and was recruited into the GRU. He was dispatched to Belgium from Moscow to join the *Grand Chef*'s Belgian circuit, but three days after he landed he was betrayed to the *Gestapo* (by whom is not recorded).[74]

While enduring savage treatment in the *Gestapo* offices in the Avenue Louise, Kruyt managed to swallow a concealed cyanide capsule. The immediate use of a stomach pump saved him, allowing the *Gestapo* to intensify their brutality in an attempt to learn the identity of a second agent who had parachuted from the same aircraft, landing in the area of The Hague. When he refused to talk, the Germans took Kruyt to the morgue at Breendonk and removed the cloth covering the corpse of his companion, who had been killed when he landed on the roof a house after bailing out.[75] Kruyt, exhausted by hardships, torture and the bitter knowledge that he had been betrayed, collapsed: the corpse was that of his son. After letting him attend the funeral, the *Gestapo* returned Kruyt to Breendonk, stood him against a wall and shot him.

What Kruyt had refused to divulge under torture, Yefremov volunteered in his role as 'adviser'. Kruyt's son had been parachuted into Holland to join the 'Hilda' group, as the Dutch circuit of the Red Orchestra was code-named. He also gave the Germans an insight into 'Hilda'. Twice a week, he informed Piepe and Giering, he met couriers in Brussels who provided liaison between the Belgian and Dutch groups.[76]

The Germans trusted Yefremov to the extent that they allowed him to go the habitual meeting point in Brussels, shadowed at a distance by members of the Secret Field Police. On the first occasion none of the couriers turned up, but a second attempt, carried out a few days later (13 August 1942), caused two couriers, who appeared simultaneously at the agreed spot, to walk into the German trap.[77] They were Maurice Peper, code-name 'Wassermann' (Aquarius), and Hermann Isbutsky, code-name 'Lunette'. Isbutsky, born in Antwerp of *émigré* Polish Jews, was an ardent Communist who had been recruited into the Red Orchestra in 1939. He worked as a courier between the Belgian and Dutch circuits, riding miles in the process on his bicycle. He refused to collaborate with the Germans after his arrest and was hideously tortured in Breendonk. In contrast Peper, shaking with fear, declared himself ready to work for the Germans and to lead them to the head of the Dutch group who operated under the code-name 'Tino'.[78]

On the strength of this Piepe, accompanied by 'Wassermann' and three Secret Field Policemen, travelled to Amsterdam. Peper knew of several 'letter-boxes' in Amsterdam but Piepe decided that this would only bag small fry and risk warning the leader of 'Hilda' that the Germans were on his trail. Peper, therefore, went to the apartment where he generally met 'Tino', but he was not there and the *concierge* said that he had been away for several days. Peper, however, left a message for his chief, requesting a meeting at five that afternoon (17 August) in a café which they used as a regular meeting point.

At the appointed time Peper went into the very large and busy café, followed at a distance by Piepe, two Secret Field Policemen and a local *Gestapo* officer. All five men sat at different tables drinking coffee, awaiting the arrival of 'Tino'. When Peper stood up to greet a very tall, powerfully built man, Pipe and his cohorts pounced and handcuffed the giant. He struggled and shouted for help, at which the café exploded in uproar, the customers taking the prisoners' part and blocking the exit of the Germans, who were unable to clear a passage to the door until they drew their revolvers.[79]

The captive, whose enormous girth explained why he was known in the Communist Party as 'The Fat Man', was driven directly to the *Gestapo* offices in Amsterdam. Piepe recalled that

He refused to answer any questions and the *Gestapo* men started beating him. Since I had no authority to stop them I decided to leave. It did not take long for the *Gestapo* to break him and force him to agree to collaborate.[80]

He was Anton Winterinck, a long-serving Dutch Comintern man who had been selected to head the 'Hilda' group by the GRU in 1939. He had soon recruited twelve agents from amongst the local Communists, including the radio operators Daniel Goulooze and Wilhelm Voegeler and the husband-and-wife team Jakob and Hendrika Rillboling, who, along with Peper and Isbutsky, worked as couriers. 'Hilda' began transmitting information to the 'Centre' at the end of 1940, and despite the fact that a continuous flow of messages had been relayed none of the transmissions were detected by the German monitoring stations until sixteen months after they had commenced. Winterinck provided Piepe and the *Gestapo* with enough information to tear the remains of the *Grand Chef*'s Dutch network to pieces. The two Rillbolings were arrested and sent to Breendonk and the short-wave transmitter hidden in Winterinck's apartment was confiscated.[81] Although nine other members of 'Hilda' managed to escape the German net – including Voegeler, Goulooze and 'Tino''s deputy, Johannes Luteraan – the Dutch circuit's links with Moscow had been completely severed.

13. *Coup de Grâce* in Brussels

Shortly after the arrest of Winterinck in Amsterdam Piepe hurried back to Brussels, concerned that the liquidation of 'Hilda' would alert the *Grand Chef* to Yefremov's treachery and that Raichmann might realize the nature of the game that Inspector Mathieu was playing. To delude the *Grand Chef*, Piepe and Giering decided to allow Yefremov to return to his apartment in Brussels and live ostensibly as a free man, although he was constantly in the company of a 'friend' from the plain-clothes *Geheime Feldpolizei*. When Yefremov learned that the *Gestapo* had released Germaine Schneider, he told Piepe that 'Schmetterling' had duped Giering, because she was in fact an important courier who frequently travelled to France and Switzerland on behalf of the *Grand Chef*. A hunt for 'Schmetterling' was immediately mounted, but without success: the 'butterfly' had flown.

Fortunately for the German sleuths, 'The Cobbler' was unaware that Yefremov had been arrested or that Mathieu was in the pay of the *Abwehr*, for he approached the Inspector requesting another identity card, this time for a woman who was on the run from the Germans. He also brought along a photograph of the woman in question. When Mathieu reported this to

Lieutenant Bödiker he alerted Piepe and Giering, who identified the woman in the photograph as the elusive 'Schmetterling'.

In an attempt to repeat the ruse that had bagged Yefremov, Mathieu was instructed to hand over the identity card to 'Schmetterling' in person. Accordingly, on 1 September 1942 Piepe and a car load of Secret Field Policemen turned up at the arranged rendezvous in the Botanical Gardens, but the 'butterfly' did not appear; instead, Raichmann appeared on her behalf.[82] The Germans were not slow to grasp the significance of this: the other side had seen through their game and, as a result, Raichmann and Mathieu had lost their value as voluntary or involuntary baits for the Red agents.[83] Consequently, on the following day (2 September) Raichmann and his mistress, the plump, matronly Czech Malvina Gruber, were arrested and incarcerated in Breendonk.

Although 'The Cobbler' said he would collaborate, he gave so little away during his initial interrogation that two of Giering's principal assistants, *Kriminalobersekretär* Willy Berg and *Kriminaloberassistent* Richard Voss, subjected him to a savage beating. Piepe arrived unannounced during the beating and immediately stopped the maltreatment of Raichmann. The unhappy man's condition distressed Piepe so much that he went out and bought him a bag full of grapes to calm him down.[84] After that Giering agreed that in future Raichmann would only be interrogated in Piepe's presence.

Piepe was undoubtedly a humane man, but his distaste for the *Gestapo*'s methods was not the only motive for treating Raichmann well. Believing that Yefremov could serve no further useful purpose, Giering had thrown him into the Saint Gilles prison, where as a last despairing effort to save his skin he provided Piepe with further information which reinstated Raichmann's importance as a contact man.[85] Yefremov reported that, after taking over the Belgian circuit from the *Petit Chef* following the Atrébates raid, he had been made aware of a firm in Brussels which had contacts with the *Grand Chef*. He had been forbidden to have any contact with the firm, called Simexco, the head office of which was situated at 192 Rue Royale. Piepe could hardly believe his ears: his bogus company office, which he used as a cover for his activities in Brussels, was of course immediately adjacent to the Simexco office. It occurred to him that he must have often passed the *Grand Chef* and his principal agents on the staircase leading up to the two offices on the second floor of number 192:

> We had always raised our hats politely to each other [Piepe recalled]. If you read this sort of thing in a novel, you would say that the author had laid it on too thick.[86] [For almost a year] Soviet espionage and German counter-espionage had shared the same landing, and the truth had never dawned on either.[87]

Piepe had caused enquiries to be made regarding the nature and credentials of Simexco when he had opened his own bogus company office in November

1941, but, as noted, he had been reassured. Now, further investigations carried out by the *Abwehr* on the strength of Yefremov's statement seemed to confirm his earlier impressions: Simexco's shareholders were perfectly innocent Belgian businessmen who were unlikely to be involved in espionage. The only remaining possibility, therefore, was that Soviet agents were making use of the firm in order to maintain courier lines and smuggle money for illegal purposes under cover of normal business activities.[88]

This theory was borne out when Piepe questioned Raichmann and Malvina about the role of Simexco. They informed Piepe that the owner of the firm, the alleged Uruguayan *Señor* Vincent Sierra, was in fact the *Petit Chef* – a Russian agent who operated under the unlikely code-name 'Kent'. In addition Malvina betrayed the fact that, following Piepe's *coup* on the Rue des Atrébates, the *Petit Chef* and his lover Margarete Barcza, a tall, blonde Czech, had fled to France. During the questioning of Malvina the Germans discovered that she too was a prize catch, for she revealed that she was a courier who had crossed the Franco–Swiss border on many occasions, carrying messages to and from a Soviet *apparat* operating in Switzerland.

The final piece of the Simexco jigsaw was provided by the senior German Commissariat officer in Brussels. When asked what he knew about the firm, he told Piepe that the Uruguayan owner had moved to France at the end of 1941 and that the Belgian manager, Nazarin Drailly, was running it in his absence. However, the Commissariat added, the key figure appeared to be another businessman who resided in Paris. He made frequent trips to Brussels – among other things to collect the firm's profits – and was present at meetings between the company's management and the Commissariat. When Piepe produced the two passport photographs discovered in the forger's workshop in 101 Rue des Atrébates and which Rita Arnould had identified as showing the *Grand Chef* and his deputy, the Commissariat confirmed that one of them showed the man whom he knew as *Señor* Vincent Sierra, the owner of Simexco, and the other – that of the *Grand Chef* – the businessman who resided in Paris.[89]

Rather than arrest the entire personnel of Simexco, thereby alerting the *Grand Chef* that they were on his trail, Piepe and Giering placed the firm's employees under surveillance while Group IIIN of the *Abwehr* (the department responsible for eavesdropping on telecommunications) tapped Simexco's telephones. The latter quickly revealed that an extraordinary number of calls and telegrams were being exchanged with Paris, which, along with the other pointers, indicated that the French capital was the centre of the *Grand Chef*'s web. Accordingly, the *Abwehr* and the *Gestapo* girded their loins to descend on Paris, using Abraham Raichmann, who professed to know a number of 'letter-boxes' in the city where he could make contact with the leader of the Red Orchestra as a pathfinder.

14. 'Case Blue'

The Belgian and Dutch circuits of the Red Orchestra were dead, but the value of the information their pianists had relayed to Moscow was such that by November 1942 it had already asserted a decisive influence on the course of the war. The Soviet counter-offensive launched on 5 December 1941 (see Chapter 3) had exhausted itself by the middle of March 1942. Although the Germans were hurled back for distances of between 100 and 200 miles, Hitler's demand that every soldier stand fast and fight with dogged resistance averted a rout, and despite being badly mauled the German front line held. However, the savage, bloody realities of 1941 dented the confidence of the German generals, who began to exhibit marked misgivings about continuing the war with Russia. They even mooted the idea that their dangerously extended forces should withdraw all the way back to the original jumping-off positions in Poland and take up a defensive position, since further offensive operations against the Red Army seemed to be beyond the strength of the *Wehrmacht*.

Hitler would not hear of a withdrawal from the one million square miles of Russian territory that he had conquered at the cost of so much German blood (casualties numbered 1,005,636 by March 1942). However, he had enough sense to realize that to anchor the German forces in their position deep within the Russian interior would invite a war of attrition that ultimately he could not win: refusing to retreat but unable to remain inert, they could only push forward, deeper and deeper into the Russian hinterland, with the aim of wiping out the entire defence potential remaining to the Soviets and to cut them off, as far as possible, from their most important centres of war industry.

The direction of the new offensive was dictated by the Reich's need for sources of crude oil, shortages of which were beginning adversely to affect the mobility of the *Wehrmacht*. As a result Hitler decided that the acquisition of the huge oilfields in the Caucasus would be the ultimate objective of the new offensive – but not the first objective. Just over 300 miles to the east of the German front line lay the huge, sprawling industrial city of Stalingrad. The ideological title deeds inherent in the name – the 'City of Stalin' – exerted a magnetic effect on Hitler's banal, obsessive mode of thought to the extent that the provocative symbolism of the name perverted the nature of his planning: the capture of the city became the first objective in the offensive while the ultimate and most important objective – the securing of the Caucasian oilfields – was deemed to depend firstly on dominating Stalingrad, ostensibly to protect the north-east flank of the drive into the Caucasus from Soviet counter-attack.

In its final form 'Case Blue', as the offensive on the southern wing of the Eastern Front was code-named, called for three consecutively launched, parallel thrusts. The first and most northerly thrust was to capture Voronezh, some 300 miles north-west of Stalingrad, and while the infantry consolidated the north-eastern flank the panzers were to wheel south-eastwards to move rapidly down the west bank of the Don river, rolling up the enemy from north to south to link up with the spearhead of the second (central) parallel thrust in the area of Millerovo, 150 miles west of Stalingrad. The two united thrusts were then to strike out eastwards along the banks of the upper Don to approach Stalingrad from the north-west, to link up with the panzer spearhead of the third and southernmost parallel thrust approaching Stalingrad from the south-west. Only after Stalingrad had been captured was the advance into the Caucasus, the ultimate objective, to be carried out. During the advance of the three thrusts the bulk of the Soviet forces were to be destroyed in a number of encirclement battles.

For the execution of 'Case Blue' Hitler amassed 54 German divisions disposed in five armies (the strongest of which was the 6th Army under General Paulus) and twenty allied divisions (six Hungarian, eight Romanian and six Italian) – in total just over one million men and 1,495 tanks. The new offensive opened on 28 June 1942 and all three thrusts made rapid progress. But it soon became apparent that the Germans were largely punching into thin air, for hardly any of the planned encircling battles, designed to destroy the mass of the Red Army, were realized. For the first time in the war the Russians systematically avoided contact, adopting an elastic, mobile defence, avoiding the German encirclements by surrendering vast tracts of territory in timely and well-planned withdrawals. Convinced that the Russians were in full flight and that the mass retreat was akin to a rout symptomatic of organizational and moral collapse, Hitler committed the cardinal tactical sin of splitting his forces and sending them off in two directions at right angles to each other. Two armies wheeled southwards into the Caucasus to capture the oilfields in the Grozny and Baku areas, one army protected the north-eastern flank along the west bank of the Don and the remaining two armies drove eastwards to capture Stalingrad. In the original plan the drive into the Caucasus was not to be attempted until Stalingrad had been secured. Now both the first and ultimate objectives were to be attained simultaneously.[90] By splitting his forces Hitler was playing directly into Stalin's hands, for the Germans were advancing straight into the jaws of the biggest trap in military history – a trap made possible by the Red Orchestra.

Stalin had expected the German summer offensive to be mounted in the centre of the front line, in an attempt to capture Moscow, and consequently the bulk of the Russian reserves were concentrated behind the lines in this area. However, the first indications that the blow would in fact fall on the southern flank were received in mid-June. During the morning of 19 June Major

Reichel, operations officer of the 23rd Panzer Division, crash-landed in a two-seat Fieseler Storch reconnaissance aircraft behind the Russian Front at Nezhegol, situated on the banks of the River Oskol east of Kharkov. Contrary to Hitler's personal instructions, Reichel was carrying in his briefcase the operational orders of the 40th Panzer Corps, which was part of the northern thrust, and the outlines of the first phase of 'Case Blue'. Both Reichel and his pilot were killed, but Soviet infantrymen who came upon the wreck retrieved Reichel's briefcase with its 1:100,000 scale map and documents.[91]

When the Reichel papers were laid before Stalin, he contemptuously swept them aside in the belief that they were a deception designed to draw Soviet reserves from the Central Front, where Stalin was convinced the real German blow would fall. Fortunately for the Russians the *Grand Chef*'s pianists were able to relay information which established the veracity of the contents of Reichel's briefcase by providing the full details of 'Case Blue', which had been obtained from sources in the German High Command. Apart from the message in 'clear' captured with Wenzel during the Laeken raid, which gave the fullest possible data on the German plans for 'Case Blue', the entire ten pages of Hitler's 'Directive No 41', which set out the strategic intentions of the summer offensive, were transmitted to Moscow by a pianist in the GRU *apparat* operating in Switzerland known as *Die Rote Drei* (The Red Three), better known in the West as the 'Lucy Ring'. This *apparat* was receiving intelligence from sources in the German High Command in Berlin on a continuous basis, often less than twenty-four hours after its daily decisions concerning the Eastern Front were made.[92] During July 1942, the first month of the German summer offensive, scarcely ten hours elapsed between the taking of a decision by the German High Command and the reception of this decision by Moscow.[93] The speed of the transmission of this information enabled Stalin to develop a strategy which ensured that the forces forming the enormous jaws of the trap he was setting were correctly placed.

Two major historians of the war on the Eastern Front, Albert Seaton and John Erickson,[94] have claimed that the collective opinion of the Soviet military authorities, despite the intelligence provided by the Red Orchestra and the Lucy Ring, remained wedded to the conviction that the German offensive would unroll on the Central Front. But these claims may be contrasted with evidence in British archives, which show that the Allied Chiefs of Staff were informed by the Soviet High Command that they expected the summer offensive to come in the south.[95] This latter appreciation is borne out by the Soviet response to 'Case Blue'.

By the beginning of September 1942 the five German, one Italian, one Hungarian and two Romanian armies involved in the offensive had been drawn into a huge 1,500-mile salient, at the centre of which stood Stalingrad.

The struggle to capture this city sucked in the whole of the German 6th Army and 4th Panzer Army, the flanks of which were manned by Romanian divisions of questionable fighting value. By employing the bare minimum of forces necessary to hold the front line in the salient, Stalin was able to husband huge forces in preparation for a counter-offensive designed to encircle the Germans fighting in the fire-blackened ruins of Stalingrad. The trap was sprung on 19 November 1942, when two concentric blows were struck at the Romanian armies holding the line north and south of the city. Employing over a million men, 1,560 tanks, 16,262 field guns and 1,327 aircraft, the Red Army not only wiped out the Romanians but encircled the German 6th Army and the bulk of the 4th Panzer Army in a huge cauldron around Stalingrad. The 269,000 doomed German troops resisted for seventy-two blood-soaked days. Devoid of adequate winter clothing, enduring temperatures of $-35°C$ on a bare, blizzard-swept steppe and with nothing to eat but scraps of bread and watery soup, the doomed Germans suffered an infinity of agonies including frostbite, dysentery and typhus. When Paulus finally surrendered on 2 February 1943, only 91,000 of the original force remained alive to be herded into Siberian prison camps.

In the meantime, commencing on 16 December 1942, Stalin had launched another offensive to the north of the besieged 6th Army which wiped out the Italian 8th Army and the Hungarian 2nd Army and threw the German front line back 250 miles, almost to the jumping-off positions of the summer offensive. These counter-attacks cost the Axis forces half a million dead and an almost equal number of wounded and prisoners, losses which effectively broke the back of the *Wehrmacht* and from which it would never recover. Coupled with the defeat of Rommel's *Afrika Korps* at the battle of El Alamein and the Anglo-American landings in North Africa (both of which occurred in November 1942), Stalingrad marked the great turning point of the Second World War, for the initiative passed out of Hitler's hands for ever.[96]

In the final analysis, the Germans were defeated at Stalingrad by the bravery and tenacity of the Russian foot soldier with his feet frozen in the snows of the steppes.[97] But there can be no doubt that the information provided by the Red Orchestra contributed enormously to the success of the Russian armed forces; and there is certainly no basis for Heinz Höhne's contention that 'the German summer offensive took the Russians completely by surprise', because the 'Soviet High Command had expected the German attack almost anywhere except in the south-west towards the Caucasus'.[98]

Höhne's premise rests on the contents of a message transmitted to Moscow by Makarov, the PTX pianist, on 12 November 1941:

Kent to Director. Source: Choro.
Plan III, directed against the Caucasus and originally scheduled for November, will

be carried out in spring 1942. All troops to be in position 1 May. Whole logistic effort directed to this purpose begins 1 February.

Deployment bases for offensive against Caucasus: Lozovatka–Balakleya–Chuguyev–Belgorod–Achtynka–Krasnograd. Headquarters in Kharkov. Details following.[99]

Höhne points out that when the summer offensive opened in June 1942 the Germans moved forward on a front three times as broad as that reported in the above message, and he cites this example to deprecate the importance of the Red Orchestra's contribution to the Russian victory at Stalingrad. But this particular message was transmitted to Moscow on 12 November 1941, before the Soviet counter-offensive was launched on 5 December, causing the Germans to abandon their planning schedule which envisaged a continuous advance after the fall of Moscow. The fact is that Makarov's message, the source for which was one of Hitler's stenographers,[100] had nothing at all to do with the 'Case Blue' planning, which did not commence until March 1942 and was not finalized until 5 April, when Hitler signed 'Directive No 41'. It was the up-to-date contents of Wenzel's message, which Piepe discovered in the Laeken raid, and the whole of 'Directive No 41' transmitted to Moscow by the Lucy Ring, which superseded Makarov's message of 12 November 1941, that made Stalingrad possible.[101]

15. Moscow's Fatal Blunder

While Piepe and Giering were beginning their investigations in Paris, the *Funkabwehr* cryptanalysts on the Matthäikirchplatz made a decisive breakthrough into the *Grand Chef*'s Berlin circuit. The cryptanalytic section of the *Funkabwehr* was under the command of the mathematician *Dr* Wilhelm Vauck, who had been drafted into the *Funkabwehr* on the outbreak of war with the rank of Lieutenant in the Reserves. Vauck assembled a team of fifteen mathematicians and philologists who were trained in the preparation of comparative tables and probability calculations.

In an attempt to break the five-figure group cipher employed by the Red Orchestra, Vauck's team concentrated on the 120 enciphered messages captured in the Atrébates raid, although some of these messages had been partially burnt when Sophie Poznanska tried to destroy them by throwing them into the fire grate. Despite employing every known mathematical combination and probability calculation, the cryptanalysts were unable to discover the key to Poznanska's enciphering table, and all they succeeded in reconstructing was one word – 'Proctor'.[102] This single word was of little use until Johann Wenzel betrayed the fact that the cipher employed by the Red Orchestra was based on key-words and sentences from works of fiction. 'Proctor', Vauck deduced, was obviously a name in a novel – but which novel? In an attempt to solve this puzzle Captain Karl von Wedel, one of the *Funkabwehr*'s senior codes and cipher evaluation officers, was sent to Brussels to interrogate Rita Arnould in the hope that she would be able to recall what books Sophie Poznanska had used. By this time Rita had been removed from the relative comfort of close arrest in a hotel room to the Saint Gilles prison, but, still frantically trying to save her skin, she racked her brains to provide von Wedel with the information he needed. She was able to recall the titles of five books from amongst the pile that Sophie kept on her desk: four of these were on sale in Belgian bookshops, but the vital proper name – 'Proctor' – did not appear in any of them.

Wedel's last hope lay with the fifth book, *Le Miracle du Professeur Wolmar* by the French author Guy de Teramond, which had been published in 1910. Wedel discovered that this book had never been on general sale but had been issued as a free supplement to subscribers of the Parisian magazine *Le Monde Illustré*. Consequently Wedel travelled to Paris, and, after a month of searching through practically every second-hand bookshop in the city, discovered a copy which, to his relief, contained the vital name.

Armed with a copy of *Le Miracle du Professeur Wolmar*, Vauck's team set to work to decipher the PTX messages. It proved to be painfully slow and laborious work, because each individual message had been based on a different key-word or sentence from the book's 286 pages; to complicate matters, only 97 of the 120 captured messages had been enciphered on fragments of the book, and Vauck's team were not aware that Poznanska had used words from Balzac's *Le Femme de Trente Ans* for the rest.

Nonetheless, the cryptanalysts slowly prised open the Soviet cipher. Although simple in conception, it was extremely difficult to break. It was based on a chequerboard system in which each letter was represented by figures from an upper horizontal column and a left-hand vertical column:

	1	2	3	4	5
1	A	B	C	D	E
2	F	G	H	I/J	K
3	L	M	N	O	P
4	Q	R	S	T	U
5	V	W	X	Y	Z

In this system each letter of the alphabet is represented by the figure from the left-hand vertical column followed by the figure from the upper horizontal column. For example, the word RED would be enciphered into the figures 42 15 14 using this system (R = 42, E = 15, D = 14).

By adding a key-word this simple cipher could be refined into a more complicated form of encipherment. For instance, if the word DIVISION were to be enciphered, this word and the chosen key-word, say SURPRISE, would first be translated into the chequerboard figures and then both sets of figures would be added together to produce the enciphered text:

Plaintext:	D	I	V	I	S	I	O	N
Chequerboard figures:	14	24	51	24	43	24	34	33
Key-word:	S	U	R	P	R	I	S	E
Chequerboard figures:	43	45	42	35	42	24	43	15
Enciphered text:	57	69	93	59	85	48	77	48

Otto Pünter (code-name 'Pakbo'), an agent working for *Die Rote Drei* in Switzerland, explains how further refinements to this basic system produced the almost impenetrable cryptographic maze employed by the Red Orchestra and the Lucy Ring.[103] For example, when transmitting a message to Moscow reporting that the *Waffen SS Division Leibstandarte Adolf Hitler* had arrived in Warsaw, Punter used the book *From Pole to Pole*, by the Swedish explorer Sven Hedin, to obtain his cipher key-word DOKUMENTAR (documentary). Pünter wrote down the key-word and, below it, on two lines, the letters of the alphabet not included in DOKUMENTAR, which were then enclosed in a chequerboard of figures:

	2	7	4	0	5	3	6	9	1	8
4	D	O	K	U	M	E	N	T	A	R
6	B	C	F	G	H	I	J	L	P	Q
1	S	V	W	X	Y	Z				

To encipher his message Pünter reduced the plaintext to the briefest form, 'Hitler Standarte in Warschau' (Hitler Standarte in Warsaw) and translated this into the figures of the chequerboard:

Hitler	=	65 63 49 43 48
Standarte	=	12 49 41 46 42 41 48 49 43
in	=	63 46
Warschau	=	14 41 48 12 67 65 41 40

In a further refinement these figures were then arranged in groups of five:

65634	96943	48124	94146	42414
84943	63461	44148	12676	54140

Pünter then added a further complication by re-enciphering these groups by writing down the whole sentence from Sven Hedin's book which commenced with key-word: 'Documentary films are withheld but will shortly be released again'. This was also translated into figures, but on a system differing from that used for the original encipherment in that the letters were represented by single figures, not the two-figure numbers of the original encipherment, by the simple device of dropping the second figure. Thus A = 1 (instead of 11), Q = 4 (instead of 41), and so on. The resulting figures were also arranged in five-figure groups. Finally Pünter added together the five-figure group of the initial encipherment and the five-figure groups of the re-encipherment, so that the plaintext was enciphered twice over. At the end of the message Pünter added a final 'indicator' group 12085, which meant page 12, line 08, word 5 of *From Pole to Pole*, so that the 'Centre' in Moscow would know where to find the key-word essential to deciphering the message. (The use of Sven Hedin's book and the numerical configuration of Pünter's chequerboard were prearranged with the 'Centre'.) To conceal the all-important 'indicator' group, Pünter added to it, by non-carrying addition, the fourth five-figure group from the beginning of the message and the fourth group from the end.

This method was the standard cipher employed by all the GRU *apparats* in Western Europe during the war, but after the Atrébates and Laeken raids a few adjustments were made in order to improve security. The messages were enciphered three times over instead of twice, and instead of just one 'indicator' group two were used. These were composed by adding the plaintext page-line-word indicator to a fixed five-figure group (69696, for example) and then, to the first enciphered indicator, the sum of the fifth cipher text group from the beginning of the message and, to the second, the sum of the fifth cipher text group from the end of the message. These enciphered indicator groups were then inserted as the third group from the beginning of the message and the third group from the end.[104]

Although relatively simple in its structure, the Soviet cipher proved to be unbreakable by deductive methods. Thus it was that, apart from the 97 messages which Sophie Poznanska had enciphered using key-words from *Le Miracle du Professeur Wolmar*, the thousands of messages transmitted to Moscow by the GRU pianists remained hermetically sealed.

Even though they had a copy of the book from which Sophie had obtained her key-words, Vauck's team only managed to decipher an average of two messages a day, slowly revealing how deep the Red Orchestra had penetrated into the political, economic and military administration of the Third Reich, whose secrets lay exposed to Moscow's gaze. A few of the messages deciphered by the *Funkabwehr* are preserved in the papers of Wilhelm Flick, and they give an indication of the quality and range of information that the Rue des Atrébates cell were relaying to the 'Centre' during November and early December 1941:

Choro to Director. Source: Maria.
Heavy artillery from Königsberg bound for front Moscow area. Heavy coastal batteries dispatched from Pillau same destination.

Choro to Director. Source: Gustav.
Material losses [German] armoured units on Eastern Front equivalent to eleven divisions.

Choro to Director. Source: Arwid.
Hitler ordered capture of Odessa by 15 September. Delaying actions southern end of front seriously upsetting line-up German attack. Information supplied by officer in OKW [German High Command].

Choro to Director. Source: Moritz.
Plan II in force past three weeks. Probable objective is to reach Archangel–Moscow–Astrakhan line by end of November. All troop movements being executed in accordance with this plan.

Choro to Director.
Tanks belonging to propaganda companies delayed in Bryansk since 19 October pending entry of German troops into Moscow originally scheduled 20 October.

Choro to Director. Source: OKW via Arwid.
Eastern Front. Majority of German divisions, sorely taxed by heavy losses sustained, have lost their normal potential. Fully trained soldiers now amount to only small percentage. Reinforcements made up of soldiers with four to six weeks' training.

All the above messages were sent to the Rue des Atrébates via couriers from the Berlin *apparat*. The following were from the French and Belgian circuits:

Source: Suzanne.
Line proposed by High Command for winter quarters to adopted by German Army early November runs Rostov–Isium–Kursk–Orel–Bryansk–Dorogobusch–Novgorod–Leningrad. Hitler had rejected this proposal and ordered sixth attack on Moscow with all available material. Should offensive fail, German troops will temporarily be without material reserves.

Source: Émile.
Two new toxic combinations discovered:
1. Nitrosylfluoride. Formula: HC_2F.
2. Kakodylisocyanide. Formula: $(CH_3)_2ASNC$.

Source: Ninette.
Germans mustering craft in Bulgarian ports for operations in Caucasus.

Source: Berlin.
Some military circles now rule out possibility of total victory in view of failure of Blitzkrieg on Eastern Front. Distinct tendency to influence Hitler toward negotiating with Britain. Influential generals OKW think war will last another thirty months and hope afterwards for compromise peace.

Source: Jacques.
Germans have lost cream of their army on Eastern Front. Superiority of Russian armour undisputed. High Command disheartened by Hitler's continual alteration of strategic plans and objectives.

Source: Paulette.
German officer reports mounting tension between Italian Army and Fascist Party. Serious incidents in Rome and Verona. Military authorities sabotaging Party indoctrination. *Coup d'état* a possibility, though not in immediate future. Germans mustering forces between Munich and Innsbruck for possible intervention.

Source: Maria.
From a German senior officer returning from Berlin. Influential military circles sceptical outcome of war on Eastern Front. Even Göring doubts military victory. German garrisons and depots empty of troops. Speculation in Berlin concerning death of Hitler and subsequent military dictatorship.

Source: Pierre.
Total strength German Army 412 divisions, 21 currently in France, chiefly second-line divisions. Numbers continually dwindling on account of frequent withdrawals. Troops previously in south and vicinity of Bordeaux along Atlantic Wall now heading east. Three divisions involved. Total strength Luftwaffe nearly a million men, including ground staff.

Source: José.
Six miles west of Madrid, a German monitoring station intercepting British, American and French radio communications. Disguised as a business firm trading under the name 'Sturmer'. Spanish Government informed and abetting scheme. One officer and fifteen men in mufti. Branch office in Seville. Direct teleprinter service between Madrid and Berlin, with relay stations in Bordeaux and Paris.

Amongst the pile of messages were a number which had been received from the 'Director' in Moscow addressed to 'Kent', the code-name of the *Petit Chef*:

Director to Kent.
Need report on Swiss Army in relation to possible German invasion of Switzerland. Strength of army in event of general mobilization. Nature of existing fortifications. Quality of munitions. Details of air force, armour and artillery. Technical resources of various armed services.

Director to Kent.
Establish production capacity of German chemical works (poison gas). Report on preparations for sabotage in factories in question.

Director to Kent.
Schneider's sources seem well-informed. Ask him to ascertain total German losses to date. Break down figures by campaigns and separate service branches.

As all of these messages had been either transmitted or received before Piepe launched the raid on the Rue des Atrébates, they were mainly of historical interest. But one of the messages sent to the *Petit Chef* from the 'Centre', which Vauck's team deciphered on 14 July 1942, gave the Germans their first and what proved to be a decisive lead into the Berlin circuit of the Red Orchestra. It was dated 10 October 1941 and read:

KLS from RTX. 1010.1725. wds qbt.
Proceed immediately Berlin three addresses indicated and determine causes failures radio links. If stoppages recur undertake transmissions personally. Efforts of three Berlin groups and transmission information vitally important. Addresses: 19 Altenburger Allee, Neu-Westend, third floor right – Choro; 26a Fredericiastrasse, Charlottenburg, second floor left – Wolf; 18 Kaiserallee, Friedenau, fourth floor left – Bauer. Remind Bauer of a book which he gave to Erdberg as a present not long before the war, and of his play Till Eulenspiegel. Password: Director. Report progress by October 20. New (repeat new) plan in force for three stations. qbt ar.
KLS from RTX.

Incredibly, the 'Centre' had committed an elementary breach of security by sending over the air the addresses of three agents belonging to the Berlin circuit of the Red Orchestra. When the *Gestapo* received a copy of the message from the *Funkabwehr* they were at first sceptical, believing it inconceivable that the GRU was capable of such a blunder. However, by acting on the information regarding the three addresses the *Gestapo* quickly discovered the true identities of 'Choro', 'Wolf' and 'Bauer' – a discovery that doomed a total of 117 agents, informers and couriers of the Berlin *apparat*.

16. Treachery in the *Funkabwehr*

By 16 July 1942, only two days after Vauck's cryptanalysts deciphered the fatal message revealing the addresses of the three Berlin agents, the *Gestapo* had identified 'Choro' as being Lieutenant Harro Schulze-Boysen, a *Luftwaffe* desk officer in the Reich Ministry of Aviation; 'Wolf' was identified as *Dr* Arvid Harnack, an *Oberregierungsrat* (senior civil servant) in the Reich Ministry of

Economics; while 'Bauer' was identified as *Dr* Adam Kuckhoff, an eminent German writer.[105] Apart from their access to highly sensitive information by virtue of their official duties, both Schulze-Boysen and Harnack were prominent members of Berlin society, rubbing shoulders with the highest-ranking members of the German High Command and the Nazi regime – which went a long way to explaining where the Red Orchestra was obtaining its information.

This revelation caused the German security agencies to call a high-level meeting, attended by Admiral Canaris, the head of the *Abwehr*; Major-General von Bentivegni, the head of *Abwehr* Section III (counter-espionage); Lieutenant-Colonel Hans Kopp, head of the *Funkabwehr*; and *SS-Oberführer* Walter Schellenberg, representing the *Gestapo*. During the meeting it was agreed that the *Gestapo* would be solely responsible for dealing with the Red Orchestra agents operating within the Reich, while the *Abwehr*, assisted by the *Gestapo*, would continue to purse the Red agents in the western occupied territories.[106] Accordingly, *SS-Gruppenführer* Heinrich Müller, the head of the *Gestapo*, appointed *Kriminalrat* and *SS-Sturmbannführer* Horst Kopkow,[107] the head of counter-intelligence in *Gestapo* headquarters at No 8 Prinz-Albrecht-Strasse, and his chief assistant, *Kriminalkommissar* and *SS-Untersturmführer* Johann Strübing, to head the investigation into the Berlin network.[108] Both these officers were seasoned experts in anti-Communist matters, having being involved in the campaign to smash the German Communist Party and the Comintern underground in the 1930s.

Kopkow and Strübing decided to proceed slowly and methodically in an attempt to discover all the agents, informers and channels of communication before sweeping them all up in one operation. To this end the telephones of the three identified agents were tapped, their letters were intercepted and read and everyone who made contact with Schulze-Boysen, Harnack and Kuckhoff was placed under surveillance. 'The result astonished even the *Gestapo* experts. Adolf Hitler's guardians of the regime found themselves watching and listening to one of the strangest espionage organizations in history.'[109] To their surprise, the Berlin circuit of the Red Orchestra – that dread spectre – turned out to be easier to dismantle than a suburban Communist Party cell. It soon became apparent to the *Gestapo* sleuths that the *apparat* did not observe the simplest security precautions: meetings were arranged over the telephone and uncoded messages were sent through the regular mail. Consequently the *Gestapo*'s blacklist grew longer every day, and by the end of August 1942 more than fifty suspects were under surveillance.[110]

The *Gestapo*'s campaign of patient observation came to an abrupt end on 30 August. Late in the evening of Saturday 29 August *Dr* Vauck was working alone in his office on the Matthäikirchplatz when, at 9.00 p.m., he heard the telephone ringing on the desk of Corporal Horst Heilmann, one of his cryptanalysts. The ringing of the phone was so persistent that Vauck decided to answer it. When he picked up the receiver he had the shock of his life: 'Schulze-Boysen here. You wished to speak to me?' Vauck was momentarily lost for words, hearing the voice of the man whom the *Gestapo* had identified as the agent working under the code-name 'Choro'. 'I'm sorry . . . I didn't quite hear . . .' Vauck blustered. 'Schulze-Boysen. My maid has just given me your message. I was to call you as soon as possible. What can I do for you?' All Vauck could think of saying was, 'I'm sorry . . . may I ask whether you spell your name with a "y" or an "i"?' 'With a "y",' came the puzzled reply. 'I think I must have the wrong number.' Vauck agreed, and with that Schulze-Boysen hung up.[111]

In consternation Vauck immediately reported what had transpired to the *Gestapo*. Kopkow and Strübing were horrified. If Heilmann, a member of the *Funkabwehr* cryptanalysts, was in league with Schulze-Boysen – and how else could 'Choro' have learned of Heilmann's extension number, which was classified? – then the enemy would have been warned that the *Gestapo* was on their trail. This left Kopkow and Strübing with no choice but to strike immediately, before Schulze-Boysen and his agents could go to ground. As a result, in the morning of Sunday 30 August the black cars of the *Gestapo* snatch squads began roaring through the streets of Berlin. They were just in time, for Heilmann was in the process of warning his co-conspirators.

Horst Heilmann had been a member of the Hitler Youth and an enthusiastic Nazi, but his allegiance changed radically when he made the acquaintance of Harro Schulze-Boysen while he, Horst, was studying languages at Berlin University. A shy, lonely youth of lower middle-class background, he quickly fell under the spell of the charismatic, worldly-wise Schulze-Boysen, who convinced Heilmann that, both intellectually and materially, the only prospect for the future lay with Marxism.[112] The naïve youth was also captivated by the vivacious feminine charms of Schulze-Boysen's attractive and promiscuous wife Libertas, with whom he became close friends.

When Heilmann graduated from University at the tender age of seventeen, Schulze-Boysen pulled strings to have him accepted into the ranks of the *Luftwaffe* Intelligence Service, where he was regarded as a first-class brain, being fluent in French, English and Russian.[113] After basic training he was posted to the *Luftwaffe* Interpreter Unit at Meissen on the outskirts of Dresden, where, being also a highly competent mathematician, he passed an examination in codes and ciphers with distinction. On the outbreak of war Heilmann's expertise came to the notice of *Dr* Vauck, who had him seconded to his cryptanalyst section in the *Funkabwehr*, where, to Schulze-Boysen's delight, he was assigned to 'Section East', which was responsible for deciphering Soviet radio traffic.

Apart from being able to keep his mentor informed on the *Funkabwehr*'s progress in their attempts to decipher the Red Orchestra's intercepted radio messages, Heilmann also became a recruiter of informers for the Schulze-Boysen circuit. An unwitting source was Warrant Officer Alfred Traxl, who worked in the same office as Heilmann and was one of the team selected by Vauck to decipher the 120 messages captured in the Rue des Atrébates raid. It was Traxl who showed Heilmann the deciphered message giving the three Berlin addresses, along with other achievements of his team, 'simply because he loved to tell a good story'.[114]

Traxl showed Heilmann a copy of the fatal message during the afternoon of 29 August. Realizing that Moscow had given the *Gestapo* an open invitation to round up the Berlin *apparat*, Heilmann immediately rang Schulze-Boysen at his private apartment on the Altenburger Allee, to warn him of the danger. Unfortunately Schulze-Boysen and his wife were spending that Saturday yachting on the Wannsee and their maid answered the call. In a state of panic Heilmann gave the maid his office telephone number and asked that Schulze-Boysen call him back the moment he arrived home – a risky proceeding since it was a punishable offence to give the telephone number of a secret agency.[115]

It was in response to this call that Schulze-Boysen telephoned Heilmann's number at 9.00 p.m. that Saturday evening and found himself talking to *Dr* Vauck. Why Heilmann did not go to Schulze-Boysen's apartment in person that evening remains a mystery. Instead, he waited until after lunch on Sunday before making his way to the Altenburger Allee, where he found Libertas Schulze-Boysen at home: Harro had gone to the Ministry of Aviation, blissfully unaware of the danger he was in. When Libertas read the deciphered message she grasped the implications at once and telephoned her husband's office to warn him. But, instead of the well-known tones of her husband, a cold-voiced stranger answered, who announced that Lieutenant Schulze-Boysen had left the Ministry a few hours previously on an official journey which would keep him away from Berlin for a few days: *Frau* Schulze-Boysen was not to worry if he did not appear for a time.[116]

Neither Libertas nor Heilmann were taken in by this: it was obvious to both of them that the *Gestapo* had beaten them to it. In a state of panic they cleared the apartment of incriminating evidence in the form of illegal anti-Nazi pamphlets, notes and other papers, all of which they bundled into a large suitcase which they took to Reva Holsey, an actress with whom Heilmann was friendly and who lived in an apartment at No 8 Hölderlinstrasse, where Heilmann lived with his parents in an apartment on another floor. The actress reluctantly agreed to hide the suitcase for a short time.[117]

Heilmann then began travelling around Berlin to alert as many of the network as possible to the danger, while Libertas went into hiding in the house of Alexander Spoerl, a friend. But escape for Libertas and the rest of the Berlin *apparat* was a hopeless endeavour, for the guardians of Hitler's totalitarian state were watching every exit from the city.

17. Rebel with a Cause

The first to be arrested in the *Gestapo* round-up in Berlin was 33-year-old Lieutenant Harro Schulze-Boysen. At midday on Sunday 30 August 1942 *Kriminalrat* Horst Kopkow entered the office of Colonel Bokelberg, Commandant of the Reich Ministry of Aviation, and explained that Schulze-Boysen was a Soviet agent. The *Gestapo* were not allowed to make arrests on military premises, and Kopkow was obliged to ask Bokelberg to make the arrest himself. Summoned to the Commandant's office, Schulze-Boysen was declared to be under arrest by Bokelberg, who then handed him over to Kopkow.

All over Berlin the arrests of the Red agents passed off equally smoothly, as the *Gestapo* swooped on them silently and unobtrusively. In less than four weeks sixty members of the Berlin *apparat* were apprehended and packed off to the cellars of *Gestapo* headquarters on the Prinz-Albrecht-Strasse. A few, warned of the danger, tried to hide or flee the capital, but they did not remain outside the *Gestapo*'s net for long. On 3 September Libertas Schulze-Boysen was arrested while boarding a train at the Anhalter Railway Station by *Kriminalkommissar* Johann Strübing: she was attempting to reach a friend's house on the Moselle. Two days later Horst Heilmann was arrested when he unwisely returned to his parents' apartment on the Holderlinstrasse.

Dr Arvid Harnack ('Wolf') and his wife Mildred were not tracked down until 7 September, when the *Gestapo* found them in the Fischerdorf Hotel, on the Kurishe Nehrung in East Prussia, where, unaware of the drama unfolding in Berlin, the Harnacks were taking their summer vacation. They were arrested while eating breakfast in the hotel's dining room. Mildred, it was reported, put her hands to her face and moaned, 'The disgrace of it, oh, the disgrace of it!'[118] The last of the three agents mentioned in the deciphered message, Adam Kuckhoff ('Bauer'), remained at large until 16 September, but the details of the place and occasion of his arrest are not mentioned in the *Gestapo* files.

The cells of the Prinz-Albrecht-Strasse were so full that the counter-intelligence section at *Gestapo* headquarters had to ask for reinforcements from other sections to deal with the interrogations. To this end the 'Red Orchestra Special Commission' was formed under the leadership of *Oberregierungsrat* Friedrich Panzinger.[119] It included twenty-five of the *Gestapo*'s most experienced interrogators, who employed every wile and had no compunction in using the most brutal methods to extract confessions from their victims. Harro Schulze-Boysen was interrogated by Johann Strübing, who recalled that

> Initially he denied any connection with foreign agents and also any treasonable activity. Even when shown a photostat copy of the deciphered radio message from Moscow he refused to confess. He stuck to his story that he and his friends had met for private purposes; occasionally they had discussed politics, but he insisted that he knew nothing of any treasonable activities.[120]

Despite these denials, however, it quickly became apparent to the Special Commission interrogators that Schulze-Boysen was the driving force of the Berlin *apparat*.

Harro Schulze-Boysen was a splendid Nordic specimen, 'tall and fair, with blue eyes and chiselled features',[121] who came from an upper-middle-class background. He was born in Kiel on 2 September 1909. His father, Commander Erich Edgar Schulze, was a naval officer who had served as Chief of Staff to the German Naval Commander in Belgium during the First World War and subsequently on the boards of various large industrial concerns. His mother, Marie-Louise Schulze (*née* Boysen) came from a well-known legal family in Flensburg and was a leading light in Kiel's exclusive society. She was related to the Tirpitz family, her mother Olga being a sister of Grand Admiral Alfred von Tirpitz.

From an early age Harro despised the upper-middle-class snobbery and the stifling, trite conventions of the hierarchical society to which his parents belonged and his youthful rebellion against their bourgeois social aspirations hardened into a lifelong, if somewhat confused, anti-establishment fervour. Strangely, for someone who disparaged upper-middle-class conventions, he adopted a pretentious double-barrel name by adding his mother's maiden name to his paternal family name, so that Harro Schulze, as he was identified on his birth certificate, became Harro Schulze-Boysen. The first serious manifestation of his rebellious nature surfaced in 1923, when, at the age of fourteen, he was arrested for taking part in demonstrations against the French occupation authorities in the Ruhr. Five years later, while studying law at Freiburg University, Harro joined the republican *Jungdeutsche Ordenern* (Order of Young Germany), whose aim was to unseat the values of bourgeois society. However, two years later, in 1930, after he had transferred to Berlin University, he lost his taste for the conservative concepts of the *Jungdeutsche Ordenern* and joined a circle of National Revolutionaries in Berlin who disparaged all the existing political parties vying for power in the Weimar Republic. According to Allen Dulles, at this stage Schulze-Boysen

> . . . was opposed to both the Nazis and Communists – the former he considered too bourgeois, the latter too bureaucratic. He concocted a political farrago around the

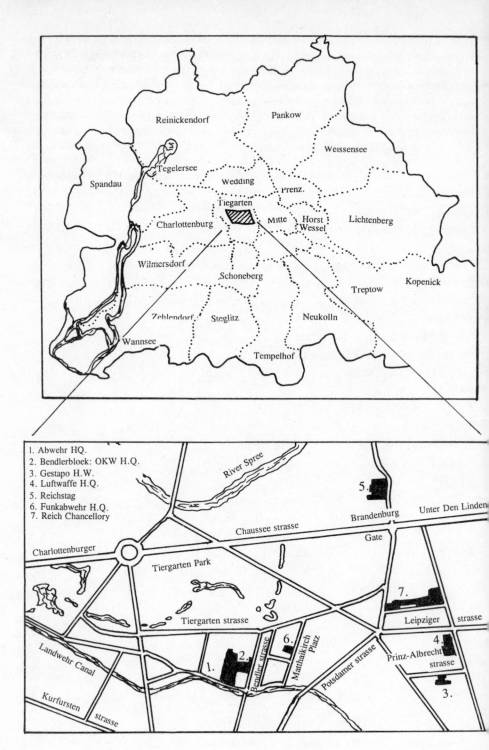

1. Abwehr HQ.
2. Bendlerbloek: OKW H.Q.
3. Gestapo H.W.
4. Luftwaffe H.Q.
5. Reichstag
6. Funkabwehr H.Q.
7. Reich Chancellory

Berlin

idea that there was no Left or Right, that political parties did not form a straight line but an incomplete circle, which did not quite close. The Communists and Nazis, of course, were at the unclosed ends of the circle. Schulze-Boysen decided his party would fill that gap and close the circle. He was young, blonde, Nordic – a product of the German Youth movement. Always wearing a black sweater, he went around with revolutionaries, surrealists and the rag-tag and bobtail of the lost generation.[122]

Shortly after becoming involved with the National Revolutionaries, Harro became the editor of the group's news-sheet, the *Gegner* (Opponent), a 64-page octavo-size periodical with a circulation of 3,000 which was first published in 1931. The *Gegner* soon became the rallying point for the discontented in Germany, attempting to recruit the disaffected from the Right and Left of the political spectrum into a third force and acting against the democrats, the totalitarians and the existing establishment.[123] However, under Schulze-Boysen's editorship the *Gegner* became more and more an anti-Nazi organ, with the result that in April 1933, a few months after Hitler seized power, its brief life came to a sudden and violent end when a squad of SS men broke into the editorial offices at No 1 Schellingstrasse, smashed up the equipment, confiscated all copies of the news-sheet and carted off Schulze-Boysen and his two editorial assistants, Adrien Turel and Henry Erlanger, to one of the 'wildcat concentration camps' on the outskirts of Berlin where the Nazi thugs dealt with their opponents.

Being a Swiss national, Turel was released unharmed, but Schulze-Boysen and Erlanger were subjected to unrestrained sadism. Shortly after they were seized the two men were dragged into the courtyard and forced to run a gauntlet formed by two ranks of SS men, who drove them forward with kicks and blows from lead-weighted whips. Three times Schulze-Boysen was forced to fight his way through the hail of blows. At the end of the third run, naked, gasping and bleeding, he suddenly rushed back uninvited through the gauntlet and, though dazed and on the verge of passing out, managed to stand upright, click his heels and shout, 'Reporting for duty! Order carried out plus one for luck!'[124] This display of reckless bravado, which impressed the SS men, probably saved Schulze-Boysen's life, for his Jewish companion, Erlanger, who collapsed during the third run, took the fury of the Nazi thugs, who beat him to death.

Harro was saved from further sadism by his mother. When she learned through her brother-in-law, the barrister Werner Schulze, that her son had been thrown into a concentration camp she travelled to Berlin from her home in Kiel. With a Party badge on her breast and making use of the fact that she was President of the women's section of the German Colonial Association, which had Nazi affiliations, she presented herself at the office of *Standartenführer* Hans Henze at 29 Potsdamer Strasse, whose SS auxiliary police commando (No 6 *SS Standarte*) were holding Harro. Henze, who had no wish to be responsible for keeping a member of the Tirpitz family in a concentration camp, ordered Schulze-Boysen's immediate release.[125] As the daughter of a lawyer, however, *Frau* Schulze had not yet grasped what the word 'law' meant in Adolf Hitler's Reich, and naïvely she filed a complaint with the police against the SS men for their brutal treatment of her son and the murder of Henry Erlanger. The SS retaliated by seizing Harro again on 30 April and throwing him back into the concentration camp. Indignantly his mother asked Admiral (retired) Magnus von Levetzow, the Berlin Police President to intervene. After a fortnight, when Levetzow persuaded *Frau* Schulze to withdraw her complaint against the SS men of No 6 *Standarte*, Schulze-Boysen was released again.

A few months later Harro bumped into Ernst von Salomon, who had written articles for the *Gegner*. Von Salomon recalled that he barely recognized him. He was very changed: half an ear was missing and his face was scored with scarlet, semi-healed wounds. He said, 'I have put my revenge into cold storage'.[126] This marked the real turning point for Schulze-Boysen. His experience in the camp 'hardened soft clay into a firm and compact entity – a solid mass of hate. He was never to forget his sufferings and humiliation. He was never to forgive.'[127] During this meeting Schulze-Boysen also told von Salomon that he intended to join the military as this profession offered the best protection against the regime's watchdogs.[128] There was nothing unusual in this, as many of the Nazis' enemies took refuge in the faceless mass of the armed forces. So it was that, in the autumn of 1933, Harro joined the Naval Air Service and underwent a twelve-month observer's course, after which he was appointed to serve in the Naval Air Headquarters at Warnemünde.

His promotion prospects were enhanced when he met Libertas Haas-Heye while yachting on the Wannsee during a spell of leave. 'Libs', as she was known to her family and friends, was a granddaughter of *Prinz* Philipp zu Eulenburg und Hertefeld (1847–1921). An attractive blonde, she was a Nazi enthusiast who was in high favour with the dignitaries of the Third Reich. Her mother, Thora Countess zu Eulenburg, who was divorced from Libertas' father, *Professor* Wilhelm Haas-Heye, lived on the family estate at Liebenberg near Berlin and was a neighbour and close friend of *Reichsmarschall* Hermann Göring. Both physically attractive, passionate and volatile people, 'Libs' and Harro fell in love. Although a more unlikely match than an enthusiastic Nazi and an anti-fascist nursing thoughts of revenge against the regime is difficult to conceive of, their romance blossomed and they married on 26 July 1936. Shortly afterwards Göring, who was a witness at the wedding, gave the young bridegroom a job in the Reich Ministry of Aviation – which involved Schulze-Boysen transferring from the Navy to the *Luftwaffe* – where he quickly obtained the rank of Lieutenant. The Haas-Heye connections had enabled Harro to get his foot in the door of one of the regime's centres of power, and, although his job in the Ministry's press office was of minor importance, it gave him the means slowly to penetrate more deeply into the Ministry's secret departments and make influential acquaintances who indiscreetly imparted highly classified information.

During the period after his release from the custody of the SS up to 1937, Schulze-Boysen gradually gathered a group of dissidents around him that was to form the kernel of the Berlin *apparat*. Amongst these were Kurt Schumacher, a sculptor whose abstract art was proscribed by the Nazi art censors, and his wife Elizabeth, who fell into the category of a half-Jewess in Nazi racial theories; and the Communist Walter Küchenmeister, who had been thrown into the Sonnenburg prison when the Nazis took power and released nine months later sick with stomach ulcers and tuberculosis of the lungs, and his female friend *Dr* Elfriede Paul, also a Communist, who had taken Küchenmeister into her home on his release from prison. In 1937 these were joined by Gisela von Poellnitz, a passionate Communist who worked on the staff of the American United Press Agency in Berlin, and Günther Weisenborn, a pacifist and left-wing democrat. This group held regular discussion evenings in their various apartments, but by the spring of 1937 these drawing-room revolutionaries had become tired of mere talk and began looking for some way to take positive action against the hated regime. By this time Libertas, under Harro's charismatic spell, had also turned anti-fascist – at least superficially so – and was ready to back any scheme. They were offered an opportunity on account of German covert operations in support of Franco's Nationalist forces, who were fighting the left-wing Republicans (supported by Moscow) in the Spanish Civil War which had broken out in July 1936.

The secret transport of German volunteers, arms and munitions to Franco's partisans was organized by a special staff set up in the Reich Ministry of Aviation. This enabled Harro to assemble a great deal of information concerning the extent of German involvement and, more importantly, the identity of *Abwehr* agents who had been infiltrated into the International Brigades. All this information was written up into reports which Gisela von Poellnitz pushed through the letter-box of the Soviet Trade Delegation at No 11 Lietzenburgen Strasse in central Berlin. As a result, a number of the undercover *Abwehr* agents were weeded out by the Republicans, stood against a wall and shot. This treachery was nearly Schulze-Boysen's undoing because the *Gestapo* had the Soviet Trade Delegation offices in Berlin under constant surveillance and Gisela von Poellnitz's frequent deposits through the delegation's letter-box did not go unnoticed.[129] She was picked up by the *Gestapo* for questioning, which threw Schulze-Boysen's group into panic. Küchenmeister and Elfriede Paul fled to Holland while Harro, Libertas and Weisenborn prepared to take refuge in Luxembourg. Fortunately Gisela managed to convince her interrogators that the material she had dropped through the Soviet delegation's letter-box was merely requests for information by the United Press Agency and she was released with a warning.[130]

Shaken but undeterred by this narrow escape, Schulze-Boysen's group began drafting a one-page anti-Nazi news-sheet which they called *Der Vortrupp* (The Advance Guard). Schumacher and Küchenmeister wrote the anti-fascist proclamations, which were printed in a rented room in No 2 Waitzstrasse and distributed by the other members of the group. Günther Weisenborn recalled that 'The news-sheets were left in bus shelters, telephone kiosks etc or sent through the post to addresses taken from the Berlin telephone directory.[131]

Gradually Schulze-Boysen's group began to expand, and an increasing number of anti-Nazis were attracted to his discussion evenings and secret propaganda campaign. They included Oda Schottmüller, a dancer and sculptress, who quickly became Harro's lover, and *Dr* Hugo Buschmann, a prominent Berlin businessman.[132] The intrinsic nature of this group was that of underground political resistance, for in the main its members were not convinced Communists, only vague sympathizers. Indeed, even as late as September 1939 Schulze-Boysen knew so little about the most elementary tenets of Communism that he borrowed books on the subject from Buschmann. On 2 September 1939, the day after Hitler invaded Poland, Schulze-Boysen threw a party in his apartment on the Altenburger Allee to celebrate his thirtieth birthday. Buschmann was one of the guests, and his recollections of the party reveal something of the ethos the Schulze-Boysen group:

It was attended by writers, actors, artists, a film producer, doctors, lawyers and a host of attractive women. It wasn't exactly a birthday they were celebrating, but the outbreak of war. What illusions those people had! They were all convinced that the end of the Third Reich was in sight; indeed, most of them thought it was imminent. Only the Luftwaffe officer, whose jaw quivered with hatred whenever the Nazis were mentioned, offered any objection; he didn't want to be a wet blanket; that little upstart Hitler, was bound to be defeated in the end, but it wasn't going to be easy. The speaker was Harro Schulze-Boysen. Then he went on dancing, something he was very good at. The women watched him admiringly. Eventually, he grew tired of all the uproar. He drew me into a corner and, fastening upon a remark of mine, he said: 'Poland is about to go under, but that's only an interlude. It will be the signal for the armies and air forces of the West to destroy one another. Those people,' he went on, with a nod toward his gaily chattering guests, 'overestimate the military strength of the West. In the first place, Britain still needs to arm herself. They have no air force to speak of, either in England or in France. But they have a breathing space until next spring, for the key operations in Poland will take the rest of the year. That lunatic Hitler still thinks he'll make mincemeat of Britain as soon as he has finished off Poland. He imagines he'll then be able to follow the plan of *Mein Kampf* and finally direct his war machine against Russia. No, the British are bound to stand up to him. They can't wriggle out of it by making concessions. One day the odds will be equal. And when that happens the established order of things will be upset from one end of Europe to the other, because the forces of the bourgeoisie will be worn out from fighting each other.'[133]

It was about this time, the autumn of 1939, that this group of idealists underwent a sudden metamorphosis into a spy-ring. The catalyst was the sinister figure of Alexander Erdberg, a GRU recruiting officer.

18. Crossing the Rubicon

It is believed that the tall, thin man who called himself Alexander Erdberg was in fact Alexander Korotkov, a Russian GRU officer who worked under diplomatic cover as a Third Secretary in the Soviet Embassy in Berlin.[134] He had been sent to the Embassy by the 'Centre' during 1935 with orders to form an espionage circuit in Germany.

On his arrival in Berlin Erdberg found an embryonic organization already in existence in the form of a small group of German informers. The principal informer in this group was *Doktor* (of law and philosophy) Arvid Harnack, who worked in the Reich Ministry of Economics. He was the son of the historian Otto Harnack and the nephew of the great German theologian Adolf von Harnack (1851–1930), Arvid himself being regarded as one of the best brains in the German bureaucracy.[135] According to Arvid's cousin, Axel von Harnack,

> Arvid had an ingenious, brooding, meditative mind. He was skilled in debating and always inclined to engage in it. A certain hardness was characteristic of him; moreover, he was inclined to be sarcastic, especially when debating with an intellectually inferior adversary. He was very ambitious, though his self-confidence was based on recognized achievements . . .[136]

Reinhold Schonbrunn recalled that

> [Arvid] was a fanatic, rigid, industrious, conspicuously energetic and efficient. He was not exactly a likeable person, not a jolly good fellow; always serious, he had little sense of humour . . . There was something puritan in this man, something narrow and doctrinaire . . .[137]

Harnack was born in Darmstadt in western Germany on 24 May 1901. In common with many young Germans who graduated from *Gymnasium* in the years immediately after the First World War, he joined the *Freikorps*. These armed paramilitary bands of nationalistic young Germans and unemployed war veterans were led by disgruntled officers of the defeated German Army and were violently anti-Communist. Originally formed to defend the disputed eastern borders of the Reich from the Poles and Balts, they became involved in the 'Kapp' *Putsch* in 1920, which attempted to overthrow the fledgeling Weimar Republic and establish a right-wing dictatorship under the reactionary Prussian politician Wolfgang Kapp.[138]

Shortly after this insurrection had been put down, Harnack grew disgusted with the bully-boy violence of the *Freikorps* and he left his unit in order to pursue an academic career, graduating four years later with honours in legal studies.[139] In 1926 he received a Rockefeller Foundation scholarship and he undertook post-graduate studies at the University of Madison, Wisconsin, where he met and married Mildred Fish, a lecturer in literature at the university. Margaret Boveri recalls that,

> With her fine blonde hair, sternly brushed back at the temples, her clear, direct blue eyes with their level gaze, Mildred embodied for me the very prototype of the American Puritan.[140]

Axel Harnack remembers that

> Mildred had bright eyes and a luminous expression. Her features were framed by blonde sleek hair. Her warm personality made her liked wherever she went. The very least one can say about her is that she was one of nature's aristocrats . . . Her direct, open ways went perfectly with the extreme simplicity of her clothes and her general style of living.[141]

Mildred, who was fluent in German, returned to her husband's native country after he had completed his post-graduate studies at Madison in 1929. A year later he was awarded a doctorate of philosophy at Giessen University, by which time both he and Mildred, after studying the history of Lenin's plan for building a Socialist state in the Soviet Union, had become fervent, if not openly avowed, Communists.[142]

However, in common with many German intellectuals in the decade before Hitler came to power, the Harnacks chose not to wear their Communist political sympathies on their sleeves by openly joining the German Communist Party. Instead Arvid, in conjunction with *Professor* Friedrich Lenz, formed the *Arbeitsgemeinschaft zum Studium der Sowjetrussischen* (Society for the Study of Soviet Planned Economy) – or *'Arplan'* for short – which received active support from the Russian Embassy in Berlin.[143] In January 1933 Sergei Bessonov, the Soviet Embassy Counsellor, arranged a trip to Russia for Harnack and twenty-three other members of *Arplan*. In Moscow they were received by senior Soviet functionaries, amongst them Osip Piatnitsky of the GRU, who induced Arvid to work for the Soviet Secret Service.[144]

Shortly after Harnack and his group returned to Berlin Hitler came to power and *Arplan* was disbanded on the *Gestapo*'s orders. Arvid and Mildred decided to leave Berlin for a while, to escape the attentions of the Nazis. However, after spending a year in Jena they returned to Berlin, where Arvid obtained a job in the foreign currency department of the Reich Ministry of Economics. This provided a perfect cover for his espionage activities, allowing him access to highly secret economic information which he passed on to his Soviet masters. To give further credence to his cover Harnack joined the Nazi Party on 8 July 1937, and soon afterwards was elected to the *'Herren Klub'*, an exclusive professional circle of prominent German manufacturers, aristocrats, bureaucrats and high-ranking officers from the Army, Navy and Air Force, many of whom became valuable sources of intelligence. Amongst these was Baron Wohlzogen-Neuhaus (cover-name 'Griechisch'), a senior representative in the technical department of the *Oberkommando der Wehrmacht*; Hans Rupp (cover-name 'Turke'), a leading accountant of I. G. Farben Industries; Tizien (cover-name 'Albanisch'), an *émigré* White Russian manufacturer with high-level contacts in the *Oberkommando der Wehrmacht*; and Harnack's step-nephew, Wolfgang Havemann (cover-name 'Italiener'), a naval intelligence officer in the *Oberkommando der Kriegsmarine* (Navy High Command).[145]

Outwardly Arvid and Mildred gave the impression of being a loyal Nazi couple, the success of their cover being confirmed by a Soviet agent in Berlin who sent the following report to the 'Centre':

> She is bold, tall, [with] blue eyes, large figure, typically German-looking, [although] a lower-middle-class American, intelligent, sensitive, loyal, very much the German *Frau*, an intensely Nordic type and very useful. He comes from a good family, German theologian and philosophy background, middle-class, well-educated, of a well-to-do family. He is also blond, blue-eyed (wears glasses), of medium height, stocky and when last seen very Nordic looking. They were intensely cautious in their technique of making contact, diplomatic in the extreme with other people, giving every impression of being highly trained and disciplined. Both of them maintain good contacts with Nazi women and men. Arvid is not suspected and has an important post in the Ministry. I am sure that, unless I have been profoundly deceived, they are completely reliable and trusted people from our point of view.[146]

Through his efficiency and zeal in his work at the Reich Ministry of Economics Arvid quickly worked his way up to the rank of *Oberregierungsrat* (Senior Government Counsellor), which gave him access to all the documentation and reports pertaining to the foreign trade of the Third Reich.[147]

The value of the information that Harnack passed on to Moscow before the outbreak of war can be judged from a contemporary summary of the information received by the 'Centre' up to June 1938:

> Valuable documentary materials on the German currency and economy, secret summary tables of all Germany's investments abroad, the German foreign debt. Secret lists of goods liable to importation into Germany. Germany's secret trade agreements with Poland, Baltic countries, Persia and others. Valuable materials concerning the secret foreign service of the German Ministry of Propaganda. The foreign policy department of the Party and other organizations. Also documentation

concerning the currency financing of the different German intelligence services, etc . . .[148]

Harnack passed his reports to Greta Lorke, an employee of the Nazi Racio-Political Office, who acted as a 'cut-out' between Harnack and the GRU couriers.[149] Greta's contact on the Berlin end of the courier line was Johannes Sieg, who passed the reports on to a Communist cell in Leipzig which then relayed them to Moscow. Sieg was also the courier for a number of other informers and contacts in Berlin, amongst whom was the writer *Dr* Adam Kuckhoff, the leader of an anti-fascist circle called Creative Intelligentsia, which included in its ranks Karl Goerdeler, the former mayor of Leipzig, Adolf Grimme, a leading Social Democrat, and *Graf* Wolf von Helldorf, the Berlin Police President.[150] It quickly became apparent to Sieg, however, that Kuckhoff understood little of the rules of conspiratorial work, and to rectify matters he introduced him to Greta Lorke. Apart from teaching Kuckhoff the ropes, Greta became emotionally attached to the writer and they eventually married, after which they began holding instructional evenings in their Berlin apartment, 'discussing, *inter alia*, Marxist doctrine and the theory of National-Socialism, so as to better oppose the Nazi regime.'[151] Regular attendants at these meetings, amongst a number of anti-fascists, included Sieg and the two Harnacks.

The informers for whom Johann Sieg was working as a courier were, in addition to Harnack, mainly industrialists, so the information he was relaying to Moscow was primarily economic. Important though this was, the GRU also needed intelligence on every aspect of the German armed forces. Fortunately for Erdberg, the reports pushed through the letter-box of the Soviet Trade Delegation by Gisela von Poellnitz gave the GRU recruiting officer a lead as to where he could obtain this kind of information. By keeping Poellnitz under surveillance Erdberg was able to identify Harro Schulze-Boysen as the source of the information delivered to the Trade Delegation offices, and he instructed Greta Kuckhoff (*née* Lorke) to make contact. Proceeding cautiously, Greta decided to bring about a meeting through an anti-Nazi lawyer, *Dr* Herbert Engelsing, who attended the instruction evenings at her apartment. Engelsing was also a producer for the Tobis film company, and, learning that Libertas Schulze-Boysen had begun working as a script-writer for the Reich Propaganda Ministry's Film Centre, he invited her and her husband to a party in his apartment in the Grünewald in south-west Berlin, ostensibly to discuss matters relating to film-making.[152] This occurred in the summer of 1939, and after the Kuckhoffs and the Schulze-Boysens had found common ground in their anti-Nazi fervour the circle was joined by the Harnacks, who in turn introduced their master – Alexander Erdberg.[153] The meeting between Schulze-Boysen and Erdberg occurred on Thursday 28 March 1940, and three days later Erdberg reported to Moscow that

[Schulze-Boysen] realizes perfectly well that he is dealing with a representative of the Soviet Union and not the [German Communist] Party. He gives the impression that he is fully prepared to tell me everything he knows. He answered my questions without an evasion or intention of concealing anything. Moreover, he had prepared for the meeting and had put down on a piece of paper certain points to pass over us.[154]

Thus it was that Schulze-Boysen, the 'drawing-room revolutionary' crossed the Rubicon, becoming an agent for the GRU.

19. A Confusion of Aims

Arvid Harnack was not very enthusiastic about the liaison among his group, which by 1940 numbered sixty strategically placed informers, and Schulze-Boysen's circle. Harnack, a convinced Communist who insisted on rigid discipline in both his espionage activities and his public life, recoiled from the buccaneer, impulsive and reckless Schulze-Boysen, who seemed to be little more than an immature nihilist leading an exotic private life in which both he and Libertas indulged in numerous love affairs. This the Harnacks and Kuckhoffs regarded as a crime against Moscow's rules of *konspiratsia* (conspiracy), while other members of their group thought that Schulze-Boysen was playing fast and loose with the rules, causing them to recoil from working with this 'drawing-room Communist'. Greta Kuckhoff stated that her husband recognized at once that 'Schu-Boy' (as he was commonly referred to by his associates) needed some discipline.[155] Hugo Buschmann recalled that

I longed to teach Harro discretion. He was terribly indiscreet. At that time it was smart, in fashionable quarters of Berlin, to tell what were known as political stories. Harro couldn't refrain from joining in. He would sit there in his Luftwaffe uniform . . . and cause an absolute sensation by making wild disclosures about the Ministry, about the various theatres of operations, about prisoners being executed, and so on. Those elegant ladies and talkative gentlemen used to prattle away until dawn; but afterwards the women never forgot to mention this radiant officer who was a god to every one of them. They did not know how dangerous it was to have dealings with him.[156]

While Harnack's group was concerned purely with espionage and stuck to the conspiratorial rules, Schulze-Boysen's circle was primarily a resistance group which also indulged in espionage, and the confusion of the two tasks added greatly to the danger of detection. For instance, Schulze-Boysen continued to be involved in the printing and distribution of anti-Nazi leaflets, posters and clandestine news-sheets, through which he hoped to change the political outlook of the German population by 'making them aware of their vital interests, by directing their thoughts to the future and to bring their attention to the hopelessness of the military situation.'[157]

The leaflets and posters were printed and duplicated in a room at No 2 Waitzstrasse by Heinz Strelow and his girlfriend Cato Bontjes van Beek, a dealer in ceramics. Schulze-Boysen generally decided on the contents of the leaflets and posters,[158] and he frequently included secret information from his office, for example the 'production capacity of the United States aircraft industry and expositions on Russian strategy'.[159] A flood of this propaganda literature was distributed all over Berlin by members of Schulze-Boysen's group, every headline announcing that the war was lost and that Hitler must be brought down before the Reich was ruined. They carried titles like 'Who Made War Inevitable?', 'Summons to Resist' and 'Why the War is Lost'. One, entitled 'Napoleon Bonaparte', described the ordeals of the German forces in Russia and foretold the fate in store for them, with supporting quotations from histories dealing with the defeat of the *Grand Armée* in 1812.

A more dramatic enterprise occurred in May 1942 in response to Goebbels' 'Soviet Paradise' exhibition in Berlin's Lustgarten, which was designed to show the German public 'startling' evidence concerning the poverty of the Russian people. Moscow ordered a small Communist resistance group under Herbert Baum, which had no connection with the Schulze-Boysen/Harnack *apparat*, to set fire to this anti-Soviet exhibition. Baum asked Schulze-Boysen for help, and Harro declared himself ready to co-operate. He set about producing posters which read, 'The Nazi Paradise – War – Starvation – Lies – Gestapo. How Much Longer?'[160] During the night of 17/18 May 1942 sixty members of Schulze-Boysen's group took to the streets to paste these posters on walls and hoardings all over the city. Hardly any of them thought the operation advisable, but Harro would brook no opposition. So determined was he that he drove his friends ahead of him with his revolver. The *Gestapo* report reads that, 'As an indication of his fanaticism – when some of his group wanted to stop, he threatened them with a loaded service revolver.'[161]

The apprehension of Schulze-Boysen's associates increased alarmingly when Baum's entire group was arrested by the *Gestapo* a few days later, after being denounced by an *agent provocateur* (they had set fire to the exhibition while Schulze-Boysen's group were pasting up their posters). Fortunately they did not betray Schulze-Boysen's group, but the entire *apparat* was on tenterhooks until all of Baum's group were finally executed.

As a result of this scare, Cato Bontjes van Beek and Strelow broke off contact with Schulze-Boysen, because they feared that this crazy gambler would eventually drive them into the arms of the *Gestapo*. The wary and secretive Harnack begged him to desist from such dangerous escapades, while Hugo Buschmann remonstrated that

Propaganda must be kept in a separate compartment from the all-important work of espionage. Experience proved that such propaganda was always discovered in the end. It would be terrible if far more vital tasks were jeopardized in this way. Harro would make promises, but he was never able to keep them. He persevered with both activities until the very end.[162]

Gilles Perrault believes that

Perhaps Schulze-Boysen felt he could perform his awesome task only if he was surrounded by the generosity and enthusiasm of pure-heartedness of those who were prepared to risk their lives for very modest results. Or perhaps, as he hammered away mercilessly at what seemed to him the monstrous features of his own country, he welcomed these paltry scraps of evidence – a leaflet here, a pamphlet there – as proof that he too was helping to fashion a new face for Germany.[163]

Wariness of Schulze-Boysen's recklessness, and indeed that of the *apparat* as a whole, was the reason why another member of his group, Ernst von Salomon, decided to sever contact, although it was his girlfriend, a Jewess called Ille, who pointed out the dangers. Von Salomon recalls that

During the spring of 1941 Harro invited Ille and myself to come with him to see a friend, a certain *Herr* Harnack, a close relative of the celebrated theologian the late Adolf Harnack. I had met *Herr* Harnack and his wife at both the Russian and the American Embassies. She was an American by birth and called herself Harnack-Fish. The young couple had an assured place in diplomatic circles. The Harnacks lived in a large, well-furnished apartment near the Halle Gate in Berlin. Ille and I went there, stayed for an hour, and then left. It was a bad habit of Ille's and mine to discuss any gathering we had attended as soon as we had left, if possible the moment the door of our host's apartment had closed behind us, at the latest as soon as we reached the street. On this occasion Ille began as soon as we were out of the apartment. 'I like that!' she said. 'There they stand, leaning against the mantelpiece, with a cup of tea in their hand, quite casually discussing things . . . things – well, any one of the things they discuss could cost them their heads.'

I said nothing. She behaved in exactly this way on our way home. Ille said: 'It sounds all wrong to me. I feel there's something very, very wrong. And I can trust my feelings, I think.' Then she said, with intensity: 'Promise me this! Promise we'll never go there again! I don't want to have my head cut off just casually. I don't want it.'

I said nothing and was glad Ille felt that way. If only she always thought so! She went on: 'I like that! They stand about there, well-dressed, decent-looking people and they talk about "cross channels of communication" – do you know what that means?'

I did, but I said nothing. Ille said: 'They describe Hitler and Himmler and Rosenburg and Frick as utter fools, and they tell me – me who has never even met any of them before except the Harnacks and the Schulze-Boysens, they tell me—'

Ille broke off in the middle of her sentence. Then, stirring an imaginary cup of tea, she said: 'They say to me, "Do you know, dear lady, I have heard from an absolutely sure source, because you see I have a direct link with Zürich . . . of course we exchange our information." And then,' said Ille, 'he suddenly catches sight of another man and says, "Excuse me for a moment, dear lady," and gives the other man a yellow envelope saying "Strictly confidential" and winks . . . And there I sit on the sofa and can hardly breathe. So I ask who the decent-looking old man is and who is the one he spoke to, and they tell me that one's a ministerial counsellor and the other's an adjutant, and that one over there is in the SS and this one here is a diplomat . . . now tell me, can you understand it all?'

I replied: 'Yes, that's the way it is. Now let's be getting home.'[164]

By trusting Ille's feelings and keeping his promise never to approach the Schulze-Boysens and Harnacks again, von Salomon escaped the scaffold.

Despite these defections, a constant flow of new members, Communists and anti-fascists, continued to swell the *apparat*'s ranks, amongst them Hans Coppi, a factory technician who had served a year's imprisonment for distributing cigarette cards with anti-fascist inscriptions and who, under the cover-name 'Strahlmann', became the *apparat*'s short-wave radio operator.[165] In 1941 Schulze-Boysen also came into contact with a large group of anti-fascist students. The leading light of this group was *Dr* John Rittmeister, Professor of psychotherapy at the Berlin Institute for Psychological Research and Psychotherapy. Rittmeister collected around him a circle of students who attended his apartment during the evenings for discussions on political matters. These too joined in Schulze-Boysen's leaflet and poster campaign, as a practical way of opposing the regime.

The Schulze-Boysen/Harnack group was still expanding when the day of decision suddenly came upon them, announced by Hitler's invasion of the Soviet Union on 22 June 1941. The invasion came as no surprise to the *apparat*. As early as 26 September 1940 Harnack had reported that Hitler was making preparations for an attack on Russia:

> An officer of the supreme command of Germany (OKW) has told [Harnack] that by the beginning of next year Germany will be ready for war with the Soviet Union. A preliminary step will be the military occupation of Rumania, which is planned for the near future. The objective of the campaign will be to occupy western European Russia along the Leningrad–Black Sea line and the creation on this territory of a German vassal state. The remainder of the USSR is to be constituted into a state which is friendly towards Germany. At a conference of the Economic Warfare Committee, its chairman, Rear-Admiral Gross, dropped hints that the general operations against England are being postponed.[166]

During the six months leading up to the invasion the Berlin *apparat* constantly warned the 'Centre' of German intentions, as a selection of the reports sent to Moscow illustrates:

> In *Herren Klub* circles the informed opinion is that Germany will lose the war [on the Western Front] and, in light of this, it is necessary to come to terms with Britain . . . in order to turn the military forces against the East. [January 1941]

> In the German Air Force General Staff an order has been issued to commence reconnaissance flights above Soviet territory on a large scale with the object of

photographing all the frontier [defence] lines. Leningrad is also included in the area of these reconnaissance missions. [January 1941]

The quartermaster departments of the Imperial Statisticians Directorate has received from OKW the order to compile maps of the industry of the USSR. [January 1941]

The practicality of anti-Soviet operational plans is being intensively discussed by the German leadership. Confirmation of this is the concentration of German troops on the eastern frontier. [March 1941]

Operations of the German Air Force in aerial photography of Soviet territory are in full swing. German aircraft are flying from airfields in Bucharest [and] Königsberg and from Kirkenes in northern Norway. Pictures are taken from a height of 6,000 metres. Kronstadt has been particularly well photographed by the Germans. [March 1941]

The question of a military attack against the USSR in the spring of this year has been decided on the basis that the Russians will not be able to burn the still-green wheat and the Germans could benefit from this harvest. Zechlin [a professor of the *Politische Hochschule* in Berlin and a member of Harnack's circle] has learned from two German Field Marshals that the attack is planned for the first day of May. [March 1941]

According to the German General Staff the Red Army will only be able to put up resistance during the first eight days, after which it will be smashed. [March 1941]

The attack on the Soviet Union is dictated by Germany's present military advantage over the USSR. When calculating the effectiveness of the anti-Soviet campaign, particular attention is being paid to the importance of the oilfield in Galicia. [March 1941]

Besides the occupation troops, the only active division [of the German Army] is presently in Belgium, which is further confirmation that combat action against the British Isles has been postponed. The German troops are concentrating in the east and south-east. [March 1941]

The preparation for a blow against the USSR has become self-evident. The location of the concentration of the German forces along the borders of the USSR confirm it. The Germans are paying particular attention to the railway line from Lvov to Odessa, which has a western European [gauge] track. [March 1941]

The German Air Force General Staff is carrying out intensive preparations for action against the USSR. Plans for bombing the most important objectives are being drawn up. The plans for raiding Leningrad, Vyborg and Kiev have just been completed. Photographs of cities and industrial targets are being regularly processed by the Luftwaffe staff. The German Air Attaché in Moscow scouts the location of the Soviet electric power stations personally in his car by driving around the areas where the generating stations are located. [March 1941]

The German Air Force General Staff has completed preparations for the air attack plan against the Soviet Union. The *Luftwaffe* is to concentrate its attack on railroad junctions in the central and western part of the USSR, on the electric power stations in the Donetsk coalfields, on aviation factories in Moscow. The airfields near Cracow are the geographic departure points for the attack on the USSR. [April 1941]

Rosenberg's expert on the USSR, Liebrandt, has advised Zechlin that the question of a military attack against the Soviet Union has been settled. Germany's total war with England . . . cannot be won. That is why a peace treaty with [England] is necessary. In order to make England more compliant, it is necessary to occupy the Ukraine. This occupation of the Ukraine will force England to make concessions. [April 1941]

It is necessary to warn Moscow seriously that the question of an attack on the Soviet Union is a settled one. The attack is planned for the immediate future. In the German Air Force General Staff, the preparations for operations against the USSR are being carried out at great speed. In conversations with staff officers, May 20 is often cited as the date for the beginning of the war. Others predict that the attack is planned for June. [May 1941]

In spite of the Soviet Government's protest note, German aircraft continue to make flights over Soviet territory on photo-reconnaissance missions. Now the photography is conducted from the height of 11,000 metres and the flights themselves are conducted with great caution. [May 1941]

All preparatory military measures including plans of Soviet airfield locations and the concentration of German air forces in the Balkan airfields are to be completed by the middle of June. [June 1941]

The commanders of [German] air bases in Poland and East Prussia have received orders to prepare to receive their aircraft. A large airfield in Instabruck [in East Prussia] is being hastily equipped. [June 1941]

The appointment of the chiefs of the quartermasters' directorate of the future districts of the occupied territory of the USSR have been made. In the Caucasus it is to be Amonn, one of the senior Nazi Party officials in Düsseldorf; in Kiev, Burandt, a former official of the Ministry of the Economy; in Moscow, Burger, the chief of the Economic Chamber [of Commerce] in Stuttgart. Schlotter, the head of the Foreign Department of the Ministry of the Economy, has been designated as General Director of the Economic Management of the occupied USSR. [June 1941]

Similar warnings were passed by the Red Orchestra circuits in Western Europe, and by the *Die Rote Drei* circuit in Switzerland. However, Stalin, despite all the evidence to the contrary, refused to heed the omens that showed a German attack to be not only inevitable but also imminent, and he refrained from mobilizing sufficient strength to prevent the *Wehrmacht* from scoring its great initial victories.

As it was impossible for the Berlin *apparat* to pass their reports on to Moscow via the courier lines after the German invasion, it was imperative that they be provided with short-range transmitters. Accordingly, shortly after the invasion began, Alexander Erdberg arranged secret meetings to hand over the required sets, each concealed in a suitcase. He handed over one to Adam and Greta Kuckhoff at an underground station and another to Schulze-Boysen at a tram stop.[167] Hans Coppi also received a transmitter, along with a radio traffic schedule giving the times, wavelengths and call-signs with which to make contact with the 'Centre' in Moscow. Silently the Germans took over their sets and silently they went on their way, while Erdberg disappeared into the shadows.

20. Choro Calling Moscow

As a precaution against being tracked down by the *Funkabwehr* short-range direction-finder squads, the three short-wave transmitters provided by Alexander Erdberg where housed in three different apartments, one with Adam and Greta Kuckhoff, one with Arvid and Mildred Harnack and the third with Kurt and Elizabeth Schumacher.[168] Each set was used at irregular intervals by Hans Coppi, who had received some basic, and as it turned out inadequate, training. He did his best, but his best was not very good. To begin with he burnt out one of the sets when he plugged it into a direct current socket; the transmitter was constructed for use only with an alternating current. The fuses were blown and other parts of the set were damaged. Replacement parts were difficult to obtain, and in the end the *apparat* had to employ Helmut Marquardt, a 17-year-old amateur radio ham, to repair the set.[169] Further difficulties arose when Coppi misinterpreted Moscow's traffic schedule. He could not understand when he was supposed to send and when to receive, and he was constantly mixing up the times, frequencies and call-signs laid down by the GRU.

The complicated instructions handed over by Erdberg would have been ideal for a virtuoso radio-operator, but they far exceeded the capabilities of Hans Coppi. The instructions required him to change his call-sign and wavelength after a certain number of 'effective communications' in accordance with a pre-arranged rhythm. This was a basic security precaution designed to baffle the German direction-finder squads. By 'effective communication' Moscow meant a radio contact in the course of which information was passed on; but Coppi interpreted the phrase to mean that any radio contact was an 'effective communication', even if it merely cleared up some technical detail. The consequence of this misunderstanding was that Moscow stayed tuned to a particular wavelength while Coppi vainly put out call-signs on a different wavelength.

After much wasted time and confusion Moscow transmitted a new set of instructions which required Coppi to employ six wavelengths and thirty different call-signs in which the first six 'effective communications' were to be made on different wavelengths, after which (for the seventh) he was to return to the wavelength he had employed for the first 'effective communication' – and so on. The same system governed the use of the call-signs; and since changes in the latter followed a separate time pattern, it would doom the *Funkabwehr* to permanent bafflement. In the event, however, it was Coppi who became baffled. He had been supplied with a list of thirty call-signs, but, as certain months of the year have thirty-one days, Moscow intended (but Coppi did not comprehend) that no transmission was to made on the thirty-first day, so as not to disturb the thirty-call-sign-and-wavelength rhythm. The upshot was that on 31 July 1941 Coppi reverted to the first call-sign on the list, and when Moscow tuned in again on 1 August they were unable to make contact because Coppi was vainly putting out calls on a completely different wavelength.[170]

Contact was re-established and then lost again with such alarming regularity that in the end the Director, General Ivan Peresypkin, lost his temper and threw caution to the wind. The result was the fatal message sent to 'Kent', the head of the Brussels *apparat*:

> Proceed immediately Berlin three addresses indicated and determine causes failures radio links... Addresses: 19 Altenburger Allee, Neu-Westend... [Schulze-Boysen's address]; 26a Fredericiastrasse, Charlottenburg . . . [Harnack's address]; 18 Kaiserallee, Friedenau . . . [Kuckhoff's address] . . .'[171]

Three days later the Berlin *apparat* was alerted to 'Kent''s imminent arrival by the following message, which Coppi received during the night of 13/14 October 1941:

> RSK from BTR. 1310.1425.54 wds qbt.
> From Director to Freddy for Wolf who will pass on to Choro. Kent arriving from BRX. Responsible for re-establishing radio traffic. In event of failure or further stoppage all material to be conveyed to Kent for transmission. Held-up material to be handed to him.[172]

'Kent', the cover-name of the *Petit Chef* of the Red Orchestra, arrived in Berlin on 15 October and rendezvoused with Schulze-Boysen in the Zoo. Harro explained the difficulties Coppi was experiencing, with the result that 'Kent' put him in touch with Walter Husemann, an elderly Communist militant who had been trained in radio telegraphy in Moscow in the 1920s. He quickly taught Coppi the ropes, but to no avail. By this time the *Funkabwehr* radio-detection squads had narrowed the search down to within a small radius of all three locations from which Coppi was making his transmissions (see Chapter 1). They were poised to strike when Fate took a hand.

In the evening of 22 October 1941, while walking to the Schumachers' apartment, from where he intended to make his nightly transmission, Coppi passed a post office canvas street shelter in which a team of men dressed in post office overalls were working. As he drew level with the tent Coppi heard one of the men say, *'Jawohl, Herr Leutnant!'* Suspicious, he paused to light a cigarette. Coppi then heard the characteristic whistle of a receiver being tuned across the wavelengths. Walking briskly away, he made his way to Schulze-Boysen's apartment to report that the *Funkabwehr* had closed in on the Schumachers' apartment. Harro immediately ordered that transmissions cease forthwith, and thereafter, for a period of five months, all the secret information gathered by the Berlin *apparat* was relayed by couriers to the *Grand Chef*'s pianists in France, Belgium and Holland for transmission to Moscow.

It was not until February 1942 that Coppi began transmitting again, but his transmissions were sporadic and he was on the air for such short periods, and always from different locations, that the *Funkabwehr* were unable to pin him down. To ensure that he was not detected, Coppi used a large number of hide-outs from which to make his transmissions, amongst them the apartment of Countess Erika von Brockdorff, with whom Coppi was having an affair, and the studio of Schulze-Boysen's mistress, the sculptress and dancer Oda Schottmuller.[173]

To improve the flow of information from the Berlin *apparat* Moscow also brought into play a group hitherto entirely separate from the Red Orchestra but more qualified to observe GRU professional standards. The leader of this group was a woman called Ilse Stöbe (cover-name 'Alta'), who worked in the Public Relations Section of the Reich Foreign Ministry. She had been recruited into the GRU in 1936 and during the following year she in turn had recruited Rudolf von Scheliha (cover-name 'Arier'), who held a high-ranking position in the Foreign Ministry. Thereafter 'Arier' passed on to Moscow a flood of highly secret information from the Foreign Office. In return the GRU paid 50,000 marks into an account set up in his name in the Julius Bar Bank in Zürich.[174] Numbered amongst the 'Arier' circuit was Kurt Schulze, a post office van driver but also a Communist espionage professional and a Moscow-trained radio operator. In addition to transmitting the information obtained by 'Arier' and other informers in his circuit, Kurt Schulze was ordered by the 'Centre' to assist Coppi by taking on a substantial part of his workload.[175] As a result the radio traffic between Berlin and Moscow began to flow more smoothly, until Schulze's short-wave transmitter, which he had been using since 1937, broke down and proved to be beyond repair, leaving Coppi alone once more to carry on his cat-and-mouse game with the *Funkabwehr*.

Despite these difficulties, the information relayed to Moscow from the Berlin *apparat* of the Red Orchestra was of major importance to the Soviets' prosecution of the war. For example, Arvid Harnack, from his position in the Reich Ministry of Economics, provided reports on the strengths and weaknesses of the German armaments industry; Rudolf von Scheliha ('Arier') was able to keep Moscow informed of Hitler's relations with his Axis allies (Italy, Romania, Hungary, Bulgaria and Finland); Libertas Schulze-Boysen was able to make use of her connections with the Reich Ministry of Propaganda to obtain access to the Ministry's secret papers, which allowed Moscow accurately to gauge the morale of the German armed forces and that of the population in general; and Harro Schulze-Boysen had, by January 1941, obtained a position in the Reich Ministry of Aviation which allowed him access to highly sensitive information.

By this stage of the war the main business of the Ministry of Aviation had been moved from the *Reichsluftfahrtministerium* (RLM, or Air Ministry) building on Leipziger Strasse in central Berlin to a large hutted camp in the Wildpark Werder near Potsdam, a few miles to the south-west of the capital. In this camp were located all the most secret sections of the *Luftwaffe*, and it was here that Schulze-Boysen was serving as an intelligence officer in Section Five of the *Luftwaffe* General Staff. This section, under the command of Colonel Beppo Schmidt, was the collecting point for all diplomatic and military reports originating from the air attachés in German embassies and legations in neutral and Axis countries. This gave Schulze-Boysen access to, amongst other things, the strategic intentions of the Axis and neutral powers, along with detailed information on the strengths and dispositions of their air forces. In addition he had access to the target maps of the *Luftwaffe* bomber force. He had no difficulty in smuggling reports out of the camp, to photograph or copy their contents, because the security guards manning the gate of the Wildpark complex were extremely lax, rarely if ever searching the briefcases or pockets of the camp's personnel.

While serving at the Wildpark Schulze-Boysen also recruited an unwitting informer in the shape of Colonel Erwin Gehrts, head of the Regulations and Instructional Appliance Section of the *Luftwaffe* Training Department. A morose, neurotic individual, feared by his subordinates for his unpredictable outbursts of rage, Gehrts was having marital troubles and he sought solace by confiding in Schulze-Boysen.[176] Learning that Gehrts had a strong interest in astrology and clairvoyance, Schulze-Boysen capitalized on the situation by recommending that Gehrts consult Anna Kraus, a fortune-teller who ran a profitable business in the Stahnsdorf quarter of Berlin. An anti-Nazi, Anna Kraus was also a member of the Schulze-Boysen/Harnack *apparat* who passed on any titbit of information gleaned from her high-class *clientele*, which included a variety of officers in the armed forces, industrialists and senior civil servants from the Reich Ministries.[177]

The gullible Gehrts quickly learned to trust Anna Kraus to the extent that, apart from paying for her oracular pronouncements on the future, he also accepted her advice on his marital problems and on his official duties: he began bringing secret files to Anna's consulting room to ask her 'professional' advice on what decision he should make in the light of their contents.[178] All the information Anna obtained from Gehrts she passed on to Schulze-Boysen via Toni Graudenz, a regular visitor to her consulting room who also acted a courier for information provided by her husband, Johann Graudenz, one of the most important informers of the Berlin *apparat*. An industrial salesman for the Blumhard company, which made undercarriages for all kinds of *Luftwaffe* aircraft, Graudenz had contact with the senior officers in the department of the Master-General of Air Ordnance in the Reich Ministry of Aviation.[179] He was on such good terms with the senior officers of this department that they loaned him secret books and reports on *Luftwaffe* production statistics, the contents of which were relayed to Moscow.

Another of Schulze-Boysen's prime informers, although an unwitting one, was Lieutenant Herbert Gollnow, a naïve young officer working in Section II of the *Abwehr*, which dealt with sabotage. An ambitious man, Gollnow decided to study English as a means of advancing his promotion prospects. To find a tutor he placed an advertisement in the personal columns of the Berlin newspapers, and he received a reply from an American lady – none other than Mildred Harnack. Gollnow went to see her in the Harnack's well-furnished apartment at 26a Fredericiastrasse, in the Charlottenburg district, and was welcomed in the most charming manner: 'I'm an American,' she said, 'and it will give me great pleasure to chat with you in English over afternoon tea.' Gollnow, greatly awed by the opulent surroundings and by this society lady, stammered a few words about prices. She waved the question aside and said smilingly, 'Don't even think of it! I wouldn't dream of charging you – I'm only too happy to have the chance to speak my own language.'[180]

Gollnow's dominant feeling in subsequent meetings was one of unease as he sat upright in the Harnacks' drawing room, teacup in hand, staring obediently at Mildred's lips as she demonstrated how to pronounce English vowel sounds. He had gone straight into the Army from a modest family background and simply did not know how to cope with the social refinements suddenly thrust upon him. One of his worst moments came when Arvid Harnack, wearing his usual stern expression, arrived unannounced half way through a lesson. By this time Gollnow had begun to consider it strange that Mildred should entertain him alone for hours on end without her husband objecting. He also felt that his teacher's amiability exceeded the limits of mere pedagogic concern. When he saw Harnack come into the drawing room he first thought that an unpleasant scene was about to take place; then he reflected that upper-class people acted according to a very strange code indeed, for Harnack was as charming as he could be, enquiring about his progress in English and the nature of his duties in the Army. Gollnow tried to deflect the question, but Harnack gave him an understanding smile, pointing out that he was an *Oberregierungsrat* at the Ministry of Economics and that he was quite used to keeping secrets.[181] This was sufficient to gain Gollnow's trust, and he let it be known that he was a desk officer for 'Air-Transported and Parachute Troops' in the Sabotage Section of the *Abwehr*.[182] Harnack then began talking about the war on the Eastern Front in sceptical and pessimistic terms, in response to which Gollnow tried to reassure him by boasting of secret operations carried out behind the Soviet lines by *Abwehr* agents. He was, after all, a young Hitler disciple, and any disbelief in ultimate victory seemed to him mere folly.[183]

When Harnack realized how pliable Gollnow could be, the relationship between pupil and teacher suddenly changed, for Mildred seduced the naïve Gollnow, who never realized that while he was in bed with the older woman he was being subtly but systematically interrogated. A highly sensitive and intelligent being, Mildred was by no means as promiscuous as many others in the Schulze-Boysen/Harnack group, and this affair was undertaken solely on her husband's urging. Under interrogation by the *Gestapo* she said that she slept with Gollnow 'because I had to obey my husband.'[184] The revelations that Mildred extracted from her young lover while they were in bed together cost the lives of dozens of *Abwehr* agents parachuted behind the Russian lines to blow up bridges and railway lines. In all, Gollnow unwittingly betrayed twelve *Abwehr* sabotage operations, which were met by the machine-gun fire of Russian ambushes.[185]

The Berlin *apparat*'s informer circuit continued to expand right up to the moment when the *Gestapo* pounced in the autumn of 1942, providing Moscow with practically every detail concerning what the Germans were thinking and planning. For example, the *apparat* reported that the *Abwehr* had captured certain British code-books and consequently the Germans knew in advance the sailing times of every Allied convoy bearing supplies to the north Russian ports,[186] and they learned of the German U-boat dispositions in the Barents Sea, designed to intercept the Allied convoys.[187] The informers also provided information on the details of new *Luftwaffe* equipment and hydrogen peroxide fuel for missiles; statistics relating to arms production; details of the German Navy's new homing torpedoes; monthly returns on the strength of the *Luftwaffe*, along with the series production of German aircraft in the occupied territories; the fuel position in Germany; reports on the production and storage of material for chemical warfare in Germany; details of the strength and disposition of individual German divisions; and reports on the locations of various German headquarters on the Eastern Front.[188]

On 14 November 1941 Schulze-Boysen reported that

The fuel supply which the German Army now has at its disposal is only sufficient to last until February or March next year. Those responsible for supplying the German Army with fuel are concerned about the situation which may arise after February/March 1942 in connection with . . . the progress of the German attack on the Caucasus and above all on Maikop, which is expected first. The German Air Force has had serious losses and now has only about 2,500 aircraft fit for action. This loss of confidence has hit the more senior section of the officer corps especially hard.[189]

During the same month the *apparat* reported that

In spite of the fact that the Germans have not yet installed generators for conducting chemical warfare in their planes, large supplies show that preparations for conducting chemical warfare are under way.

Hitler's headquarters often changes its location and its precise whereabouts are known only to a few. Supposedly Hitler is now in the vicinity of Instabruck. Göring's HQ is now in the area of Instabruck.

The Germans possess the USSR's diplomatic cipher, which was captured in Petsamo; however, the cipher has reportedly not yet yielded to the extent that there is an opportunity to decipher any large volume of Soviet documents. The chief of German Intelligence, Admiral Canaris, has for a large sum of money recruited a French officer [on] General de Gaulle's staff, to work for the benefit of the Germans. [His] recruitment was effected in Portugal. [He] was also in Berlin and Paris, and, with German help, has exposed General de Gaulle's espionage network in France, where important arrests have been made mainly among the officer corps. The Germans decipher a greater part of the telegrams sent by the British to the American Government. The Germans have also uncovered the entire British intelligence network in the Balkans. That is why [Schulze-Boysen] warns us that it is dangerous to contact the British for joint work in the Balkan countries. The Germans have the key to all the cryptograms sent to London by the Yugoslav representatives in Moscow.[190]

In addition, Schulze-Boysen was indefatigable in his efforts to answer the Director's demands for information on German strategy. A message dated 22 September 1941 read:

OKW regards all intelligence about a special Russian winter army as false. OKW convinced that Russians have thrown everything into defeating present German offensive and have no further reserves left.[191]

A month later Schulze-Boysen reported that 'Senior Generals in OKW now reckon on a further thirty months of war, after which compromise peace possible.[192]

During the dark days of 1941–42, when the tide of German conquest seemed invincible, every report from the Berlin *apparat* gave the Soviet General Staff fresh hope; every message relayed over the air by Coppi and Kurt Schulze revealed weaknesses in the German war machine, opening up the possibility for the Russians that, despite all their defeats and discouragements, one day they would gain the upper hand and drive the invader back.[193] By throwing caution to the wind and sending the fatal message of 10 October 1941, giving Schulze-Boysen's, Harnack's and Kuckhoff's addresses, the Director sacrificed a source of intelligence unique in the history of espionage, dooming its members to the tender mercies of the *Gestapo*.

21. Treason *en Gros*

By the end of September 1942 sixty members of the Berlin *apparat* of the Red Orchestra had been packed into the subterranean cells of the *Gestapo* headquarters on the Prinz-Albrecht-Strasse. To begin with, the inquisitors of the 'Red Orchestra Special Commission' employed a humane approach to obtain confessions from the Red agents.

When interrogating Harro Schulze-Boysen, *Kriminalkommissar* Johann Strübing tried the technique of inveigling him in conversations on a number of general and abstract subjects, then deftly slipping in a small question regarding his espionage activities in an attempt to catch him unawares. But, despite hours of 'friendly conversation', Schulze-Boysen never dropped his guard, adamant that he had not been involved in any treasonable activities.[194]

Kriminalobersekretär Reinhold Ortmann had no better luck while employing this technique on Johann Graudenz, the industrial salesman for the Blumhard company and one of the *apparat*'s most important informers. Ortmann recalled that

> I questioned Graudenz on several occasions without any success at all. All he would tell me was that he was a close friend of Schulze-Boysen and that they had once spent a summer holiday together.[195]

Similar negative results were obtained by the other inquisitors. For example, Adam Kuckhoff and Arvid Harnack were both obstinate in their refusal to admit anything or to assist the *Gestapo* by saying anything of substance.[196] Initially, all of the arrested members of the *apparat* maintained a common front, impervious to the sophisticated ruses of the *Gestapo*'s interrogators – all except one.

Libertas Schulze-Boysen was interrogated by *Kriminalobersekretär* Alfred Göpfert, who soon realized that she had naïvely believed that her husband's conspiratorial activities were nothing more than a game. Present at the interrogations was *Frau* Gertrüd Breiter, a typist in the Prinz-Albrecht-Strasse, who took down a record of Göpfert's questions and Libertas' answers in shorthand. Göpfert decided to employ a ruse whereby he would leave the two women alone in his office, which resulted in what Gertrüd Breiter termed as 'just conversations between ourselves'.[197] Late one afternoon Libertas asked, 'Well now, how do you come to be here?', to which Gertrüd shrugged her shoulders and replied, 'One doesn't have to be in one hundred per cent agreement with what goes on to be here. After all, it's wartime.'[198] As the conversation progressed, Gertrüd, having been primed by Alfred Göpfert, managed to convince the naïve Libertas that, provided she turned 'State's evidence' against her friends at the forthcoming trial, the *Gestapo* would ensure that she received a lenient sentence. Grasping this chance to save her life, Libertas immediately betrayed Hans Coppi, the Berlin *apparat*'s pianist, who was arrested that very night. Subsequently, on twenty-five occasions Gertrüd and Libertas had 'conversations between ourselves' and twenty-five times Libertas blabbed out the secrets of the Red Orchestra, betraying, amongst others, Jan Bontjes van Beek and his daughter Cato, Wolfgang Havemann, Countess Erika von Brockdorff and Hugo Buschmann.[199] Had it not been for Libertas the *Gestapo* would never have known that these people were connected with the *apparat*. 'Why did she betray us?' Hugo Buschmann ruminated after the war. 'Well, she was a nice young girl and simply wanted to go on living. Libertas was a charming person who loved life and basically understood very little of Harro's activities.'[200] Pastor Harald Poelchau believed that 'She was a person without much willpower, highly irresponsible, devoid of critical sense and very easily led.'[201]

Libertas' revelations proved to be only the beginning of the moral collapse amongst those languishing in the *Gestapo* cellars. After a week of trying to break the conspiracy of silence by subtle ruses, without success, the *Gestapo* resorted to the more persuasive methods for which they were infamous. Exasperated by the lack of progress, Friedrich Panzinger, the head of the 'Red Orchestra Special Commission', issued the strictest instructions that henceforth the interrogators were to show no mercy in extracting confessions. As a result the prisoners were kept handcuffed day and night, the handcuffs tightened to the extent that they tore the skin, and the interrogations were accompanied by beatings and trips to the 'Stalin Room', as the torture chamber in the cellar of the Prinz-Albrecht-Strasse building was known.[202] There they were 'tortured with the soulless, pedantic application of bureaucratic method which the *Gestapo* considered to be proof of propriety'.[203]

In the Third Reich even sadism was reduced to paper in the proper form. Application was made in writing to Heinrich Himmler, the Chief of the Security Police, requesting permission to apply 'intensified interrogation'. Once the authorization had been signed, an official authorized to apply torture set to work on the unfortunate individuals. In attendance was an SS medical officer who testified to the effect of the torture on the prisoners' health, which information was duly filed in the prisoners' records. In most cases a whip was used, but some prisoners were subjected to lengthy and repeated exposure to ultraviolet rays which burnt their skin raw.[204] Kurt Schumacher wrote: 'Can any man conceive of the depths of pain, affliction, distress, misery and despair which these unfortunates had to endure . . .'[205] Indeed, the *Gestapo*'s methods were more than some could endure. *Dr* Hans-Heinrich Kummerow, who had passed to Moscow the plans for a *Luftwaffe* night-fighter guidance system amongst other secrets, smashed his spectacles and swallowed the glass. When that did not work he slashed his wrists, but he was saved by the prompt action of the guards.[206] Walter Husemann, who assisted Coppi with his radio problems, tried to jump out of an open window from an office on the top floor of the Prinz-Albrecht-Strasse building and carry Friedrich Panzinger to his death with him; they were caught just in time.[207] Johann Sieg and Herbert Grasse both succeeded in killing themselves, the latter by throwing himself from the fifth floor of the Berlin Police Presidency on the Alexanderplatz. In total six of the prisoners committed suicide and a number of others, including Mildred Harnack, made unsuccessful attempts.[208]

Not all captives were tortured: in a large number of cases the mere threat of 'intensified interrogation' was unnerving enough to extract full confessions. There was another element which led prisoners to confess and betray others whom the *Gestapo* had overlooked, in a process which David Dallin had termed 'treason *en gros*'.[209] With its members in solitary confinement, cut off from the outside world and maltreated by the sophisticated interrogators of the totalitarian police machine, the anti-fascist front cracked because it was composed of disparate elements – idealists and adventurers, spies and resistance fighters, anti-Nazis and opportunists, and chance adherents – incapable of withstanding the ultimate and most brutal test.[210] The moral collapse, under torture or the threat of torture, caused the prisoners to betray a further fifty-seven members of the *apparat* or unwitting informers who had so far escaped the *Gestapo*'s net. Schulze-Boysen betrayed Colonel Gehrts, Lieutenant Gollnow and Anna Kraus the fortune-teller;[211] Adam Kuckhoff betrayed, amongst others, Johann Sieg and Adolf Grimme.[212] Greta Kuckhoff was horrified by what her husband had done:

> Finally they [Adam Kuckhoff and Arvid Harnack] told everything and gave away all the names in the belief that people had made themselves scarce. I was speechless when I heard that Adam had confessed; even his death sentence did not shake me so much as this news.[213]

In a letter to her mother dated 2 March 1943, Cato Bontjes van Beek complained that 'As far as I can see, Schulze-Boysen and many other leaders [of the *apparat*] have behaved shamefully and have brought an enormous number of people to their deaths.'[214]

One who held firm under the *Gestapo*'s whips and endured the blinding glare of the lamps while being interrogated was Günther Weisenborn, a well-known German dramatist. On Schulze-Boysen's instructions he had joined the German broadcasting service, where he had attended secret conferences. It was through Weisenborn's efforts that the speeches of Stalin, Churchill and Roosevelt, which were censored by the Nazis, had been distributed in leaflets to the German public. He denied every allegation, but he was denounced by another member of the *apparat*.

However, he did not give up hope, because under German law two prosecution witnesses were needed to obtain a conviction. Then he learned, during the course of a further interrogation, that the sculptor Kurt Schumacher had also incriminated him. Luckily Schumacher was held in the adjoining cell to Weisenborn, and Weisenborn used a pencil to tap on the wall in an attempt to communicate with him. He used the simple code of one tap for 'a', two taps for 'b', three taps for 'c' and so on. The sculptor replied with an incoherent hammering: he had failed to grasp the simple code. Desperate, Weisenborn kept at the task all night long, with an eye on the peephole in the cell door, in constant fear that a guard might burst in and subject him to a beating. At dawn he threw himself on to his bunk, exhausted and in despair: he had still not succeeded in making Schumacher understand. The following night he returned to the attack. Suddenly the taps from the other cell acquired a distinct pattern and rhythm. Weisenborn made out the word 'understood'. Enormously relieved, he sent the following message: 'Essential you retract your statement. Second deposition against me will mean death sentence.' Schumacher replied: 'Did not know. Will retract.' This desperate fight for life and Schumacher's subsequent retraction saved Weisenborn from the scaffold.[215]

Despite the seeming hopelessness of his situation, Schulze-Boysen also attempted to escape the executioner. During an interrogation carried out at the end of September he hinted to Johann Strübing that he had smuggled German official documents to friends in Sweden which, if they were published, would prove highly embarrassing to the leaders of the Third Reich. The contents of these documents, he alleged, were tantamount to a bucket full of mire, blood and excrement, being evidence of the Nazi crimes of torture, mass executions and the death camps;[216] he also hinted that his friends had been instructed that, if he were executed, they should send copies of these incriminating documents to London and Moscow. Strübing, Kopkow and Panzinger were so concerned by this threat that when Schulze-Boysen offered to tell them more about the contents of the documents on condition that he be allowed a visit from his father the *Gestapo* readily agreed.

Captain Erich Edgar Schulze, who had been recalled to the colours on the outbreak of war, was serving as Chief of Staff to the German Naval Commander in Holland. He recalls that, when he arrived at the *Gestapo* headquarters in Berlin,

Kriminalrat Kopkow, Panzinger's colleague, conducted me to a first-floor room, which was apparently not ordinarily occupied. There was a bare desk in a corner and a sofa against a wall, two armchairs and a small table. I waited alone for a minute or two. Then a concealed door opened and Harro came in, accompanied by Kopkow and another officer. He lumbered forward as though he were no longer used to walking; but he held himself very erect, with his hands behind his back, so that I thought they must be handcuffed, which wasn't the case. His face was colourless and terribly thin, with rings under his eyes. Apart from this he looked almost well-groomed, as if he had prepared himself for this meeting. He was wearing a grey suit and a blue shirt. I took his hand, drew him to one of the chairs and sat down in the second, drawing it close to his. I took both his hands and kept them in mine throughout our conversation. This pressure of our hands was like a long, intimate dialogue between us.

The two officers sat down at the desk and kept an eye on us. One of them seemed to be taking down what we were saying.

I told Harro that I had come to him full of fatherly feelings, to help and fight for him, to hear from his lips how I could help him and why he had been arrested. At the same time I gave him the affectionate wishes of his mother, who was also in Berlin, and of his brother. They had not been allowed to come and see him. He replied calmly but firmly: it was impossible to help him; any fight would be hopeless. For years he had been knowingly betraying his country. In other words, he had been fighting the present regime in every possible way and on every possible occasion. He was perfectly aware of the consequences and fully prepared to bear them.

One of the officers – they had remained silent until then – asked a question concerning a matter which Panzinger had already mentioned to me and which seemed to be worrying the *Gestapo*. Certain clues had led them to suppose that, prior to his arrest, Harro might have smuggled some vitally important secret documents out of the country – very likely containing revelations about Nazi crimes – with the probable, or even certain, aim of providing himself and his friends with a form of security in case they were discovered. Until now, Harro had refused to breathe a word about this; but perhaps now he would be prepared to discuss it. Harro firmly rejected their demand.

The rest of our conversation was of a personal and intimate nature, but in view of the presence of the two officers Harro and I refrained from expressing our feelings outwardly. However, at the end, grief got the better of me and I stood up, saying: 'The road before you is a hard one. I don't wish to make it even more painful. I'm going now.' Harro stood up too. He drew himself very erect and looked at me proudly, but for the first time tears came to our eyes. I only managed to say to him, 'I have always loved you.' He answered softly, 'I know.' I held out my hands to him and at the door I turned around, looked at him once more and nodded. We both felt that we were seeing each other for the last time.[217]

After his father had left, Schulze-Boysen proposed a deal: he would hand over the papers in Sweden if the *Gestapo* promised not to carry out the anticipated death sentences on him and his friends earlier than December 1943. Irrational to the end, Schulze-Boysen thought that the war would be over by this time.[218] Cynically, Kopkow agreed to the deal, knowing full well that the authorities responsible for executing the death sentences would not honour such a promise. Schulze-Boysen then elicited a further concession, stating that he would only tell his father where the papers had been deposited. Once more Captain Schulze was summoned to the Prinz-Albrecht-Strasse, and during the visit Harro had to admit that there were no documents in Sweden: he had merely invented the story in order to see his father and help his friends.[219] Captain Schulze enquired anxiously, and rather naïvely, whether the *Gestapo* would nevertheless honour their promise not to execute his son before December 1943, to which Kopkow replied that he was not authorized to give such a promise.[220] Harro Schulze-Boysen had played his last card and lost.

22. Last Echoes in Berlin

While the members of the Schulze-Boysen/Harnack *apparat* were suffering in the inferno of subterranean corridors, steel doors and cells of the Prinz-Albrecht-Strasse, the *Funkabwehr* cryptanalysts made another breakthrough by deciphering a message from Moscow which ordered 'Kent' to make contact with the 'Arier' group through an agent with the cover-name 'Alta', resident at No 37 Wielandstrasse in the Charlotenburg district of Berlin.[221] When this message was conveyed to the *Gestapo* they quickly identified 'Alta' as Ilse Stöbe, although she had by then moved from the Wielandstrasse to No 36 Saalestrasse.[222] Ilse was arrested on 12 September 1942. Her first interrogation lasted uninterruptedly for three days and three nights, during which time she was not allowed to sleep, eat or drink.[223] But she saw it through, and despite suffering *Gestapo* brutality for a further several weeks, she refused to betray the identities of 'Arier' or any other members of the group.

At this time Hermann Wenzel was playing the radio play-back game for the *Gestapo* in Brussels (this was before his dramatic escape – see Chapter 9), and Panzinger asked *Kriminalkommissar* Ampletzer, who was supervising Wenzel's transmissions to Moscow, if he could help. As a result Ampletzer caused Wenzel to transmit a message to the 'Centre' asking the Director to dispatch a parachute agent at once since 'Alta' was experiencing difficulties, primarily because of a lack of money.[224] Moscow fell for the ruse and they dispatched Heinrich Koenen, a German GRU agent who had fled to Russia in 1933 and had been trained as a parachutist and radio operator. He was dropped near Osterode in East Prussia during the night of 23 October 1942, carrying a short-wave radio transmitter, a quantity of German money and false papers made out in the name of Heinz Köster.[225] Making his way to Berlin, Koenen reached Ilse Stöbe's apartment in the Saalestrasse at about 5.00 p.m. on Wednesday 28 October. Ilse was in *Gestapo* custody, and he was met by Gertrüd Breiter, the *Gestapo* secretary, who was posing as 'Alta'. Koenen's visit was brief. He left the radio transmitter, hidden in a suitcase, in the apartment and asked 'Alta' to meet him later at the Savignyplatz tram stop.

Gertrüd was convinced that Koenen had seen through the ruse, but she kept the appointment and to her surprise found the agent waiting for her. During a tram ride to the Tiergarten, Koenen tested the woman out with a catch remark: 'I bring you greetings from your husband Rudi,' he said. This referred to Rudolf Herrnstadt, Ilse Stöbe's lover, who had recruited her into the GRU before he was forced to flee to Russia. Well briefed by her masters, Gertrüd corrected Koenen by pointing out that Rudi was not her husband but her boyfriend. By the end of the tram ride Gertrüd had convinced Koenen that she was the real 'Alta', and he asked her to buy him two shirts and meet him the next day at the Café Adler in the Wittenbergplatz, where he would hand over the money provided by Moscow.

When Koenen arrived at the rendezvous at midday on 29 October the *Gestapo* were waiting for him. In his inside jacket pocket they found the wad of German banknotes and, more importantly, a clue to 'Arier''s identity. Moscow had given Koenen a photostat copy of a receipt of the 'Centre''s first payment of 5,000 marks to Rudolf von Scheliha, Counsellor First Class at the Reich Foreign Ministry, which was to be used as an instrument of blackmail since, for some time, 'Arier''s reports to Moscow had become increasingly infrequent. Koenen had been instructed to threaten to hand over the receipt to the *Gestapo* if von Scheliha failed to provide a regular supply of secret information. This receipt not only betrayed 'Arier''s identity but also offered the *Gestapo* proof that von Scheliha had been in Soviet pay as a GRU agent since February 1938.[226]

However, when the *Gestapo* swooped on the Foreign Ministry to arrest the diplomat, they found that the bird had flown: von Scheliha was in Switzerland. Panzinger jumped to the conclusion that 'Arier' had been tipped off that Ilse Stöbe had been arrested and had fled, but in fact von Scheliha was merely taking a short vacation in a hotel overlooking Lake Constance. Unaware of this, Panzinger alerted *Abwehr* agents operating in Switzerland, who tracked down the errant diplomat and placed him under surveillance. Within a day or two they reported that 'Arier' had left Lake Constance and was waiting at the Badische station in Basle for a train back to Germany. The moment he received this report Panzinger flew to Konstanz on the German–Swiss frontier, and the moment the train bearing 'Arier' crossed into Germany Panzinger boarded it and arrested him.

With the arrest of 'Arier' the *Gestapo* considered the case closed, and Heinrich Müller, the head of the Secret State Police, proposed to Himmler that the members of the Berlin *apparat* be brought before the 'Peoples' Court' forthwith.[227] The total bag was 117 members of the Berlin *apparat*, and the *Gestapo* report on the case concluded, with Teutonic thoroughness, that the occupations of those arrested were: academics and students – 29 per cent; authors, journalists and artists – 21 per cent; professional soldiers, civil servants and government officials – 20 per cent; wartime recruits to the armed forces – 17 per cent; and artisans and labourers – 13 per cent.[228] The Berlin *apparat* of the Red Orchestra was dead, but Soviet records show that those arrested constituted less than half those involved in the Schulze-Boysen/Harnack circuit.[229]

23. Swift and Severe Punishment

At the end of September 1942 Hitler was in Berlin, having recently returned to the Reich capital from his headquarters in Vinnitsa in the Ukraine where he had been directing the German advance into the Caucasus and on Stalingrad. When Himmler presented him with the full facts of the round-up of the Berlin *apparat* the *Führer* was beside himself with rage, ordering that 'the Bolsheviks within our own ranks' be dealt with by swift and severe punishment.[230] Hitler also called for absolute secrecy. The case was classified as a 'state secret.' Merely talking about it made anyone liable to the death sentence, the reason being that the regime could not allow such a scandal to be made public, because the accused were not Jews, nor persons of low mentality, nor social failures. On the contrary, they were members of the Aryan élite.[231] Consequently no reference was made to the Schulze-Boysen/Harnack *apparat* in German radio broadcasts or in the newspapers. Schulze-Boysen's colleagues in the Reich Ministry of Aviation were told that he had been sent on a mission abroad, while Walther Funk, the Reich Minister of Economics, was not told that his subordinate, Arvid Harnack, was a Soviet agent until the trial began, and even he was sworn to secrecy. However, despite the secrecy surrounding the affair, the news finally leaked out and was circulated by word of mouth. For example, the diplomat Ulrich von Hassell recorded in his diary that

A vast Communist conspiracy has been discovered at the Air Ministry and in other departments. Fanatics, it would seem (motivated by hatred of the regime), they claim their purpose was to set up a standby organization to meet the possibility of a Bolshevik victory.[232]

At social gatherings, in the anterooms of the various Reich Ministries and along the corridors of the armed services headquarters there was talk of this evil-smelling abscess suddenly discovered at the heart of the Third Reich. Everyone claimed to know the whole story, and what people did not know they invented. Myth took shape and the wildest suspicions flourished – the inevitable price of secrecy, unless that secrecy be absolute.[233]

If Himmler had hoped that Hitler would place him in charge of the proceedings to bring the Red agents to trial, he was disappointed. The task was allotted to the Deputy *Führer* and Himmler's rival, Hermann Göring. The reasons why the Commander-in-Chief of the *Luftwaffe* and not the Chief of the German Police was chosen for this task are not difficult to determine: Göring was a close friend of Libertas Schulze-Boysen's family; he had been a witness at Libertas and Harro's wedding; he had been responsible for advancing Harro's career in the Reich Ministry of Aviation; and several other *Luftwaffe* officers were involved in the affair. However, in an attempt to exonerate himself, Göring tried to apportion the blame, as Ribbentrop, the Reich Foreign Minister, recalled in his memoirs:

> Whenever I was with the *Führer* and Göring, the latter would monopolize Hitler's attention and I did not exist; I used to suffer as a result of the repercussions which this had in the field of foreign policy. Göring knew just how to exert his influence on Hitler. I remember a characteristic scene which was enacted at Klesheim Castle. In his anxiety to give Hitler a touched-up picture of the espionage affair known as the 'Red Orchestra', in which several *Luftwaffe* officers had been implicated, Göring tried to throw the blame on to an innocent official at the Reich Foreign Ministry. Hitler, who disliked the staff at the Wilhelmstrasse, took Göring's side as usual; it was only by protesting vehemently that I re-established the truth.[234]

On 17 October 1942 Göring, as convening officer, appointed *Oberstgerichtstrat Dr* Manfred Roeder, the *Luftwaffe* Judge Advocate-General of Air Region III, as the prosecuting council in the trial of the 117 Red Orchestra prisoners. Roeder was the natural choice because Air Region III included Berlin, with its aviation ministries and headquarters, within its boundaries and so all *Luftwaffe* court-martial cases of major importance or political significance had been dealt with by Roeder, whose fanatical zeal to the Nazi cause had earned him the nickname 'Hitler's Bloodhound'. Indeed, Roeder was regarded as one of the sternest and most loyal officers in the military legal service.[235] Possessed of a harsh, boorish manner tinged with cynicism, Roeder was disliked by his fellow officers and superiors. According to Judge Eugen Schmitt,

> There was something lacking in Roeder's temperament: he did not possess the normal man's sympathy for the sufferings of others, so that he did not mind witnessing an execution or undertaking unpleasant tasks.[236]

It was the original intention to try the accused in the notorious *Volksgerichtshof* (People's Court), presided over by the merciless Nazi 'hanging' judge Roland Freisler, but Roeder pointed out that the People's Court was not the correct orum since this was a case of military espionage and, in accordance with Paragraph 2, Section 4, of the special wartime legal code, the sole competent authority was the *Reichskriegsgericht* (Reich Court Martial), the highest military tribunal in the Third Reich.[237]

After Göring obtained Hitler's permission to change the forum for the trial, Roeder set about drafting the case for the prosecution, using the *Gestapo* files on the accused for the purpose. He was assisted by another Judge Advocate, *Kriegsgerichtsrat* Werner Falkenberg, and two secretaries, Adelheid Eidenbenz and Erika Strey. They worked at a frantic pace, because Hitler insisted that the main trial and the executions had to be over before the Christmas period.

By the end of November 1942, after little more than a month of work, Roeder and Falkenberg had put together an 800-page prosecution brief, which was approved by the President of the Reich Court Martial, Admiral Max Bastian.[238] Of the 117 persons arrested six had committed suicide, and of the remaining 111 Roeder decided that prima facie evidence only existed in 76 of the cases.

Amongst the 35 'suspects' subsequently released by the *Gestapo* was Wolfgang Havemann (Arvid Harnack's step-nephew) who, as a naval intelligence officer in the *Oberkommando der Kriegsmarine*, had provided the Berlin *apparat* with top secret naval information. His full involvement was never uncovered by the *Gestapo*, but his uncle's guilt was cause enough for his transfer from the German Navy to an infantry division on the Eastern Front. When his unit was overrun by the Red Army in November 1943 Havemann was taken prisoner, and after identifying himself he was able to provide the 'Centre' in Moscow with the full details of the break-up of the Berlin *apparat*.[239]

For procedural reasons Roeder divided the 76 accused into twelve groups who were arraigned in seven separate trials. Since the proceedings were to be held *in camera*, only lawyers accredited to the Reich Court Martial were permitted to act for the defence, which resulted in only four defence counsels being appointed to represent all 76 defendants. These were Dr Kurt Valentin, Dr Rudolf Behse, Dr Heinz Bergmann and Dr Bernhard Schwarz, all of whom had to swear total silence regarding the sensitive nature of the proceedings.

The first trial commenced at 9.15 a.m. on Monday 14 December 1942, in the main court room of the Reich Court Martial at No 4-10 Witzlebenstrasse, Berlin-Charlottenburg, with Military Judges Dr Alexander Kraell and Dr Gerhard Ranft and three officers presiding. Roeder produced only two defendants at this hearing, the diplomat Rudolf von Scheliha ('Arier') and Ilse Stöbe ('Alta'). The evidence against them was overwhelming, the trial lasted only a few hours and on a count of treason both defendants were condemned to death.

Two days later, on Wednesday 16 December, Roeder brought before the court the second and most important group of defendants: Harro Schulze-Boysen and his wife Libertas; *Dr* Arvid Harnack and his wife Mildred; the radio operators Hans Coppi and Kurt Schulze; Kurt and Elizabeth Schumacher; Countess Erika von Brockdorff; the *Funkabwehr* cryptanalyst Horst Heilmann; the industrial informer Johann Graudenz; the unwitting informer Colonel Erwin Gehrts, who had discussed *Luftwaffe* secrets with the fortune-teller Anna Kraus; and Lieutenant Herbert Gollnow, the naïve young officer who had unwittingly betrayed *Abwehr* secrets to the Harnacks. The trial lasted four days, but once again none of the thirteen defendants could dispute the prosecution's evidence, which was based on the confessions obtained by the *Gestapo*.

Throughout the trial Roeder lived up to his infamous reputation. His speeches were savage; his accusations and insults echoed through the courtroom; he constantly interrupted the defendants when they made their statements; and he denigrated their motives. All that was required of him as prosecutor was to prove that the accused had been engaged in treasonable activities, but Roeder, the strict bourgeois moralist, could not resist the opportunity to defame reputations by subjecting the court to highly detailed sketches of the group's dissolute sexual mores. He made great play on the fact that Harro Schulze-Boysen had been intimate with Oda Schottmüller, Countess von Brockdorff, Elizabeth Schumacher and two shorthand typists in the Ministry of Aviation. Neither did he tire of showing the court a collection of nude photographs of Libertas Schulze-Boysen which had been taken by Kurt Schumacher.[240] Roeder also had a field day with Countess Erika von Brockdorff, who, it appears, had slept with nearly every male member of the *apparat*, causing the prosecutor to refer to her as the 'Red Orchestra prostitute'.[241]

Nevertheless, the accused held their heads high before the court and before history during the proceedings. One after another they proclaimed proudly that what had brought them all together was their disgust and hatred of the vile Nazi regime. Arvid Harnack, speaking in a tired, subdued voice, proclaimed that he acted in the conviction that the ideals of the Soviet Union were paving the way for the world's salvation and that his aim was the destruction of the Hitler regime by every available means.[242] Harro Schulze-Boysen fought like a lion, denying every detail that was not positively proved. He turned himself from accused into accuser and pilloried Roeder with a whole series of proud and fiery interjections.[243] Erika von Brockdorff maintained a subtle smile throughout the trial which was beyond fear or hope, and she constantly interrupted the proceedings with interjections and laughter, so that the President of the court (Kraell) admonished her: 'To me this case is too serious for laughter; you too will have the smile taken off your face in the end.' To which Erika von Brockdorff yelled, 'And even on the scaffold I'll laugh in your face.'[244]

Only one of the thirteen defendants lost composure. This was Libertas Schulze-Boysen, who up to the time of the trial had lived on the illusion that since she had turned State's evidence her statements and testimony against her husband and his accomplices would gain her a light punishment. It was only during Roeder's summing up, when he demanded the death penalty for all thirteen accused, that she finally understood the true worth of the *Gestapo*'s promises. When she heard Roeder demand the death penalty she broke down and her defence counsel, *Dr* Rudolf Behse, had to request an adjournment.

But neither tears nor defiance made any difference to the outcome of the trial. Harro and Libertas Schulze-Boysen, Kurt and Elizabeth Schumacher, Arvid Harnack, Horst Heilmann, Kurt Schulze, Hans Coppi and Johann Graudenz were all condemned to death. But, surprisingly, in four cases the court refused to accept Roeder's demand for the death penalty. Sentence on Colonel Erwin Gehrts was postponed until medical reports could be prepared, after his defence counsel, *Dr* Rudolf Behse, put in a plea of diminished responsibility on account of his client's curious personality and belief in all kinds of occult powers; moreover, Behse argued, by discussing official secrets with the fortune-teller Anna Kraus, Gehrts had not considered this to be an act of resistance since he had no idea that Kraus was passing the information to Schulze-Boysen.[245]

Dr Behse also defended Lieutenant Herbert Gollnow of Section III of the *Abwehr*. In Gollnow's case Behse maintained that although he had given away official secrets to the Harnacks, mainly when he was in bed with Mildred, he had not realized that he was thereby collaborating with an enemy espionage organization. Gollnow was, Behse argued, a loyal National Socialist and had only been trying, by producing concrete information, to bring the sceptical Harnacks to believe in an ultimate German victory. Nevertheless, the court considered it proven that Gollnow's information had contributed to the death of numerous German soldiers operating behind the Soviet front line and he was, accordingly, condemned to death for military indiscipline, though not for treason. For this reason the court petitioned the *Führer*, recommending that the death sentence be commuted to one of imprisonment.[246]

In the case of Mildred Harnack and Countess Erika von Brockdorff, the prosecutor's preoccupation with eroticism rebounded on him. The court ruled that the Countess had become embroiled with the Red Orchestra solely to satisfy her own personal sexual cravings and was therefore judged merely to be an accessory to espionage because 'in the last analysis the motive for her actions was not political'.[247] As a result the she received a sentence of ten years' hard labour. Mildred Harnack, on the other hand, was sentenced to only six years' hard labour for being an accessary to espionage and not for complicity, since the court considered that 'she had acted more out of loyalty to her husband than [of] her own volition'.[248] Judge Kraell later confessed that this relatively light sentence was influenced by the court's sympathy for 'a highly educated woman interested in all questions of public and particularly social affairs, and the hesitancy of the court to impute to *Frau* Harnack any traitorous intent in the questions she put to Lieutenant Gollnow'.[249]

Theoretically, the sentences were subject to confirmation by Admiral Max Bastian, the President of the Reich Court Martial: he had the right to ratify or reject them. But in this particular instance Hitler had reserved the privilege for himself, and when, a few hours after the trial had ended, he was informed of the outcome by his aide-de-camp, Admiral Karl von Puttkamer, he confirmed the death sentences, refused the recommendation to commute the death penalty in the case of Gollnow and annulled the prison sentences passed on Mildred Harnack and Countess Brockdorff, ordering a retrial for the two women.[250]

The retrial did not take place until 12 January 1943, when both women appeared before a court presided over by Military Judge *Dr* Karl Schmauser. To Schmauser a more decisive argument was that

> ... their own ideology and their own political views had led the defendants Mildred Harnack and Countess Erika von Brockdorff to approve and participate in the efforts of the Schulze-Boysen/Harnack circle in favour of Russia. [Consequently] ... instead of being mere accessaries to preparations for treason as accepted [in the first trial], it must be accepted that the defendants are guilty of preparation for treason in complicity with the other accused.[251]

On this basis Schmauser overturned the original sentences and condemned both women to death.

Shortly thereafter Schmauser also condemned Colonel Erwin Gehrts to death, because the medical report pronounced him fully responsible for his actions. Neither was Schmauser prepared to consider as a mitigating circumstance the fact that Gehrts had not realized that the secrets he discussed with Anna Kraus were being passed on to Schulze-Boysen: it was sufficient, Schmauser contended, that the Colonel had handed to a Soviet agent secret material which was his duty to keep under lock and key.[252]

Two days later, on Thursday 14 January 1943, the fourth trial commenced, when Roeder arraigned a further nine prisoners. Military Judges Kraell and Ranft presided. All the accused belonged to *Dr* John Rittmeister's group of anti-fascist students who had joined in Schulze-Boysen's leaflet and poster campaign. They were Heinz Strelow and his girlfriend Cato Bontjes van Beek, who had disassociated themselves from Schulze-Boysen in May 1942; Fritz Rehmer and his fiancée Liane Berkowitz; Fritz Thiel and his wife Hannelore; *Professor* Werner Krauss and his girlfriend Ursula Goetze; and Otto Gollnow (no relation to Lieutenant Herbert Gollnow of the *Abwehr*).

Although the majority of this group were Communists, their resistance to the regime had consisted in nothing more than printing and distributing anti-fascist literature and an involvement in discussion evenings in which they voiced their hatred of the regime. But none of them had been involved in espionage: their resistance to the Third Reich had been limited to moral protest. Nonetheless, Roeder demanded the death sentence on the basis that they were all guilty of 'treasonable activities against the government, which was tantamount to treason against the country in the sense of "furnishing aid and comfort to an enemy" under paragraph 91b of the Criminal Code, because the object of their activities was to damage the war effort'.[253] As a result seven of the defendants were condemned to death and two, Otto Gollnow and Hannelore Thiel, received terms of six years' hard labour on account of their age (both were 18).

On 19 January Roeder arraigned Hilde Coppi (the radio operator's wife), Karl Behrens and Rose Schlösinger. Although all three had merely rendered small services to the *apparat*, they all received the death penalty – as did Oda Schottmüller, the dancer and Schulze-Boysen's mistress. She was brought before the court on the 26 January, the main charge against her being that she had allowed Hans Coppi to work his short-wave radio transmitter from her apartment.

The penultimate trial took place on Wednesday 27 January 1943 when the dentist *Dr* Hans Helmuth Himpel and his fiancée Rosemarie Terwiel, both members of the Rittmeister group, were condemned to death for taking part in Schulze-Boysen's leaflet and poster campaign. The final trial commenced on 28 January when Roeder arraigned a total of 46 defendants, a combination of resisters and those who had knowingly engaged in espionage. Amongst the accused were Adam Kuckhoff (condemned to death); his wife Greta Kuckhoff (who received the surprisingly light sentence of five years' hard labour on account of a legal technicality); Anna Kraus the fortune-teller (condemned to death); and *Dr* John Rittmeister (condemned to death). By the end of the proceedings a total of 46 of the 76 accused had been condemned to death, while fifteen had received sentences of hard labour and fifteen terms of imprisonment. Hitler's demand for swift and severe punishment had been well and truly discharged.

24. The Men in Top Hats and Tails

On the evening of 21 December 1943 the eleven prisoners condemned to death in the first two trials – Harro and Libertas Schulze-Boysen, Arvid Harnack, Kurt and Elizabeth Schumacher, Horst Heilmann, Kurt Schulze, Hans Coppi, Johann Graudenz, Rudolf von Scheliha and Ilse Stöbe – were transferred from the cellars of the *Gestapo* headquarters on the Prinz-Albrecht-Strasse to the Plötzensee Prison in the Königsdamm in Berlin-Charlottenburg, where they were to be executed on the following morning. They were housed in a building at the rear of the main prison which contained the condemned cells and the execution chamber.

Monday 21 December was cold and dismal. A howling, icy east wind rattled the barred windows of the condemned cells as the doomed prisoners wrote their farewell letters. Harro Schulze-Boysen wrote to his parents:

So the time has come; another few hours and I shall be parting company with my 'self'. I am perfectly calm, and I beg you to be so too and to accept the news unperturbed. Such important things are now at stake on this earth that the extinction of a single human life is of small account.

I do not wish to say anything further about what is past and what I have done. Everything I have done, I have done with the full knowledge of my head and heart, and by conviction. That is the light in which you, my parents, must accept them. I beg you to do so.

This way of dying suits me. Somehow, I always knew it would be like this. It is, in Rilke's phrase, my 'personal way of dying'.

It is only when I think of you that I feel heavy hearted, my dear ones. Libertas is close to me and will be sharing my fate at the same hour. You two are now suffering both a loss and a feeling of shame, and this you have not deserved. Time will soften your sorrow – not only do I hope it, but I am convinced of it. I am only a pioneer, with my impetuous impulses and my sometimes rather confused intentions. Try to believe, as I do, that time, which is just, will bring all things to ripeness.

I shall be thinking until the very end of the last look my father gave me – I shall be thinking of my darling Mama's tears at Christmas. It has taken these last months to bring me so close to you – I, your prodigal son, now completely returned to the fold. After so much impulsiveness and passion, after following so many paths which seemed so strange to you, I have finally found my way home . . . I conjure up the memory of a full and beautiful life, for which I owe you so much – so much that was never returned.

If you were here – you are here, even if invisible – you would see me laughing in the face of death. I conquered my fear of it long ago. In Europe, blood usually has to nourish ideas. It is possible that we were only a pack of fools. But when death is so close, one is surely entitled to a little self-delusion.

Yes, and now I reach out my hand to you all, and in a little while I shall deposit a tear here (just one) as a seal and as a token of my love.[254]

The prison chaplain, Harald Poelchau, only learned by chance that eleven prisoners under sentence of death had arrived at Plötzensee. When he visited them in their individual cells he found that Harro betrayed no sense of fear, but he expressed a certain bitterness at all the opportunities for action against the hated Nazi regime he would be losing. Just as a vanquished soldier suffers at having to surrender his weapons, so Harro Schulze-Boysen was having difficulty in accepting the fact that the fight was over and that he must now deliver his courage and strength into the hands of death.[255] A poem which he had hidden in his cell expressed his frustration:

> With death at your throat,
> How you love life . . .
> And your mind is brimming over
> With all that used to propel it.[256]

Libertas Schulze-Boysen spent her last hours wrestling with herself and against her fate. She wrote to her mother:

I had to drink the bitter cup of finding that I had been betrayed by a person in whom I had placed complete trust, Gertrüd Breiter [the *Gestapo* secretary].

> Now harvest what you have sown
> For whosoever betrays shall himself be betrayed.

Through selfishness, I betrayed my friends. I wanted to be free and come back to you – but, believe me, I would have suffered immensely for the wrong I had done. Now they have all forgiven me and we go to our end with a sense of fellowship only possible when facing death.[257]

Pastor Poelchau found Arvid Harnack calm and serene. He was ready to die for his convictions, although he knew that such a sacrifice would not save Germany. He told the chaplain of his anguish for the German people, whose souls had been corrupted by Hitler. Then he asked the chaplain to recite the lines from Goethe's *Orpheus*, followed by the accounts of the Nativity from the Gospels of Matthew and Luke (a strange request from a convinced Communist).[258] To his relatives he wrote:

I shall be departing this life within the next few hours. I would like to thank you once again for all the love you have given me, especially in these last days. The thought of that love has lightened my burden. I am also thinking of the wonders of nature, to which I feel so close. This morning I recited aloud:

> The sun, in accordance with ancient rite,
> Mingles its voice with the harmonious choir of the spheres,
> And runs its prescribed course with thunderous step.

But above all I think of humanity in its evolution. These are the three foundations of my strength. I was especially happy to learn that there is soon to be an engagement in the family. I should very much like my signet ring, which was once my father's, to be given to F. This would mean that L. could wear his own. My ring will be sent to you with my effects.

This evening I shall give myself a small Christmas celebration by reading the story of the Nativity. And after that it will be time for me to be on my way. I would have loved to see you all once more. Alas, it is not possible. My thoughts go out to you, and I shall not forget anyone – you must each know that, especially Mother. For the last time I embrace you all.

P.S. You must celebrate Christmas as usual. This is my last wish. And be sure to sing 'I Invoke the Power of Love'.[259]

Hans Coppi, the Berlin *apparat*'s pianist, no doubt spent his last hours thinking of his baby son, born on 27 November in the prison where his wife Hilde was being held. As soon as the news of the child's birth had reached him, Hans had written Hilde a letter begging her not to worry about the future but to enjoy the great happiness which the present had bestowed on them. For Hans Coppi this happiness lasted just twenty-six days.[260]

Horst Heilmann, the *Funkabwehr* cryptanalyst, who had vainly tried to warn Schulze-Boysen when the fatal message from Moscow was deciphered, wrote to his parents:

> . . . My life has been so beautiful that even in my death I hear the echoes of a divine harmony. I have asked that my body be sent to you; I would like to be buried with my friends. I am so grateful to you for all your love and kindness. Remember me with love, with as much love as I have always had for you. I die strong and sure of 'myself'.[261]

Early in the morning of Tuesday 22 December the prison guards entered the cells and began preparing the prisoners for execution. Their hair was cropped short and they were given a change of clothing. The first to be executed were the eight men. They trod their last road along the corridor which led from the condemned cells to the execution chamber. They walked with a firm step, holding their heads high – all except Rudolf von Scheliha, who collapsed and rolled around on the concrete floor, crying that he did not want to die. He found it harder to accept his fate than the others, for 'Arier' was dying for 50,000 marks, not ideology. The execution chamber measured about eight metres by four and was divided in half by a black curtain. Behind the curtain was the guillotine and eight hooks suspended from an iron girder running the width of the ceiling. Hitler had decreed that the women should beheaded and the men hanged by the neck. In accordance with the law, the President of the Reich Court Martial, the two judges and three officers of the court which had passed the death sentences, Roeder the prosecutor, the prison governor and the prison chaplain had all gathered to witness the executions. Pastor Poelchau took the opportunity to complain to Roeder that he had not been officially informed of the impending executions, to which the cynical prosecutor replied, 'The participation of a clergyman was not provided for!'[262]

When the procession reached the execution chamber it halted, a corner of the black curtain was raised and Johann Reichhart, the principal German executioner (who held the post from 1922 to 1945), and his two assistants – all three dressed in tailcoats and top hats and wearing white gloves, as was the German tradition – stepped forward to take delivery of their first victim. After the President of the Reich Court Martial had read out the death sentence, he instructed the executioner to do his duty and the prisoner was made to stand on a stool, his hands handcuffed behind his back. One of the assistants slipped the noose of a rope around his neck and the executioner pulled the stool away. This form of hanging was known as the 'Austrian' method, which, without a measured drop, resulted in the slow strangulation of the victim rather than the breaking of the neck and instant death as with the British scaffold and trapdoor system. After the first sentence had been carried out a smaller black curtain was drawn around the hanging body to conceal it from the view of the next victim. All except von Scheliha, who struggled to the very end, met their end calmly and with dignity, causing Roeder to remark, 'Schulze-Boysen died like a man.'[263]

While the bodies dangled in the cubicles formed by the black curtains, Libertas Schulze-Boysen and Ilse Stöbe were marched into the chamber. As Libertas' head was placed in the stock of the guillotine she screamed, 'Let me keep my young life!' Further cries were cut short by the razor-sharp blade of the guillotine.[264] Pastor Poelchau recalled:

> Afterwards there was silence. The guards dispersed, and the officials went away. The guard on duty walked along the corridor jangling his bunch of keys; he closed the doors of the now empty condemned cells and turned off the lights one after the other. There was darkness everywhere.[265]

No further executions took place until the conclusion of all seven trials, the remaining 35 condemned Red Orchestra prisoners being executed in Plötzensee between 19 February and the end of August 1943. The first to go was Colonel Erwin Gehrts, who was hanged on 19 February. Two days later Lieutenant Herbert Gollnow of the *Abwehr* was executed by firing squad – the only 'favour' granted to him by the *Führer*, since he had been convicted of military indiscipline rather than treason. Four days later Gollnow's lover, Mildred Harnack, was guillotined. By this time her hair had turned grey and she was terribly emaciated. The last words of this American intellectual were, 'And I loved Germany so much!'[266] Pastor Poelchau later wrote to one of her relatives:

> She was very brave, well aware of all that was happening, but she had obviously already finished with this world. She had erected a wall around herself to shut out painful thoughts and to exclude all sentimental feelings. Only her mother's photograph brought her out of this state for a few moments. She would hold silent but passionate dialogues with her mother while her eyes filled with tears. Then she covered the photograph with kisses and calmed down.[267]

While waiting for her end she translated some lines of the German poet Goethe into English, in effect her own requiem:

Thou who comest from on high
To calm suffering and grief,
Thou who doubly soothes,
Who doubly knows unhappiness,
I am tired of all this woe!
What good is sorrow and happiness?
Gentle peace come,
Come to my heart![268]

It was not until Thursday 13 May that the next batch of prisoners, thirteen in number, kept their appointment with the men in tailcoats, top hats and white gloves. These were Countess Erika von Brockdorff, Wilhelm Guddorf, Hans Helmuth Himpel, Walter Husemann, Karl Behrens, Walter Küchenmeister, Fritz Rehmer, Philip Schaeffer, John Rittmeister, Heinz Strelow, Fritz Thiel, Richard Wüsstensteiner and Thomfor (Christian name not known).[269] From the condemned cell Countess von Brockdorff wrote to her mother:

. . . No one will be able to say of me, without lying, that I wept, that I clung to life or trembled because of it. It is in laughter that I shall end my life, just as it is in laughter that I have loved life and that I love it still . . . [270]

True to this attitude, she waved away August Ohm, another of Plötzensee's chaplains, when he tried to offer her words of comfort. Ohm recalled that 'Even at the very door of the place of execution, she said to me that she did not care if her body was to be turned into a cake of soap in a few hours' time.'[271] Walter Husemann, who had tried to throw himself out of the window at *Gestapo* headquarters, and to take Panzinger with him, wrote his farewell letter to his father:

Be strong. I shall die as I have lived, as a fighter for the working class. It is easy to call oneself a Communist when one is not called upon to shed blood. It's only at the testing time that one proves one is really a Communist. Father, I am a Communist. I am not suffering, Father, you must believe that. No one will see me weaken. To die well is my final duty. Be proud of your son, overcome your grief – you still have a task to perform. You must do it doubly, even trebly, since your sons are no more. Poor Father, happy Father, you have had to sacrifice to your ideals all that has been most dear to you. But the war won't last for ever and your time will come. Think of all those who have already taken this road and those who still will. And remember this about the Nazis: every sign of weakness they see will cost pools of blood. That is why you must remain strong. I regret nothing in life, except perhaps not having done enough with it. But my death will reconcile those who have not always agreed with me. Oh Father, my dear Father, if only I knew that you wouldn't break down because of my death. Be tough, tough, tough! Now is the time to prove that you have always, from the bottom of your heart, been a fighter for the working class . . .

I shall die easily, for I know the reason. Those who are about to murder me will soon meet with a painful death, I'm convinced of it. Be tough, Father, be tough! Don't give way! At each moment of weakness think of the last wish of your son Walter.[272]

The executions of the largest group of Schulze-Boysen's adherents took place three months later, on Thursday 5 August 1943. There were sixteen in all, and, apart from Emil Hübner, Stanislas Wesolek and Adam Kuckhoff, they were all women: Liane Berkowitz (aged 20, who had given birth while in prison and whose baby was taken from her – to die in an SS hospital before Liane was executed), Cato Bontjes van Beek, Eva-Maria Buch, Hilde Coppi, Ursula Goetze, Else Imme, Anna Kraus, Ingeborg Kummerow, Klara Schabbel (who had been a courier between Berlin and Brussels), Rose Schlösinger (who had hidden a transmitter in her home), Oda Schottmüller, Rosemarie Terwiel and Frieda Wesolek.[273]

Hilda Coppi, who gave birth to a son in prison twenty-six days before her husband Hans was executed, wrote to her parents: 'I'm very calm, even content, and happy for each day I can spend with my son. And he laughs so much, he is so gay – why should I cry?'[274] The dancer Oda Schottmüller wrote to her mother: 'That all should now be over is entirely according to plan for me. I have never wanted to grow old – there is nothing nice about getting slowly stiffer and stiffer.'[275] Cato Bontjes van Beek was not so resigned: 'It is only sad that I do not know why I have to die. Mama, there is no great glory attached to involvement in this business.'[276] The writer Adam Kuckhoff's chief concern was for his five-year-old son, Ule, who would be left fatherless. Just before being taken to the scaffold he scribbled a verse on a piece of paper:

> For Ule.
> My beloved son, my great and final happiness,
> I am going away and leaving you fatherless.
> No! A whole people – no, that's not enough –
> The whole of humanity will be a father to you.[277]

And to his wife Greta, serving a sentence of five years' hard labour, Kuckhoff wrote:

> I know that this is more painful for you than if you had gone with me, but I must be glad that you are staying – at least I hope so; for your son, for everything that is so alive in you, I feel so clearly in advance – yes, I know it – how you will live when you are free once again . . .
> How many human beings can say that they have been as happy as we? What else? Nothing remains of the way we walked together . . . It was that way when we saw each other for the last time, and nothing has changed . . . It is three o'clock, not much time left before I must go. I write my last farewell.[278]

A few weeks later Wilhelm Schürmann-Horster, Wolfgang Thiess and Eugen Neutert, the final three, were hanged in Plötzensee, bringing to end the whole grisly process. The Berlin *apparat* had passed into history.

25. Set-Back in Paris

While the *Gestapo* were scoring their *coup de grâce* against the Berlin *apparat*, Harry Piepe and Karl Giering began centring all their resources in Paris, with the specific intention of tracking down the *Grand Chef*. During October 1942 the two sleuths occupied offices on the fourth floor of No 11 Rue de Saussaies, the past and future location of the French Security Police headquarters. They were joined by twenty *Gestapo* officers who, along with Piepe and Giering, formed the *Rote Kapelle Sonderkommando* (Red Orchestra Special Squad).

When the French author Gilles Perrault interviewed Harry Piepe in the 1960s, the latter pulled no punches when describing the nature of his *Gestapo* colleagues:

> *Willy Berg* – Giering's right-hand man. Fifty or thereabouts. Tiny, practically a dwarf. He was hard as nails, unscrupulous. A real butcher.
>
> *Richard Voss* – Physically . . . Berg's opposite: extremely tall and broad-shouldered, with fair hair. A butcher.
>
> *Otto Schwab* – A small man. He had a pliant, conciliatory nature. He preferred guile to force.
>
> *Ella Rempka* – The secretary. Rather a pretty blonde. She attended every one of the interrogations, without showing the slightest feeling; she had seen plenty of others in Berlin, where she worked at *Gestapo* headquarters.
>
> *Eric Jung* – Tall, slim, athletic-looking. He was always very pleasant to me. Far from pleasant to the prisoners though. A butcher.
>
> *Rolf Richter* – Hard! Terribly hard! Even with women he was merciless.[279]

In their search for the *Grand Chef* the *Sonderkommando* had precious little to go on. After fifteen months of investigation all Piepe and Giering had was the photograph of the elusive leader of the Red Orchestra which had been found at the Rue des Atrébates and the knowledge that he operated under a number of cover-names, one of them being Jean Gilbert. And that was all. Although the Germans had destroyed three networks, in Brussels, Amsterdam and Berlin, the Red Orchestra's internal security system was so strict that not a single line led to the master spy of the organization.

The *Sonderkommando*'s main hope of obtaining a lead rested on Abraham Raichmann – 'The Cobbler' – and his mistress, the courier Malvina Gruber, both of whom had agreed to collaborate with the Germans. Having set the couple up in a comfortable apartment in Paris, the Germans unleashed them on to the streets where, unsupervised, they were to visit all the known 'letter-boxes' of the *apparat*, leaving the same message in each case: asking the *Grand Chef* to meet them at the earliest possible moment, even naming a time and place.[280]

To report on progress Raichmann agreed to meet Piepe every morning at the Café Viel in the Boulevard Italien, where he made his reports over breakfast. But, despite approaching every contact offering the slightest prospect of gaining touch with the *Grand Chef*, both Raichmann and Malvina drew a blank. Piepe and Giering were forced to recognize that Raichmann's Paris contacts were either suspicious or inadequate to the task.

The Germans' second line of approach was provided by Simone Phelter, who worked in the Paris office of the Franco-Belgian Chamber of Commerce. Following the Rue des Atrébates raid Piepe had discovered that the woman in charge of the typing pool in the Brussels *Bourse* was interpolating cryptic messages with official *Bourse* correspondence, and that these messages were being relayed to Simone Phelter. Both women had been kept under surveillance, and Piepe and Giering decided to capitalize on the situation. They instructed Raichmann to write a message asking Simone to arrange a meeting with the *Grand Chef* and then instructed him to travel to Brussels so that Simone would receive the message through the normal channel via the contact in the Brussels *Bourse*. The ruse worked: back came a message from Simone informing Raichmann of the date and hour of the meeting, which was to be held in a Paris restaurant.[281]

On the appointed day the *Gestapo* mingled with the customers in the restaurant and took up positions on the street. However, the moment Simone Phelter entered the restaurant to ascertain that the coast was clear, in advance of the *Grand Chef*'s arrival, she sensed immediately that the Germans had set a trap and she stole away to give the warning.[282]

Foiled in this attempt, the *Sonderkommando* had only one other small clue to work on: the frequency of the communications between Simexco – the firm in Brussels which Yefremov had betrayed as being a cover for the Red Orchestra's agents – and a company in Paris called Simex. Since September 1942 the *Abwehr* had kept Simexco's employees under surveillance, while Group IIIN of the *Abwehr* (the department responsible for eavesdropping on telecommunications) had tapped the firm's telephones and intercepted its incoming and outgoing mail. The nature of the intercepts showed that the main subject of discussion was the supply of building materials for the German paramilitary Todt Organization.

However, the similarities in the names of the two firms, and the regularity of the communications between them, gave rise to the suspicion that Simex was also a cover firm for the activities of the Red Orchestra.[283] This suspicion was confirmed when Giering inspected the records of the Seine District Commercial Court, where Simex had been registered on 16 January 1941. Sure enough, the managing director of Simex was registered as *Monsieur* Jean Gilbert (the *Grand Chef*'s cover-name), and amongst the shareholders was a certain Léon

Grossvogel, whom Giering knew, from Yefremov, to be one of the lieutenants of the *Grand Chef*.

Originally situated on the Champs Élysées, the offices of Simex had moved (on 20 February 1942) to a luxury suit on the third floor of 89 Boulevard Haussmann, just opposite the church of St Augustin in central Paris. As the firm was doing a considerable amount of business with the Todt Organization, Giering and Piepe decided to make inquiries at the organization's headquarters in the Champs Élysées. There they interviewed *Hauptsturmführer* Wilhelm Nikolai, the *Gestapo* liaison officer responsible for contacting and supervising French firms supplying the Todt Organization and working as subcontractors on *Wehrmacht* installations.[284]

Nikolai was well acquainted with Simex, which he described as a reliable firm with which the Todt Organization had conducted a lot of trade during the past year: it was supplying material for the construction of the Atlantic Wall, designed to resist an invasion force launched from the United Kingdom.[285] When Piepe showed Nikolai the photograph of the *Grand Chef* discovered during the Rue des Atrébates raid, he identified him as *Monsieur* Jean Gilbert, the managing director of Simex. Piepe then divulged to the liaison officer that he had, in fact, been doing business with the head of Soviet espionage in Western Europe.[286] After recovering from the initial shock, Nikolai revealed that he was expecting a visit from the *Grand Chef* within the next few days, because his travel permit, which allowed him to travel to the unoccupied zone in the south of France, was due to expire and it was Nikolai's responsibility to renew it. All Piepe and Giering had to do was wait for the *Grand Chef* to make his expected appearance, but Nikolai wrecked the plan by overenthusiasm. Hardly had Piepe and Giering left his office than he wrote a letter to the managing director of Simex, asking him to call since his pass was due for renewal. The wily *Grand Chef* obviously smelt a rat, for he did not appear. Piepe and Giering could hardly conceal their fury, and they had to think of another way of contacting the *Grand Chef* without alerting him.

Piepe and Giering prepared a new plan. They decided to make contact with Simex themselves, posing as businessmen from Mainz who were in search of industrial diamonds – a scarce and much sought-after commodity in wartime Europe. Piepe was convinced that this would work: 'Diamonds for one and a half million marks – that must attract anybody.'[287] They asked Nikolai the best way to go about proposing the deal to Simex, and he suggested that they contact *Madame* Maria Likhonin, who handled many of the commercial transactions between the firm and the Todt Organization.[288]

When they approached the ageing but elegant *Madame* Likhonin at Simex's office on Boulevard Haussmann, she showed extreme interest in the proposed diamond deal and betrayed not the slightest hint of suspicion when Piepe and

Giering pretended to be ultra-cautious businessmen who insisted that they would only deal with *Monsieur* Jean Gilbert in person: they were, after all, sinking enormous assets into the transaction and they needed sound guarantees on the quality of the diamonds. *Madame* Likhonin promised to arrange a meeting with *Monsieur* Gilbert within a few days, and Piepe gave her the telephone number of the apartment he was renting in Paris as the point of contact.[289]

The reply, when it came a few days later, was negative. The head of Simex was unable to sign the contract personally because he was suffering from a serious heart condition and was undergoing treatment. This sounded fishy to Piepe and Giering, but Nikolai confirmed that the *Grand Chef* did indeed have heart trouble and frequently convalesced at the Château des Ardennes in Spa. The two Germans immediately dispatched a squad from the *Sonderkommando* to the château, but there was no sign of the elusive spy.[290]

When Piepe and Giering pressed *Madame* Likhonin about the deal, she contacted them after a few days to tell them that *Monsieur* Gilbert would meet them in Brussels. This sounded promising, and the Germans decided to arrest the *Grand Chef* as soon as he stepped off the train at the Gare du Sud railway station in Brussels. They sealed off every exit from the station and had a *Gestapo* squad with them on the platform:

> I have to admit [Piepe recalled] that we were very nervous as we waited for the train: we were convinced there would be trouble, and possibly shooting – the *Grand Chef* wouldn't allow himself to be captured just like that. Even Giering was uneasy.[291]

But when the train from Paris arrived at the Gare du Sud, the *Grand Chef* did not alight. *Madame* Likhonin stepped off the train unaccompanied, explaining that *Monsieur* Gilbert was not well enough to travel and had given her full powers to sign the contract on his behalf. 'He had a good nose!' Piepe lamented, never suspecting that *Madame* Likhonin had warned the *Grand Chef* that she suspected a trap. The tortuous trail had led nowhere.

26. The Marseilles Connection

Raichmann and Malvina's efforts in Paris had failed to give the Germans a single lead that would put them on the trail of the *Grand Chef*; but their efforts were not totally negative – far from it. While making their rounds of the Paris 'letter-boxes' Malvina had learned that the *Petit Chef* ('Kent') had fled to Marseilles after the Rue des Atrébates raid, taking his mistress, Margarete Barcza, with him.[292]

At that stage of the war Marseilles was beyond the reach of the German security forces. In the terms of the armistice following the collapse of France in June 1940, the Germans had left the French Government an unoccupied zone in the south and south-east which the French were, ostensibly, free to govern. As Marseilles was in the Free Zone, the *Sonderkommando* could not follow up Malvina's lead. But the situation suddenly changed during the second week of November 1942, when, following the Allied landings in French North Africa, Hitler ordered the occupation of the Free Zone to protect his southern flank.

Following in the wake of the German Army as it overran southern France was a squad from the *Sonderkommando* headed by *Sturmbannführer* Boemelburg, accompanied by Raichmann and Malvina. In Marseilles the two collaborators were quick to discover the trail of their old friends from the now defunct Brussels *apparat*. Within only two days they managed to track down the *Petit Chef* and his mistress to a luxury apartment at 85 Rue de l'Abbé de l'Épée.[293]

The couple were arrested on the morning of Thursday 12 November 1942 when five French policemen, acting on the *Gestapo*'s behalf, burst into their apartment. They were taken to the police station at the Gare Saint-Charles, charged with spying and handed over to the *Gestapo* the following day. Late in the afternoon of 13 November 'Kent' and Margarete left Marseilles in a pair of *Gestapo* cars bound for Paris. Boemelburg travelled in the car carrying 'Kent' while one of his lieutenants was in the other car with Margarete; the other seats in the two cars were filled by half a dozen French police officers. They were heavily armed, for Boemelburg was afraid that the network might stage an ambush to free the prisoners; for although the German Army has moved into the Free Zone several days previously, it had not yet established full control of the region.[294]

When the convoy reached Paris the prisoners were taken to the *Sonderkommando* office in the Rue des Saussaies, where they were subjected to their first interrogation by Piepe and Giering. 'Kent' refused to say anything, and Margarete Barcza denied any knowledge of espionage activities. Then, for some reason which is not clear, Piepe and Giering decided to escort the two prisoners to the *Gestapo* offices in the Avenue Louise in Brussels, where they interrogated them for several days. 'Kent' still refused to co-operate, and Margarete remained adamant that the first she knew of her lover's role in the Red Orchestra was when the French police charged them both with spying: she had always believed, and still believed, that 'Kent' was nothing more than a successful South American businessman. This was later confirmed by 'Kent', who told his interrogators that he had concealed his espionage activities from Margarete to protect his cover.[295]

At the end of November *Gestapo* headquarters in Berlin ordered Giering to transfer the two prisoners to the Prinz-Albrecht-Strasse. They made the journey in a black Mercedes. The right-hand rear door was sealed from the outside by a thick rope wrapped around the handle which was stretched between the front and back bumpers. 'Kent' was instructed to sit next to this sealed door while Margarete sat in the middle of the back seat, a *Gestapo* man on her left. In the front sat two *Gestapo* men, one driving and the other with a sub-machine gun on his lap. The Mercedes was full of parcels that members of the Brussels *Gestapo* were sending home to their families, and both 'Kent' and Margarete spent the long journey to Berlin with piles of presents on their knees.[296]

When they arrived in the German capital the couple were separated. The *Petit Chef* was incarcerated in the cellars of the Prinz-Albrecht-Strasse while Margarete was locked in a cell in the Berlin Police Presidency on the Alexanderplatz. After four days in *Gestapo* headquarters 'Kent' suddenly broke his silence, offering to collaborate on condition that he be allowed regular visits from Margarete and that she would not be harmed: she was, after all, a Jewess. Margarete recalled that

> The *Gestapo* made a deal to leave us alone all day together, on the condition that 'Kent' spent the evenings making full disclosures concerning the Red Orchestra at night. Kent agreed, and so I was able to see him every day.[297]

Having devoted his days to love, the *Petit Chef* devoted his nights to betrayal, disclosing everything he knew about the French *apparat* in Paris, Marseilles and Lyon and the role of Simexco and Simex. He was not, however, *au fait* with the *Grand Chef*'s present whereabouts or immediate plans.

He also disclosed his true identity to the Germans: he was Victor Sukulov-Gurevich, a captain in Soviet Military Intelligence. As a cover the 'Centre' had provided him with a forged passport, ostensibly issued in New York on 17 April 1936, which turned Sukulov-Gurevich into Vincent Sierra, a citizen of Uruguay, born on 3 November 1911 and living at No 9 Calle Colón, Montevideo. To cover his tracks Sukulov-Gurevich actually flew to Montevideo in order to start his journey to Belgium to join the Red Orchestra.[298]

The son of a Leningrad workman, educated at a good school and exhibiting a gift for languages, Victor Sukulov-Gurevich joined the Red Army after matriculating and fought in the International Brigade with the rank of Captain during the Spanish Civil War. On his return to Russia he was recruited into the GRU, and he was dispatched to Brussels via Montevideo during July 1939. He was known to the 'Centre' as 'Kent', a code-name of his own choosing. When he was eighteen he had read a novel by the Russian author N. G. Smirnov called *The Diary of a Spy*. The hero of the novel was a fictional British agent named Edward Kent, and Sukulov-Gurevich became so enamoured with the astute, fearless, audacious character that he called himself 'Kent' thereafter.

The 'Centre''s initial intention was for 'Kent' to stay in Brussels for about a year, studying commercial law in the university and perfecting his knowledge of foreign languages, before proceeding to Copenhagen to set up a GRU network in Denmark. But when war broke out in September 1939, only two months after his arrival in the Belgian capital, Moscow instructed 'Kent' to stay put and place himself at the disposal of the *Grand Chef,* who ordered him to continue with his studies while at the same time begin establishing contacts amongst the Brussels business fraternity.[299] To this end 'Kent' moved into a luxurious apartment on the fourth floor of No 106 Avenue Émile Béco, and by virtue of GRU funds he established a lavish life style, making contacts with rich entrepreneurs in the exclusive night clubs of the Belgian capital and entertaining in his apartment. During May 1940, when the Germans invaded the Low Countries, he met and fell in love with Margarete Barcza, who lived on the sixth floor of the building where 'Kent' resided. They made acquaintance while sheltering in the cellar of the apartment block during a German air raid on Brussels. A tall, 28-year-old, curvaceous blonde, Margarete was a Czech and the widow of a Czech millionaire seventeen years her senior who had died of a heart attack only two months before she met 'Kent'. She and her late husband were both Jews and they had fled to Brussels when the Germans annexed Czechoslovakia in 1938. Margarete recalled that

> No one would call him ['Kent'] handsome: he was much shorter than I, with fair hair and thick, fleshy lips. But he was so thoughtful and considerate – madly charming. He dressed divinely, and not only did he have plenty of money but he knew how to spend it. We went out almost every evening and did plenty of dancing.[300]

What Margarete did not know, until the pair were arrested in November 1942, was that Vincente Sierra, her rich Uruguayan lover, was in fact a Russian GRU agent.

During the latter months of 1940 the *Grand Chef* ordered 'Kent' to abandon his studies in Brussels University and set about canvassing his unsuspecting Belgian business contacts to support a procurement firm which was to be formed with the intention of supplying the German occupation authorities. He soon collected nine Belgian shareholders, who between them put up capital of 288,000 Belgian francs to fund the Société Importation-Exportation – Simexco – with its head office at 192 Rue Royale, which was registered with the Belgian Chamber of Commerce on 13 January 1941. The firm not only provided a cover for the Belgian *apparat*; it also gave the Red agents a means of getting on good terms with the German authorities so as to infiltrate their ranks and collect information.

Within a short time the Third Reich's construction army, the Todt Organization, was receiving regular supplies of building materials, bulldozers and even railway tracks and bicycles from Simexco.[301] The Germans were so trusting that they allowed Simexco's people to move about freely inside *Wehrmacht* installations. Without a qualm the *Abwehr* issued passes to senior Simexco employees and called them in for consultation on secret building projects, allowing 'Kent' and his associates to travel around in German-occupied territory without restriction.[302]

By November 1941, by which time the unsuspecting Harry Piepe had set up his own cover firm in the office adjoining Simexco's at 192 Rue Royale, 'Kent''s firm had become to successful that he set up branches in Marseilles, Rome, Prague and Stockholm, forming subsidiaries in the German protectorate of Bohemia-Moravia and in Romania.[303] Under cover of these business connections 'Kent' was able to organize new bases for the Red Orchestra, linking Communist agents in Central Europe, including the Berlin *apparat* and *Die Rote Drei* network in Switzerland with the *Grand Chef*'s circuit in the West.[304]

With the profits from Simexco 'Kent' was able to move from Émile Béco to a magnificent 27-room apartment on the Avenue Slegers, where he set up home with the by now jewel-laden Margarete Barcza, becoming the centre of an exclusive society of conservative and right-wing Catholic fops – the perfect cover for a GRU agent. By this time the *Grand Chef* had moved his centre of operations to Paris and 'Kent' was thereby appointed the *Petit Chef* (Little Chief), responsible for supervising the Belgian *apparat*, based on the group of agents operating from the Rue des Atrébates.

Narrowly escaping arrest by the *Abwehr* following Piepe's raid on the Rue des Atrébates during the night of 13/14 December 1941, 'Kent' and Margarete escaped to Paris. The *Grand Chef* quickly decided that 'Kent' was now a liability. After his numerous trips to Germany, Czechoslovakia and Switzerland he knew too much to be exposed for a single minute to the possibility of arrest.[305] Moreover, the *Grand Chef* was concerned that 'Kent' seemed to have been badly affected psychologically by the Rue des Atrébates raid and had lost his nerve.[306] As a result the Big Chief decided to bundle him off to Marseilles, where 'Kent' had already opened a branch of Simexco. There he was to set up a local network with its own transmitter. The unoccupied zone was well suited to such an enterprise, for surveillance was obviously less strict in that part of France.

But the *Grand Chef* did not pitch his hopes too high: 'Kent' had been weighed and found wanting. He was also concerned about his deputy's relationship with Margarete Barcza: 'Kent' was so passionately in love with her that he was even more afraid for her safety than for his own. She was softening him and wasting his time. The *Grand Chef* offered to get her into Switzerland, where she could wait safely for the end of the war and a more propitious time for their love affair. But 'Kent' would not hear of it: he had no intention of going to Marseilles without her.[307]

From the moment he set foot in the relative safety of Marseilles, the *Petit Chef* was lost to the Red Orchestra. He invented a thousand and one reasons for not using his short-wave transmitter to establish regular contact with Moscow. He claimed it was always breaking down, but when the *Grand Chef* called in some technicians attached to a local Resistance group they declared that it was in perfect working order. Even then 'Kent' balked. The best the *Grand Chef* could hope for was that the *Petit Chef* would be content to wallow in defeatism and his luxurious life style, funded by Simexco, without exposing the network to the attentions of French Vichy counter-intelligence.[308]

But no one had bargained for the treachery of Abraham Raichmann and Malvina Gruber, which led to the arrest of 'Kent' and Margarete – the woman for whom 'Kent', in turn, decided to betray his comrades.

27. *Wo ist Gilbert?*

'Kent''s statements to the *Gestapo* in Berlin gave the Germans their first in-depth picture of the French *apparat*'s scope, personnel and methods – enough in fact to enable Piepe and Giering to plan a synchronized onslaught on what remained of the *Grand Chef*'s circuit.[309] The offices and employees of Simexco in Brussels and Marseilles and those of Simex in Paris, along with agents in Lyon, were kept under constant surveillance, while the *Sonderkommando*'s flying squads prepared to make a round-up in all four cities, timed for 24 November 1942.[310] But the plan went awry when *Kriminalobersekretär* Eric Jung, who had taken over temporary command of the *Sonderkommando* in Paris while Piepe and Giering were in Brussels, attempted to bring the *Grand Chef* to book single-handed. On Thursday 19 November 1942 Jung, acting entirely on his own initiative, launched a premature strike in the French capital.[311]

Jung arranged for *Hauptsturmführer* Nikolai, the Todt Organization's liaison officer, to lure Alfred Corbin, the manager of Simex, to his office on the Champs Élysées under the pretext of renewing his pass for travel in prohibited areas. Corbin, who was a member of the Red Orchestra, turned up for the appointment accompanied by Vladimir Keller, a Swiss national who worked as the firm's interpreter and was blissfully unaware that Simex was a cover operation for espionage. Hardly had they entered the foyer of the Todt office building than they were confronted with Jung and other members of the *Sonderkommando*, backed up by four uniformed German soldiers brandishing sub-machine guns. Handcuffed, Corbin and the bewildered Keller were bundled into the back of a black Mercedes and driven away to the Rue des Saussaies.[312]

In the *Sonderkommando*'s offices both men were subjected to an interrogation, the only question being *'Wo ist Gilbert?'* ('Where is Gilbert?'). The questions were accompanied by hard slaps and punches, but to no avail because neither man had the slightest idea where the *Grand Chef* was hiding. By eight o'clock that evening, realizing that his hope of finding some clue which would lead to the *Grand Chef* was not going to be realized, Jung had both men transferred to Fresnes prison, where they were separated and placed in solitary confinement, their wrists kept handcuffed tightly behind their backs.[313]

Meanwhile at 10.00 a.m. that same day another squad from the *Sonderkommando* raided the offices of Simex at 89 Boulevard Haussmann. The twelve offices were ransacked, all the company's files were confiscated and all the staff present were carted off to prison – though all were as ignorant as Vladimir Keller of the espionage connection, save one, Suzanne Cointe, a Communist militant of long standing.[314] This raid also proved totally unproductive in unearthing the *Grand Chef*, so the following day Jung and his cronies paid a visit to Alfred Corbin's home. Informing *Madame* Corbin that her husband was being held in connection with a trivial black market offence, Jung assured her that he was sure *Monsieur* Jean Gilbert would be able to clear up the matter if he could be found. This ruse produced equally negative results, for *Madame* Corbin had no idea of Gilbert's whereabouts. Jung then reassured her that there was no question of interfering with her freedom or that of her daughters, but he asked her to stay indoors for a few days and advised her that he was obliged to leave two of his men on duty in the house in case *Monsieur* Gilbert should turn up.[315]

When Giering learned of Jung's premature action he flew into a fury and hurried back to Paris to call his unruly minion to order. He arrived in Paris on 23 November, where Jung tried to excuse his precipitancy, saying that he had feared that the birds might fly.[316] Giering's temper did not improve until the following day, when, trying to salvage something from his wrecked plan, he paid a visit to *Madame* Corbin and shrewdly brought psychological pressure to bear on the worried woman. He told her frankly that, far from a matter of black-marketeering, her husband was mixed up in espionage. He was, however, more than ready to believe in Alfred Corbin's innocence, but the tragedy was that he might suffer for the real culprit – Jean Gilbert. It was, then, imperative that she help them discover Gilbert's whereabouts. The distraught woman protested that she had no idea where Gilbert could be found, but then suddenly she remembered that in the course of one his visits Gilbert had complained of toothache and that her husband had given him the address of the family dentist, *Dr* Maleplate – 13 Rue de Rivoli, near the Hotel de Ville.[317]

This information gave Giering a one in a million chance of capturing the *Grand Chef*, but with no other clue to go on he decided to follow it up. From the Corbins' home Giering and Jung drove to *Dr* Maleplate's dental surgery. They asked the dentist to read out all his appointments for the week. Maleplate recalled:

I did so, and they listened carefully, without showing any reaction. When I had finished they asked me to go through it again. So I recited all the names a second time, noticing that I had made a mistake. At 2.00 p.m. on Friday 27 November I had booked an appointment for a *Madame* Labayle, but she had later cancelled the appointment and I had offered it to another client, but I had forgotten to cross out *Madame* Labayle's name – the name of the substitute was *Monsieur* Jean Gilbert.[318]

From his office on the Rue de Saussaies Giering telephoned Piepe, who had remained in Brussels, to tell him the electrifying news. Piepe prepared to fly back to Paris, but in the meantime he led a raid on Simexco, conveniently situated in the adjoining office to his own bogus company office above the tailor's shop at 192 Rue Royale. All of Simexco's employees were arrested by the *Geheime Feldpolizei*, including Nazarin Drailly, the manager. Further arrests took place all over Brussels as the innocent Belgian shareholders in the firm and anyone remotely connected with the employees of Simexco were carted off to the Saint Gilles prison.[319]

Raids were also launched on the Simex branch office in the Rue du Dragon in Marseilles, where all the employees and the manager, Jules Jasper, were arrested; and in Lyon, where Isidor Springer, the diamond merchant who had fled from Brussels after the Atrébates raid, had been operating a short-wave radio transmitter. Along with Springer the *Sonderkommando* also arrested Germaine Schneider ('Schmetterling'), the courier, who had fled from Brussels.[320]

Having smashed the reminder of the *Grand Chef*'s circuit in Brussels, Piepe flew to Paris and in the morning of 27 November he accompanied Giering and Jung to *Dr* Maleplate's surgery in the Rue de Rivoli. Informing the dentist that they intended to arrest Gilbert, they outlined their plan. The dentist was to ensure that his assistant was absent from the surgery at the appointed time, and when Gilbert arrived he was to commence his treatment as if nothing was amiss.[321]

Shortly before 2.00 p.m. Giering and Piepe concealed themselves in the dentist's office, behind a door which opened into the surgery. *Dr* Maleplate recalled that

When *Monsieur* Gilbert arrived I sat him in the chair. He was perfectly relaxed. I chatted to him and went through the motions of selecting my instruments. He smiled and said, 'Things are looking up, aren't they? Did you hear the news on the radio?' [The German 6th Army had been surrounded at Stalingrad.] I was in a cold sweat, for at that very moment I heard the jingle of handcuffs just beyond the door. Time was beginning to drag, so I placed some cotton wool in his mouth and began to adjust my drill; but at long last the Germans made up their minds to burst into the surgery.

They came at him fast, pistols in hand. He put his hands up and told them he was unarmed. He was very pale, but perfectly calm. As for the Germans – all I can say is that they were the ones who were in a panic![322]

Piepe confirms this:

The dentist was shaking, and Giering and I were in a terrible state of nerves. The *Grand Chef* was the calmest man in the room. He didn't turn a hair! 'Bravo!' he said as Giering slipped on the handcuffs. 'You've done a good job.' I replied modestly: 'It's the result of two years of searching.'[323]

Bundled into a black Mercedes, the *Grand Chef* was driven at high speed to the *Sonderkommando* offices, handcuffed between Giering and Piepe – between *Gestapo* and *Abwehr*.[324]

28. The Road to Kropotkin Square

The *Grand Chef* – alias Jean Gilbert – was a Polish Jew called Leopold Trepper. He was born on 23 February 1904 in Novy-Targ, a small town of some 3,000 inhabitants near Zakopane, which is situated close to the present day Polish–Slovakian border. His parents were poor, debt-ridden Jews eking out a living by running a small shop at No 5 Sobieski Street. The customers seldom paid for their purchases with money but exchanged them for some product of their land.[325] His father, worn out by the daily battle against poverty and misery, died of a heart attack when Leopold was barely thirteen years of age.

Forced to abandon his education to support his starving family, Trepper found work wherever he could – first in an ironworks, then in a soap factory and finally in the coal mines of Katowice.[326] As a reaction to the anti-semitism of the right-wing Pilsudski dictatorship which ruled Poland after the First World War, he joined the Jewish youth movement, the *Hashomer Hatzair* – a Zionist inspired organization which proposed to find the definitive solution to the destiny of the Jewish people in Palestine.[327] In addition, on account of the atrocious working and living conditions afforded the miners in Katowice, Trepper also played a part in the militant actions of a Communist youth group. Meetings, demonstrations and writing and distributing leaflets culminated in his role as a ringleader of a workers' rebellion which erupted in 1923. The rebellion was quickly crushed by Polish lancers, and Trepper was arrested and jailed for eight months. On his release he found himself blacklisted and unable to find work of any kind. Turning for help to the *Hashomer Hatzair* movement, he was put in touch with the *Hechalutz* organization, a Zionist body financed by wealthy American Jews whose aim was to promote Jewish immigration to the Promised

Land. In April 1924, funded by *Hechalutz*, Trepper was put on a train with a group of fifteen other Jewish immigrants which took them by way of Vienna and Trieste to the Italian port of Brindisi, where they boarded an old Turkish freighter bound for Palestine.[328]

Hunger and poverty followed Trepper to the Promised Land: they accosted him like a staunch old friend almost as soon as he stepped ashore at Haifa. The organization in charge of finding employment for newly arrived immigrants assigned Trepper to a Jewish orange plantation owner, who put him to work with a gang draining swampland. Trepper recalled:

> We lived in tents and worked from dawn to dusk knee deep in muck; at night we lay awake, devoured by thousands of mosquitoes. Each day three of four of us came down with malaria.[329]

It soon became apparent to Trepper that rich Jewish landowners, who lived very comfortably, were exploiting the newly arrived immigrants and the Arab agricultural workers. This discovery profoundly disturbed his serene idealism. As a young immigrant who had come to Palestine to build a new world, he soon realized that the Zionist bourgeoisie, imbued with its privileges, was trying to perpetuate the very social injustice Trepper had tried to escape.[330] Leaving the orange plantation, he joined a *kibbutz* in Emek-Israel in Galilee, where some of his friends from the *Hashomer Hatzair* movement in Poland were working. Most of these had also become disillusioned by Zionism and had joined the Palestinian Communist Party (founded in 1920 by Joseph Berger), and Trepper followed their example early in 1925.

From its inception the Communist Party in Palestine, which numbered only a few hundred militants and a few thousand sympathizers, struggled to wean the mass of Jewish workers away from Zionist ideology and win over the Arab population so that Jews and Arabs could unite to lay the foundations of a socialist state.[331] But Trepper quickly discovered that finding work in Palestine (which was under British mandate) was virtually impossible for a known or even suspected Communist, and for the remainder of 1925 he was reduced to living in a shack in Tel Aviv which he shared with eight other Communists who included Sophie Poznanska, Leo Grossvogel and Hillel Katz, all future members of the Red Orchestra. They lived on the idea of revolution and a few tomatoes.[332]

At the end of 1925 things improved for Trepper when he eventually found work in an electrical engineering factory in Tel Aviv, giving him the means to rent a small room which he shared with Luba Brojde (whom he eventually married). Luba, a Jewess born in the Polish town of Drohubucz in 1908, was working in a chocolate factory in Lvov when she began engaging in militant activities with a Communist youth group. A member of this group shot and killed an *agent provocateur* who had betrayed a number of militants to the police, and, hunted by the police as an accessory to murder, Luba was forced to flee to Palestine, where she worked in a *kibbutz* and then as a house painter before encountering Trepper during a Communist Party meeting.[333]

Both Trepper and Luba were arrested during 1927 for taking part in demonstrations against the British administration, after which the Communist Party appointed Trepper secretary of the Haifa section, which was one of the most powerful in Palestine, being well established in the factories and among the railway workers.[334] He organized political work, wrote tracts and manifestos and presided over meetings, which brought him to the attention of the police so that he was forced to live a clandestine existence: he could only go out after dark and he had to take a thousand precautions to elude the authorities.[335] His luck ran out in December 1928 when he was arrested while holding a secret meeting. Incarcerated in the medieval fortress of Saint-Jean d'Acre, where he endured extremely unpleasant conditions, he was eventually deported on the orders of Sir Herbert Samuel, the British Governor of Palestine.[336]

Trepper landed in Marseilles at the end of 1929, with few belongings but one precious resource – a recommendation from the Central Committee of the Palestinian Communist Party. After spending a fortnight in Marseilles, where he worked in the kitchen of a small restaurant, he made his way to Paris. There he made contact with Alter Ström, a Communist militant who had left Palestine a year before Trepper was deported. Ström introduced him to Isaiah Bir, a Polish Jew who had set up a *Rabcor* circuit in France. (The *Rabcor* was a system whereby workers provided the Soviet Union with industrial secrets.) Working by day as a house painter for a small Jewish firm, Trepper spent his evenings and free time as one of Bir's agents, collecting information from French Communist workers which was passed to Moscow via the Soviet Embassy in Paris. He was joined in 1930 by Luba and the couple rented a small apartment in the Nineteenth *Arrondissement*. Their first son, Michel, was born in April 1931.[337]

Trepper lapped up Bir's teaching, which was later to turn him into an expert at covering his tracks: he learnt the art of disguise, how to deceive his opponents and how to escape from a tight corner. Bir's nickname among the sleuths of the Paris *Sûreté* (Security Police) was 'Phantomas' (Phantom-Man), owing to his ability to disappear like a ghost whenever the police closed in on him. He seemed to know the back door of every house in Paris, every cellar, every hide-out. He was continually evading his pursuers, and to the very end they were puzzled as to who 'Phantomas' really was. When they finally caught him in June 1932 they were almost disappointed: instead of the super-spy whom they expected, they found themselves confronted by an unassuming student who ran a sort of spy youth club (at 28 years of age, Trepper was the oldest).[338]

While under arrest Bir and his agents were interrogated by Charles Faux-Pas-Bidet, an official from the *Sûreté*, who made it clear that they had been betrayed by one of their own *Rabcor* agents. At the end of 1933 Bir, Ström and five other agents were sentenced to three years' imprisonment by a Paris court.[339]

Trepper escaped the police haul by hurriedly boarding a train for Germany. When he reached Berlin he made contact with the Soviet Embassy, where, on the strength of his recommendation by the Central Committee of the Palestinian Communist Party, arrangements were made for him to travel to Moscow by train. When he arrived in the Russian capital he was provided with a room in the Woronzowe-Pole, a large building where political *émigrés* were housed – mainly militant exiles from Poland, Hungary, Lithuania and Yugoslavia, with a few militants on the run from the authorities of other European countries.[340]

After he had been interviewed by Communist officials Trepper was enrolled in the Marchlevski University (one of four Communist universities in the Russian capital), where militants were trained with the intention of spreading revolutionary activity abroad. Trepper underwent three cycles of study. The first involved social sciences and economics, which included the history of the Soviet Union, the history of the Bolshevik Party and of the Comintern and the study of Leninism. The second cycle was devoted to the study of his native country, the workers' movement and the Communist Party. Languages, at which Trepper excelled, formed the third cycle. The work was intense – an average of twelve to fourteen hours a day. He was also given military training, with the emphasis on the handling of weapons and shooting practice.[341]

When he fled France Trepper had been forced to leave Luba and his son behind, but at the beginning of 1933, through arrangements made by the Soviet Embassy in Paris, his family joined him in Moscow. On their arrival Luba was also enrolled at the Marchlevski University, and after three years of study she became a political commissar involved in agricultural planning.[342]

During 1936 Isaiah Bir ('Phantomas') and Alter Ström were released from prison in France, and they demanded asylum in the Soviet Union. Until their arrival in Moscow the heads of the Soviet Intelligence Directorate had accepted the French version of the 'Phantomas' case, which maintained that it was a journalist on the French Communist newspaper *L'Humanité* by the name of Riquier who had betrayed Bir's *Rabcor* group. Bir and Ström, however, were convinced of Riquier's innocence, and to establish who the guilty party really was the Intelligence Directorate decided to dispatch Trepper to Paris. He was chosen because he was fluent in French and had first-hand knowledge of the case.[343]

Thus it was that on 26 December 1936 Trepper took the train to Finland and by way of Sweden travelled to Antwerp and took a train to Paris, arriving on

1 January 1937. He travelled with a forged passport made out in the name of 'Sommer'. Pretending to be a relative of Alter Ström, he began his investigation by conferring with the two principal lawyers who had prosecuted and defended the accused in the 'Phantomas' trial. After a few months he came to the conclusion that Riquier was definitely innocent. It was an important conclusion, for it cleared the French Communist Party of harbouring an informer. Moreover, after further probing, Trepper unmasked the real traitor, who turned out to be a Dutch Jew named Svitz, the former head of a Soviet spy ring in the United States. Svitz had been arrested by the FBI in America, and to escape being charged and imprisoned he had agreed to become a double-agent for American counter-intelligence. He continued to feed the Americans with information even after Moscow had transferred him to France; and the denunciation of the 'Phantomas' network had come to the *Sûreté* from Svitz via the FBI.[344]

When Trepper returned to Moscow and presented his findings, the Intelligence Directorate was sceptical and demanded proof. This required Trepper to make a second trip to Paris. He returned to Moscow in June 1937 with documents which provided irrefutable proof of Svitz's guilt – letters the double-agent had written to the US Military Attaché in Paris.[345]

The success of Trepper's investigation brought him to the attention of the Director of Soviet Military Intelligence, and he was summoned to the GRU headquarters on Kropotkin Square in Moscow. According to Trepper, the Director told him:

> I propose that you come and work with us, because we need you. Not here in the central organization; this is not your place. I want you to lay the basis of our activity in Western Europe.[346]

The Director reasoned that no one seemed better qualified to take up the post of Resident Director of the GRU in Western Europe than Trepper. He knew the French arena; his Polish friends of the Bir *apparat* were either still in France or had gone to ground in Belgium; and not only could he speak French like a Frenchman, he could also speak German – the language of the perceived principal enemy.[347]

As a cover the 'Centre' provided Trepper with a Canadian passport, No 43671, issued to a certain Michael Dzumaga born in Winnipeg on 2 August 1914, which had fallen into the hands of the Soviet Secret Service during the Spanish Civil War. This was altered to bear the name Adam Mikler, a French-speaking Canadian industrialist. To make his cover story watertight – a Canadian industrialist intent on setting up business in Belgium – Trepper took minute pains to acquaint himself with his Canadian background. He briefed himself most carefully on the Canadian official and business world and on life in Canada in general. He even obtained detailed reports on Canadian industry, economy, food supply, agriculture and forestry.[348]

Thus armed, Trepper set out in the spring of 1938 on his great venture to form a GRU *apparat* in Western Europe. As his Canadian passport could obviously not show a Soviet visa, he embarked on a roundabout journey to Belgium using a series of false papers. One passport took him to Finland and Sweden and another was used to gain entry into Denmark and then Antwerp, where he received his Canadian passport from a representative of the Soviet Trade Delegation, its stamps proving that the holder, Adam Mikler, had just arrived in Belgium direct from Canada.[349]

A few months later Luba and their second son Edgar, who was eighteen months old, joined Trepper in Belgium. Luba travelled with a the passport of a French schoolteacher, receiving another, which identified her as Anna Mikler newly arrived from Canada, when she reached Belgium. Michel, the elder son, remained in a boarding school in Moscow: it was the habit of the Soviets to keep at least one member of a spy's family in Russia as an insurance policy against defection.[350]

The scene was set for the formation of the Red Orchestra.

29. The Road to Brussels

Trepper, alias Adam Mikler, arrived in Belgium with 10,000 Canadian dollars, provided by the GRU, to set up a commercial enterprise as a cover for his clandestine activities. Belgium was chosen because it provided an ideal observation post on Nazi Germany. Belgian law attached only lenient penalties for espionage, provided it was not directed against the country itself; and her geographical situation permitted rapid communications with Germany, France and the Scandinavian countries. A further point in Belgium's favour was the fact that it was the only country with which the Moscow 'Centre' maintained a smooth flow of radio traffic.[351] This was provided by Johann Wenzel, a GRU agent who had been infiltrated into Belgium in 1936, where he set up a small *apparat* called 'Group Hermann', which specialized in collecting information on the armaments industries of the Western European powers. Trepper made contact with Wenzel shortly after he arrived in Belgium; and 'Group Hermann' became the embryo of the Red Orchestra.[352]

The $10,000 provided by the GRU, which was far from a modest amount by 1938 standards, allowed Trepper to engender the image of a well-to-do Canadian industrialist by renting a comfortable apartment in the Avenue Richard-Neuberg in a fashionable part of Brussels, where he set up home with

Luba and his baby son. Trepper's next step was to set up his commercial cover. For this he made contact with Leo Grossvogel, his old friend from the Palestine Communist Party.

Grossvogel came from a line of prosperous Jewish burghers who had lived in Strasbourg for generations. As a teenager Leo had been sent to study in Berlin, but, seized with Zionist idealism, he had abandoned his studies in 1925 and emigrated to Palestine. Like Trepper, he quickly became disillusioned with Zionism and he joined the Palestinian Communist Party. Unable to stand the grinding poverty of his situation, Leo returned to Europe in 1928 and joined two members of his family who had set up the business called Le Roi du Caoutchouc (The Raincoat King) which specialized in all kinds of rainwear.[353]

Leo was appointed the firm's commercial director, but he did not repudiate his Communist convictions. As a respectable businessman, well known in industrial and commercial circles in Brussels, he had the perfect cover to act as liaison between the Comintern and the Communist parties of the Near East. Trepper did not have much difficulty, however, in persuading Grossvogel to give up this very important function and devote himself to espionage for the GRU. To this end he helped Trepper set up a cover firm. Since Le Roi du Caoutchouc made raincoats, Leo came up with the idea of creating an import–export company that would market Le Roi du Caoutchouc's products through numerous branches in foreign countries.[354]

The resulting company, which was given the unidiomatic English name 'Foreign Excellent Trench Coat Company', was floated in the autumn of 1938. The management of the firm was entrusted to a plump, jovial Belgian in his late fifties, a *bon vivant* with a white moustache and ruddy cheeks called Jules Jaspar. The Jaspar family was one of the country's outstanding bourgeois dynasties: Jules' brother had been Prime Minister of Belgium, and Jules himself had served as Belgian Consul in both Indo-China and Scandinavia. Armed with such a figurehead, the firm was above suspicion – although Jules had no inkling of the dark secrets lurking beneath the trench coats. Another of Leo's long-time acquaintances, Nazarin Drailly, was made head of the accounting department.[355]

Thanks to the *savoir-faire* of Grossvogel, Jaspar and Drailly the firm prospered and expanded rapidly. Branches were established in Sweden, Denmark and Norway, and trading relations were established with outlets in Italy, Germany, France and Holland. All of the branch officers were run by respectable businessmen who had no idea that the profits were funding a Soviet espionage *apparat*.[356]

As soon as the commercial cover was deemed sufficiently reliable, the 'Centre' began sending Trepper additional trained personnel. In April 1939 Mikael Makarov, the radio operator, arrived from Moscow posing as Carlos

Alamo, a citizen of Uruguay. He was followed in July 1939 by Victor Sukulov-Gurevich (alias 'Kent'), also posing as a Uruguayan citizen, and two months later by Konstantin Yefremov, posing as Eric Jernstroem, a Finnish student. These were joined at the end of 1939 by Sophie Poznanska, the cipher expert who was already resident in Belgium and operating under the cover-name of Anna Verlinden, and the Palestinian Jew David Kamy, a radio operator working under the cover-name Albert Desmets, who had been living in Paris since the early 1930s.[357] To this group of professional GRU agents was added Isidor Springer, a German Jew and successful diamond merchant who had fled to Belgium from Frankfurt in 1933: he was introduced to the *Grand Chef* by Grossvogel, who had met Springer, a convinced Communist, through his business contacts. Springer in turn brought along other friends: Rita Arnould, the German *émigré* and Springer's mistress, whom Trepper employed as a courier; Hermann Isbutsky, courier; Augustin Sesee, reserve radio operator; and Simone Phelter, an employee in the Franco-Belgian Chamber of Commerce.[358]

Through Wenzel the *Grand Chef* was also able to extend his network into Holland. Wenzel made contact with Daniel Goulooze, a Dutch Communist radio operator and an old comrade of his in the Comintern. Goulooze was in contact with other Comintern men in Amsterdam, amongst them Anton Winterinck ('Tino'), whom the *Grand Chef* appointed head of the Dutch group, code-named 'Hilda'. Winterinck quickly gathered together a group of twelve agents, including radio operators, couriers and informers, and by the end of 1940 'Hilda' had begun relaying radio messages to Moscow.[359]

Wenzel also put the *Grand Chef* on to Abraham Raichmann – 'The Cobbler' – who was at that time on remand in a Belgian prison awaiting trial for forgery. To obtain his expertise Trepper instructed Grossvogel to employ the best lawyers available to assure Raichmann's acquittal.[360] His mistress, Malvina Gruber, a plump, matronly Czech, also joined the *apparat* as a courier.

Throughout this period of formation the Red Orchestra kept radio silence. Trepper thought it more important to recruit informers and organize contacts with business circles, diplomats and the military than send information over the air to Moscow. The Red Orchestra would only really start work in the event of a Russo-German conflict.[361]

In May 1940, when the German forces began their westward march of conquest, they demolished one of the most important strategic assumptions on which the Soviet espionage campaign was based. The Red Orchestra's strategy had rested on the principle that the intelligence assault on the Third Reich would be directed from neighbouring neutral countries, out of reach of the German counter-espionage agencies. As a result of the German invasion of France and the Low Countries, however, Trepper's *apparat* was suddenly confronted by the physical proximity of Hitler's field-grey legions and the *Abwehr* and *Gestapo*: the hunted and the hunters were now next-door neighbours.[362] Moreover, on the day the Germans invaded Belgium a weakness in Trepper's cover came to light. The 'Centre' had decided to give Trepper the German-sounding cover-name 'Mikler' as a way of explaining his slight foreign accent when speaking French. That the name 'Mikler' suggested German ethnic origins had unfortunate results, as Trepper recalled:

> At dawn on 10 May 1940 the *Wehrmacht* moved on Western Europe. German aircraft bombed Brussels. I had gone to see 'Kent' to write my first coded dispatch on the military operations. During my absence three Belgian police officers presented themselves at my apartment on the Rue Richard-Neuberg, where Luba and I had been living as Adam and Anna Mikler since 1938, both of us very busy with the first phases of organizing the *apparat*. They told her that they had orders to arrest us and send us to an internment camp. We were to take a change of clothes and sufficient food for a few days. The reason they gave was that, in their opinion, although we were naturalized Canadians, our surname suggested people of German descent and the Belgian authorities had decided to lock up all nationals of the Third Reich and their relatives residing in Belgium. The moment was critical, to say the least.
>
> Fortunately Luba did not lose her nerve and she invited the three policemen to enter the apartment and sit down. She explained that the town we came from, Sambor, was in Polish territory, and she pointed out its position in a Larousse Encyclopedia. Uncertain what to do, the three policemen decided to go back to their superiors for further instructions.
>
> I arrived home a short while later. When Luba told me what had happened I congratulated her on her initiative and decided to break camp without delay. The police would certainly be back, and this time they would not pass us by. We hastily packed our bags and left the premises.[363]

They sought refuge in Leo Grossvogel's apartment at 117 Avenue Prudent-Bols. Trepper equipped himself with new identity papers, prepared by Raichmann, which changed his cover to that of *Monsieur* Jean Gilbert, an industrialist born in Antwerp. He then decided to get Luba and Edgar to safety, and they were repatriated to Russia, travelling in the diplomatic cars of the Soviet Trade Delegation which was withdrawn from Brussels back to Russia via Marseilles.[364]

While the *Wehrmacht* swept through Holland, Belgium and northern France, the *Grand Chef* and his agents set out to observe German strategy and tactics. Trepper followed the victorious Germans in a car, witnessing at first hand the breakthrough by the panzers at Sedan and the fighting around Abbeville and Dunkirk. Back in Brussels, he wrote an eighty-page report at the beginning of June in which he summed up everything that he and his agents had learned and witnessed of the German *Blitzkrieg* in the west – the deep penetration by tanks behind enemy lines, the aerial bombardments of strategic points and the mechanisms of communication between the rear and the front.[365]

Up to the German occupation of Belgium, Trepper had kept in touch with the 'Centre' through the Military Attaché at the Soviet Trade Delegation in Brussels. The withdrawal of the delegation cut off Trepper's line of communication, forcing him to activate the *apparat*'s radio operators. The main radio team was installed in a villa on the Avenue Longchamp in the Ukkel district of Brussels. It consisted of Mikael Makarov (alias Carlos Alamo) and David Kamy (alias Albert Desmets), who worked the short-wave radio transmitter; Sophie Poznanska (alias Anna Verlinden), who did the encoding and Isidor Springer's mistress Rita Arnould, who, somewhat unwillingly acted as housekeeper and courier. Wenzel, meanwhile, acted as reserve radio operator from an apartment in the Laeken district. At this stage the radio in the Avenue Longchamp was only activated on very few occasions, to receive instructions from Moscow and to keep the 'Centre' informed of the *Grand Chef*'s progress; Wenzel, meanwhile, maintained strict radio silence.[366]

In August 1940, two months after the defeat of France, Trepper decided to expand his *apparat* by setting up a network in Paris. Appointing 'Kent' – the *Petit Chef* – as his deputy, he placed him in charge of the Brussels *apparat* with funds and instructions to set up another cover firm, which resulted in the formation of Simexco. The *Grand Chef* then embarked on the road to Paris.

30. The Road to Paris

The *Grand Chef* arrived in Paris at the end of August 1940. He was accompanied by his pregnant mistress, Georgie de Winter, and Leo Grossvogel. Trepper had started an affair with Georgie de Winter during the autumn of 1939. She was a 20-year-old, auburn-haired beauty 'with sparkling eyes, graceful bearing and a perfect figure'[367] when she fell for the charms of the 35-year-old, thick-set Trepper, who had no scruples about betraying his wife Luba's fidelity. The daughter of a Belgian mother and an American father, who was working at the Paramount Studios in Hollywood, Georgie had been studying classical dancing in Brussels when she met the man who would eventually introduce horror and tragedy into her life. She recalled:

> I was overjoyed when we moved to Paris. There we really lived a magnificent life. You cannot imagine the kindness of that man [Trepper], his sensitivity and attentiveness. Whenever he had to travel he used to reserve me seats at concerts and plays for every evening he would be away. He was always buying me things. Because of the danger he kept urging me to return to America, offering me a small nest-egg in dollars to live on. But I loved him too dearly and I was ready to die for him. He never discussed his activities with me. All in all he was very secretive – not that I had any real desire to

know what he was up to. I was very young and carefree, we loved each other, life was marvellous, and that was all that mattered. Whether he was a spy or a raincoat salesman, my feelings for him were exactly the same. I used to go to the Place Clichy in Paris every day for dancing lessons. In the evening – almost every evening – we used to go to a restaurant and then wind up in a cabaret; he had a passion for cabaret singers. What a wonderful life we had! I can honestly say I've never been so happy.[368]

Trepper also enjoyed the benefit of Leo Grossvogel's business acumen and powers of organization in setting up the cover-firm Simex and forming the new espionage circuit in the French capital. Grossvogel rented apartments in the Rue Fortuny and Rue de Prony for the *Grand Chef*, and later a villa in Vésinet for Georgie, shortly after her son Patrick was born, where she lived under the cover-name of Elisabeth Thevenet with forged papers provided by Raichmann. Grossvogel also rented some twenty flats in the suburbs of Paris as hide-outs for the *apparat*.[369]

Trepper and Grossvogel were assisted in the recruitment of agents, couriers, 'letter-boxes' and informers by Hillel Katz, a Polish Jew and a Communist whom both men had known in Palestine. Of medium height, with keen, intelligent eyes behind thick spectacle lenses and possessing a high forehead crowned by an abundant head of curly hair, Katz was instrumental in persuading Alfred Corbin to become the manager of Simex, which was registered with the Seine District Commercial Court on 16 January 1941. Katz also recruited the Communist militant Suzanne Cointe, who became office manager, and Vladimir Keller as the firm's translator; the latter, who had been born in Russia but had become a Swiss national, had no idea that his employers were involved in espionage.[370]

At its inception Simex occupied offices in the Lido building on the Champs Élysées and the firm did its principal business with the Todt Organization, whose offices were conveniently situated in the requisitioned Marbeuf Cinema directly across the street. One of the firm's unsuspecting employees, Emmanuel Mignon, recalled that

> Simex was amusing; we used to get a lot of fun out of our work. The firm dealt almost exclusively in black-market goods. People would turn up from all over the place, offering the most extraordinary merchandise, and we would ask the Boches [Germans] if they were interested. They never said no. Some of the junk we managed to unload on them was simply unbelievable. On one occasion we received several bales of some so-called Oriental rugs. We opened one bale, to take a quick look, and were driven back by a cloud of moths. We wrapped it up again and decided to sell the whole consignment to the Todt just as they were. They paid up without a murmur. The Todt Organization was our chief customer, and the men in charge knew perfectly well that our merchandise came from the black market, but they did not seem to mind. Once we sold them a disused railway that someone had approached us about. They bought the rails and the ties were sold off as firewood. We also sold them several hundred

thousand oil drums. At first they were of good quality, but after a while we could get only damaged ones. It was my job to supervise the repair operations. I used to roam around the repair yard chalk-marking all the holes that needed patching. Then the welders would move in and conscientiously solder them, well to the side of the holes! Truck-loads of oil drums full of holes were dispatched to Germany, day after day, and we never received one word of complaint.[371]

The net profits of Simex and Simexco amounted to 1,616,000 francs in 1941 and 1,641,000 francs in 1942, after deducting the operating costs of the Belgian, Dutch and French networks. Trepper kept a strict account of all income and expenditure, for, like all other Soviet network chiefs, he knew that eventually he would have to submit his accounts to Moscow. He and his associates were paid in dollars (the dollar had always been the monetary unit employed by the 'Centre').

In 1939, the *Grand Chef* received $350 a month. This was reduced to $275 when Luba and Edgar returned to Moscow. 'Kent', Makarov and Grossvogel at first received $175 a month. But after the outbreak of the German-Russian conflict in June 1941 all the Red Orchestra agents, from the biggest to the smallest, were paid a uniform wage of $100 a month: this was war, and they were regarded as troops on active service. Naturally, they were allowed unlimited expenses.

At first glance the expenses seem light. In the period from 1 June to 31 December 1941 the Belgian *apparat* cost $5,650 and the French *apparat* $9,421. From 1 January to 30 April 1942 $2,414 went to the French network and $2,042 to the Belgian network, while 'Kent', in Marseilles, received $810. From 1 May to 30 September 1942 the figures are given in francs: 593,000 for France, 380,000 for Belgium and 185,000 for 'Kent'.

But these figures cover only routine expenses – agents' pay, rent, etc – and do not reflect the total expenditure involved in lavish entertainments laid on for German officers and officials. For these occasions the *Grand Chef* could afford to splash out, for, thanks to the activities of Simex and Simexco, the money spent on entertaining the Germans actually came out of their own pockets. The Third Reich was subsidizing the Red Orchestra, just as a living organism will nourish the cancer which is eroding it. Trepper kept his accounts hidden inside a large clock in a rented apartment at Verviers, while Katz hoarded a thousand gold dollars at his home as a reserve in case of a crisis.

Although Simexco and Simex had been set up primarily to serve as a cover and to finance the Red Orchestra, Trepper soon realized that they allowed himself and his agents to penetrate the official German services in an unhoped-for manner. Because of their business relations with the Todt Organization in Brussels and Paris, the principals in Simexco and Simex received *Ausweise* (passes) which allowed access to restricted areas.[372]

In the course of good meals washed down with plenty of wine the Germans talked readily while Trepper and his associates, with glasses in hand and smiles on their lips, exuding an approving air, listened to their revelations. The information they accumulated in this manner proved to be considerable. For example, Ludwig Kainz, one of the engineers of the Todt Organization, who became very friendly with Leo Grossvogel, gave the Red Orchestra the first indications of the German build-up in the east. Kainz had worked on the construction of fortifications on the German≈Russian border in occupied Poland and he had observed the *Wehrmacht*'s preparations for the offensive against Russia.[373]

Trepper also established liaisons with the French resistance organizations. Amongst these was Henry Robinson, who had years of service in the Comintern to his credit. Born in 1897 in Frankfurt, he had been involved in the left wing socialist 'Spartacist' attempt to proclaim a soviet republic in Germany during 1918. He was later a Comintern instructor in Paris, becoming responsible for industrial espionage in France early in the 1930s.[374] Robinson brought into Trepper's embryo French organization an intelligence circuit whose informers worked in numerous government agencies; they even had links with the Vichy cabinet governing the French Free Zone, and with the French Army's secret service. The Robinson circuit was also in close touch with the French Communist Party and the GRU's *Die Rote Drei apparat* in Switzerland.[375]

A second group of agents, initially regarded with some suspicion by Trepper but finally accepted into the Red Orchestra, brought the *Grand Chef* into contact with another section of French society – the church, the aristocracy, and Russian *émigrés*. Heading this group were Baron Vassily Pavlovich Maximovich, a mining engineer, and his sister Anna Pavlovna Maximovich, a neurologist. Their father had been a general in the Tsar's army and the family had been forced to flee to France from Russia after the October Revolution in 1917 when the Bolsheviks seized power. They had initially belonged to the 'Young Russia' movement, an association of White Guard *émigrés* in France with somewhat fascist tendencies, but by the early 1930s they had drifted into Soviet service since the money enabled Anna Maximovich to open a private clinic and nursing home at Choisy-le-Roi.[376] This clinic became a repository of highly important information since it was frequented not only by Russian *émigré* leaders but also by *Monsignor* Chaptal, Bishop of Paris, and Darquier de Pellepoix, Commissioner-General for Jewish Affairs in the Vichy government; the latter's brother was the clinic's head doctor.[377]

Trepper, however, was primarily interested in the Maximovichs because of their relations with the German occupation authorities. As a general's son Vassily was on good terms with officials in the German military administration in Paris, particularly since he had formed a romantic liaison with 44-year-old

Anna-Margaret Hoffman-Scholtz (code-name 'Hoscho') of the German Women's Auxiliary Service, who was serving as a secretary to *Militärverwaltungsoberra* Hans Kuprian, a senior military administrative officer on the staff of the German Commandant of Paris.[378] Vassily, a White Russian *émigré* and thus ostensibly an anti-Communist, was trusted by the Germans to the extent that they provided him with a permanent pass for entry into the Hotel Majestic, where the Germans had set up their General Headquarters. He made a habit of turning up at the hotel every evening to meet Anna-Margaret when she finished her duties, where she would hand over copies of the most important documents that had passed through her hands that day, which Vassily then passed to the *Grand Chef* over a courier line.[379] Later – exactly when is not clear – Anna-Margaret was transferred to the secretariat of the German Ambassador in Paris, Otto Abetz. 'Hoscho''s industriousness soon earned her the trust of the entire embassy staff, together with access to the most confidential documents. Through her efforts, Moscow was kept informed of political deals with the Vichy government, of the feelings and attitudes of the French people and of Germany's plans and set-backs.[380]

Another source of inside information was recruited by Anna Maximovich. Among the patients at her neurological clinic was 35-year-old Käthe Völkner, a secretary to the president of the French branch of the Sauckel Organization, which was in charge of the procurement of foreign workers for the Third Reich. Anna had divined that Käthe, at heart, was anti-Nazi, and her instinct paid off. Käthe began supplying first-hand information on the manpower needs of German industry and the economic problems of the Third Reich. In addition, she procured blank forms and certificates of employment for the members of the Red Orchestra; in the event of an inspection, these certified that the bearer, a worker in Germany, was currently on vacation.[381] Käthe also introduced into the *apparat*'s ranks a Frenchman employed in the *Wehrmacht*'s Central Billeting Office in Paris. At first sight he did not appear to have much to offer, but in fact he was to prove one of the most important recruits acquired by the *Grand Chef*. He worked in an agency known as the Jeip-Fahrer. 'Jeip' was a name made up from the first letters of the phrase *Jeder einmal in Paris* ('Everyone to Paris once'), a propaganda and morale-boosting exercise which tried to ensure that every German soldier paid one visit to the occupied French capital. As it was impossible to pull whole units out of the front line, the Jeip-Fahrer would be informed that private A, serving with unit B, was due to arrive from point C for a spell of leave in Paris. From these lists the French informer in the Jeip-Fahrer was able to provide Trepper with a more or less complete picture of the German order of battle.[382]

Trepper also managed to induce a group of French telephone technicians to set up a monitoring board on the telephone lines of the Hotel Lutetia, the headquarters of the Paris *Abwehr*, allowing the *apparat* to monitor the calls between the German counter-espionage section in Paris and *Abwehr* headquarters on the Tirpitzufer in Berlin.[383]

Another method of extracting information from the Germans involved the use of prostitutes in Parisian nightclubs which were frequented by the enemy. One of the guides employed by the Jeip-Fahrer to show the German soldiers around Montmarte and the Eiffel Tower was also in Trepper's pay, and he steered them towards certain bars where they were introduced to 'ladies' who took a 'real' interest in the soldiers' lives and troubles. With the aid of liquor and feminine charm, the 'ladies' were able to provide Trepper with many interesting facts – the strength of German divisions and their location, casualties, supply problems and the morale of the troops.[384]

In the early months of 1941 the *Grand Chef*'s network of agents, informers and couriers, which was rapidly spreading over the whole of France, Belgium, Holland, Germany and neutral Switzerland like a great spider's web, noticed that the German preparations in the Channel ports for an invasion of Great Britain were being wound down. The vessels which had been assembled to transport the invading army to the beaches of southern England were being withdrawn, along with the mass of troops that had been billeted in the French and Belgian coastal areas. In addition, informers and agents working for the French, Belgian and German railways reported a great shift of German forces to East Prussia and Poland – a sure indication that Hitler had abandoned his plans to invade Great Britain and was preparing for an attack on the Soviet Union.[385]

Trepper sent detailed dispatches to Moscow giving the exact number of German divisions being withdrawn from the west to the east. During the first week of May 1941 he also learned of the proposed date on which the invasion would be launched, 15 May, which was later revised to 22 June. The 'Centre' was also receiving accurate warnings of the German intentions from the British and American Governments, the Berlin *apparat* and the *Die Rote Drei* circuit in Switzerland, and from Richard Sorge, a GRU agent in Japan. Yet Stalin chose to ignore the warnings. Marshal Golikov, writing in a Soviet historical review thirty years after the war, confirmed the value of the information received by the 'Centre':

> The Soviet Intelligence Service had learned in good time the date of the attack against the USSR and had given the alarm before it was too late ... The intelligence services provided accurate information regarding the military potential of Hitler's Germany, the exact number of divisions and aircraft involved, the quantities of arms, and the strategic plans of the commanders of the *Wehrmacht* ...[386]

So why did Stalin choose to ignore the warnings? Trepper believed that

He who closes his eyes sees nothing, even in the full light of day. This was the case with Stalin, who preferred to trust his political instinct rather than the secret reports piled up on his desk. Convinced that he had signed an eternal pact of friendship with Germany, he was content to go on sucking on the pipe of peace.[387]

Because Stalin chose to ignore the warnings, it took the sacrifices of the whole of the Soviet Union for four long and terrible years to reverse the defeat of the summer, autumn and winter of 1941, at a cost of twenty million Russian lives. The moment Hitler's field-grey legions poured over the Bug and Niemen rivers into the Soviet Union, the Red Orchestra's short-wave radio transmitters burst into life. Such was the flood of information that had to be relayed to Moscow that the pianists Makarov, Kamy and Wenzel in Brussels, Goulooze and Voegeler in Amsterdam and Coppi in Berlin were obliged to tap away on their Morse keys for up to five hours a night. Trepper's invisible network had raised its periscope in a sea of field-grey uniforms, giving the Germans their first indication of the existence of the Red Orchestra, when the long-range radio monitoring station at Kranz intercepted one of Makarov's PTX transmissions in the early hours of 26 June 1941.

Ironically, however, Trepper's French *apparat* did not possess a single transmitter. Shortly before the German invasion of the USSR the Military Attaché in the Russian Embassy in Vichy had promised to hand over two short-wave radio transmitters to the *Grand Chef*, but, owing to the hurried departure of the embassy staff, he had not found time and the French *apparat* were left without radio communication to Moscow.[388] Consequently they had no choice but to relay all their messages via the transmitters in Brussels and Amsterdam, which not only overworked the pianists but also put a heavy strain on the courier lines linking the three cities. Matters were made worse by the difficulties experienced by Hans Coppi, the Berlin pianist, which necessitated the three Brussels pianists' also having to cope with the bulk of the Berlin *apparat*'s messages. One of the couriers carrying the enciphered messages from Berlin to Brussels was the very beautiful Ina Ender, a fashion model in the Salon de Couture, where Hitler's mistress Eva Braun and the wives of Nazi dignitaries bought their clothes![389]

So overworked did the three Brussels pianists become, tapping their Morse keys non-stop night after night, that it aided the German security forces in their hunt for the clandestine transmitters, culminating in the Rue des Atrébates raid during the night of 13/14 December 1941. Apart from capturing Mikael Makarov, David Kamy, Sophie Poznanska and Rita Arnould, the Germans also came close to capturing the *Grand Chef* himself. Makarov, Poznanska and Arnould had moved into 101 Rue des Atrébates only a month or two before the raid, leaving Kamy to operate his set in the Avenue Longchamp. Hardly had the group taken up residence in the new abode when Sophie Poznanska sent an anxious message to Trepper, asking him to come and restore discipline because Makarov had began bringing ladyfriends back to the apartment who had no connection with the *apparat*. Trepper arrived at the Rue des Atrébates on the day following the raid. In his memoirs he recalled how near he came to being arrested:

It was noon when I rang the doorbell. A German policeman opened the door. We were face to face. I had the definite sensation that my heart stopped beating. With some effort I pulled myself together, and, adopting an assertive manner, inquired when the garage across the street opened. The policeman grabbed my arm and pulled me inside. The house had been searched from top to bottom, and the disorder was indescribable – the classic image of a police raid. This was a tight one. I was in a large room; through the glass partition that separated me from the stairway I saw Kamy. I got out my papers without waiting to be asked, in a deliberate way, with an air of confidence, and handed them to the German. His jaw dropped in astonishment. The document I handed him, which was covered with official stamps and signatures, said the bearer, *Monsieur* Jean Gilbert, had been commissioned by the president of the Todt Organization in Paris to look for strategic material destined for the *Wehrmacht*. The president requested the different branches of the army of occupation to facilitate *Monsieur* Gilbert's search in any way they could.

To break the silence, and by way of further explanation, I said: 'There's a garage across the street where I thought I might find some old cars for scrap iron. It's closed, and I rang this bell to find out what time it opens.' A little more pleasantly the German replied: 'I believe you, but you'll have to wait until the chief [Piepe] gets back.' I replied that it was impossible as I had to catch a train back to Paris, because the president of the Todt Organization was expecting me to report back that afternoon. The policeman hesitated for a few moments, then decided to call Captain Piepe. I can still hear the thunder of abuse that crackled in the receiver: 'Imbecile! Why are you holding this man? Release him immediately!' The German grew pale and looked as if the sky had fallen on his head.[390]

Having so narrowly missed falling into the clutches of the *Abwehr*, Trepper rushed off to warn 'Kent' of the danger. After the word had been spread for the Belgian *apparat* to suspend their activities and lie low, Trepper ordered 'Kent' and Springer to make their way to Paris, from where they eventually moved to the Free Zone. 'Kent' went to Marseilles, where, with Jules Jaspar, he set up a branch office of Simexco with the intention of forming a new espionage circuit, while Springer went to Lyon in company with his wife Flore on a similar mission.

The loss of two of the Brussels pianists and the necessity of the third (Wenzel) to remain silent until the storm had blown over made it all the more imperative for Trepper to find a pianist and transmitter for the French *apparat*. Accordingly he requested the 'Centre', via the Dutch transmitters, to put him in touch with the head radio man of the French Communist Party. The 'Centre' complied, but it was not until February 1942 that Trepper was able to establish contact with a French Communist agent calling himself 'Michel'. He arranged for Trepper to make temporary use of the Party's transmitters, limiting the messages to some 300 cipher groups a week pending his being able to place a set at the *Grand Chef*'s sole disposal.

The French Communist Party was in fact so short of sets that Fernand Pauriol, its radio expert, had to rig up a set himself for Trepper's French *apparat*. It proved to be too weak to send messages directly to Moscow, but its wattage was sufficient to reach the Soviet Embassy in London, whence the French *apparat*'s messages were passed on to the 'Centre'. The set was worked by the Polish husband and wife team Hersch and Myra Sokol, who had been recruited by the Military Attaché in the Soviet Embassy in Paris during the summer of 1940. They began transmitting on Pauriol's rigged-up transmitter at the end of February 1942, but after relaying some 600 lengthy messages their transmissions came to an abrupt end when they were arrested by the *Gestapo* during the night of 9/10 July (see Chapter 10).

Radio communication now became the Red Orchestra's Achilles' heel, for without the means of relaying messages to Moscow the intelligence-gathering activities of the *apparat* were worthless. A week before the Sokols were arrested Trepper's only remaining Belgian pianist, Johann Wenzel, had also fallen into the hands of the Germans (see Chapter 8), a disaster compounded by the break of the Dutch *apparat* a month later (see Chapter 12) and the round-up of the Berlin *apparat* in September. For the remaining two months of the French *apparat*'s activities, which ended when Trepper was arrested in Dr Maleplate's dental surgery on 27 November, the only means of communication with Moscow was provided by the limited use of the transmitters of the French Communist Party.

At the beginning of 1942, with his network in ruins and the knowledge that the *Sonderkommando* were poised to strike, Trepper, along with Leo Grossvogel and Hillel Katz, retreated to a villa in Antony, a suburb of Paris. There they decided that the fifty-odd members of the French *apparat* should suspend their activities, while they themselves should acquire new identity papers and go to ground in the south of France. As a way of covering his tracks, Trepper – whom the Germans knew as Jean Gilbert – prepared a funeral service in Toyat, a little town near Clermont-Ferrand. A death certificate and a memorial plaque were duly readied in the name of Jean Gilbert;[391] but, before he could 'die', *Monsieur* Gilbert had a dental appointment to keep.

31. The Road to Perdition

During the short drive from *Dr* Maleplate's dental surgery to the *Sonderkommando*'s headquarters in the Rue des Saussaies, the *Grand Chef*, handcuffed between Piepe and Giering, calmly announced that the game was up and that he was prepared to collaborate. Piepe and Giering were stunned by this unhoped-for statement, for if the *Grand Chef* were true to his word they believed that it would mean the end of Soviet espionage in the West.[392]

Capitalizing on the possibilities, the Germans did their best, during the preliminary interrogations of Trepper, to establish an atmosphere of mutual trust. Incarcerated in an improvised cell on the ground floor of the Rue des Saussaies, where he remained for two and a half months, he was not mistreated and was well fed and supplied with as many cigarettes as he wanted. As he had heart trouble he was examined by an Army doctor twice a week. The interrogations were carried out in an informal manner and usually took place after lunch, for the members of the *Sonderkommando* were not at their best in the mornings on account of hangovers. Every evening of the week they set off on heavy drinking bouts, their favourite haunt being a nightclub in the Rue Saint-Anne, where the French singer Suzy Solidor sang 'Lily Marlene' and other wartime favourites in a husky, suggestive voice.[393]

By this time Giering was visibly wasting away and his voice had become hollow as the cancer which had first manifested itself as a tumour in the throat continued its relentless spread. Thus it was that when Giering and Piepe conducted their interrogations of the *Grand Chef* they did so over a bottle of brandy and endless cups of coffee, which Giering consumed in large quantities to relieve his symptoms. They chatted away like old comrades exchanging reminiscences as Trepper betrayed the remains of his *apparat*.[394]

In the eyes of the moralists, the fact that Trepper was prepared to collaborate indicated 'a level of moral degradation and treachery which represents the most shocking chapter in the three-decade history of Soviet espionage'.[395] But that is easy to say by someone who was not facing the prospect of 'intensified interrogation' by the masters of the craft, and ultimately execution if he refused to co-operate. Trepper's behaviour, Heinz Höhne suggests, was motivated by a whole complex of circumstances – the instinct of self-preservation, the hope of escape in an unguarded moment and, above all, the insatiable curiosity of the professional who longed to know how his adversary set about solving his problem.[396] As for the Germans, they were astute enough to realize that in Trepper's case they would be unable to extract the truth by physical methods of pressure: under torture he would only answer leading questions but never give away his real secrets.[397]

To begin with, Trepper assisted the *Sonderkommando* in rounding up the few leading agents of the French *apparat* who were still at large. Hillel Katz was the first victim of the master whom he had regarded with almost religious veneration. On Giering's orders Trepper telephoned Katz and arranged to meet him at the Madeleine Metro station. Giering sent a couple of his men to the rendezvous and Katz was arrested on one of the platforms. Driven to the Rue des Saussaies, he was brought face to face with Trepper. His whole world collapsed around him when he realized who had betrayed him, but Trepper remained quite unmoved, saying, 'Katz, the game is up: we must work with these gentlemen.'[398]

But, unlike his chief, Katz refused to collaborate, and during his preliminary interrogations he was beaten up by *Kriminalobersekretär* Eric Jung, who smashed his spectacles with a blow from his fist which lacerated Katz's cheeks and eyelids. When beatings and threats failed to loosen Katz's tongue the *Gestapo* tore out his fingernails, but still Katz refused to talk.[399] Trepper also divulged his contacts with the German headquarters in Paris, as a result of which Vassily Maximovich was arrested on 12 December 1942 and Vassily's sister Anna Maximovich and his mistress Anna-Margaret Hoffmann-Scholtz (who was serving on the secretariat of the German Ambassador in Paris) shortly thereafter. Because anything relating to the German military administration in Paris was technically the preserve of the *Abwehr*, Piepe conducted the interrogations of the two Maximovichs, who betrayed Käthe Völkner, secretary to the President of the French branch of the German Sauckel organization, and her lover, an Italian named Podsialdo, who had acted as a courier between the Frenchman working in the Jeip-Fahrer billeting office and the *apparat*.[400] Trepper also betrayed the fact that Ludwig Kainz, the engineer with the Todt Organization, had been an unwitting informer, and he received a prison sentence for military indiscipline.[401]

Only two of the French *apparat*'s leading agents now remained at liberty – Leo Grossvogel and Henry Robinson, the representative of the Comintern. They too became victims of the *Grand Chef*'s treachery. Although he did not know Grossvogel's precise whereabouts, Trepper was able to give the *Sonderkommando* a vial clue: Grossvogel regularly made contact with Simone Phelter, the secretary in the Franco-Belgian Chamber of Commerce in Paris. In the second week of December Simone was arrested and under interrogation she revealed that she was expecting Grossvogel to make telephone contact with her at her office in the Chamber of Commerce. Occupying the office, the *Gestapo* forced Simone to continue to answer her telephone as usual, and when Grossvogel duly rang on the 16 December Simone, as instructed by the Germans, arranged to meet him at the Café de la Paix near the Paris Opera at 7.00 p.m. that evening.[402] Grossvogel was arrested as he approached the café, he *Gestapo* being able to identify him by way of a recent photograph provided by Simone Phelter.

In the hunt for Henry Robinson, Trepper gave Giering the address of Medardo Griotto, an Italian engraver and forger whose apartment Robinson frequently used as a rendezvous with Comintern agents.[403] Under Giering's orders Trepper telephoned Griotto, instructing him to summon Robinson to a meeting at the Palais de Chaillot, where he was to collect an important message from the *Grand Chef*. Robinson turned up at the rendezvous and was identified by Trepper, who was sitting in the back of a *Gestapo* car. Both Robinson and the unsuspecting Griotto were arrested and driven to the Rue des Saussaies.[404]

Robinson had covered his activities by posing as a journalist. He lived in a small hotel room which was filled with books and papers. In the midst of this jumble the *Gestapo* discovered five passports which had been forged by Griotto, three of them made out in the name of Henry Robinson. All three had been recently used for journeys to Switzerland, as was shown by the date stamps of the frontier control. This infuriated the *Gestapo* because Henry Robinson had been on their wanted persons list since 1933, yet none of the German border guards had apprehended him. The number of passports was understandable: by alternating them when crossing the frontier into Switzerland, he did not arouse suspicion by the frequency of his journeys, as shown by the tell-tale date stamps in any one passport. But for them to be in Robinson's own name was incomprehensible to the *Gestapo*. Trepper, however, saw it as typical of the amateurism of the Comintern in general and of Robinson in particular.[405]

Thanks to the *Grand Chef*'s treachery, at the end of December 1942 Karl Giering and Harry Piepe reported to their masters in Berlin that their hunt was finally at an end. Moscow's greatest espionage organization in Hitler's empire had been eliminated. Piepe's role in the affair ended at this point and he returned to Brussels, where he served in the local *Abwehr* until the Allies liberated the city in September 1944. Giering, however, despite his rapidly deteriorating health, was not finished with the *Grand Chef*.

32. Last Echoes in Brussels and Paris

On 18 February 1943, only three weeks after he had prosecuted in the last of the Berlin trials, Manfred Roeder arrived in Brussels to condemn the Red spies of the Belgian network in accordance with German martial law. However, Roeder would not be prosecuting because he had now donned the mantle of Judge Advocate-General, to head a special tribunal with the sonorous title

'Special Field Court Martial of the Commanding General and Commander-in-Chief of Air Region III'.[406]

The trials lasted a fortnight and resulted in death sentences being passed on the three surviving members of those captured during the Rue des Atrébates raid – David Kamy, Mikael Makarov and Rita Arnould. The last-named's attempt to save her neck by betraying everything she knew to the Germans was no more successful than Libertas Schulze-Boysen's decision to turn State's evidence. Death sentences were also passed on Augustine Sesée (the reserve radio operator), Hermann Isbutsky and Maurice Peper (couriers), Leo Grossvogel's wife Jeanne (who had given birth to a son only three months before the trial) and Nazarin Drailly (manager of Simexco). Makarov's death sentence was later commuted when the Germans discovered that he was a nephew of Molotov, the Soviet Foreign Minister.

In addition Bill Hoorickx, who had rented apartments for the *apparat*, and Henry Rauch, a Czech relative of Margarete Barcza who had been forcibly conscripted into the *Wehrmacht* and became an informer, were sentenced to terms of hard labour, along with Renée and Josephine Clais, who had worked as couriers. Roeder also passed terms of imprisonment on the shareholders of Simexco, most of whom had no idea of the firm's espionage connection, and on Maurice Beublet, the company's legal adviser. Amongst the shareholders were Jean Passelecq, a businessman; Robert Christen, a nightclub owner; Louis Thevenet, the owner of a cigarette factory; Henry de Ryck, a publisher; Henry Seghers, a businessman; and Charles Drailly, Nazarin's brother.[407]

On 8 March 1943 Roeder's court moved to an office block opposite the Élysée Palace in Paris, where he opened a new series of trials to condemn the members of the French *apparat* of the Red Orchestra. The improvised courtroom was set up in a requisitioned office on the sixth floor of the building. In total, Roeder passed eleven death sentences: on Alfred Corbin, Leo Grossvogel, Vassily and Anna Maximovich, Henry Robinson, Käthe Völkner, Suzanne Cointe, Medardo Griotto, Simone Phelter, Giuseppe Podsialdo and Flore Springer (whose husband, Isidor Springer, had committed suicide in Fresnes prison while awaiting trial). Marie Corbin (Alfred's wife), Germaine Schneider ('Schmetterling'), Vladimir Keller (the interpreter), Jules Jaspar and his wife Claire, Marguerite Marivet (secretary of the Marseilles branch of Simexco) and Anna-Margaret Hoffmann-Scholtz were all sentenced to terms of hard labour.[408] Hillel Katz was not arraigned before Roeder because the *Sonderkommando* had other plans for him.

A sentence of imprisonment with hard labour had a particularly sinister connotation in Hitler's Reich: what it in fact meant for the majority who received this sentence was merely an alternative and agonizing form of death. At dawn on 15 April 1943 all those who had been sentenced by Roeder were

riven from Fresnes prison to the Gare du Nord railway station, where they
ere bundled on to a train bound for Berlin. They were seated six to eight
 a compartment: the doors and windows were locked and armed SS guards
atrolled the corridor of the carriage. Later that day the train stopped at
russels, where the French prisoners were horrified to see a group of wretched
en and women, little more than skin and bones, being led by guards towards
e train, some of them with large, festering sores on their legs. These unhappy
reatures were members of the Dutch and Belgian *apparat*s who had been
rought from the Breendonk *SS-Auffanglager*. The most pitiful were David
amy, Hermann Isbutsky and Nazarin Drailly, all of whom had been
articularly cruelly tortured; Drailly was so changed that his wife did not
ecognize him among the others on the platform. The guards distributed the
russels contingent among the others and the train continued its journey to
erlin with a total of 68 members of the Red Orchestra on board.[409]

The train reached Berlin's Anhalter railway station in the morning of 17 April,
orty-eight hours after leaving Paris. The exhausted prisoners had the impression
f setting foot on another planet. It was a Saturday and the railway station was
rowded with Berliners gaily going off to picnic in the woods outside the capital.[410]
he *Gestapo* sorted out the herd and dispatched those who had been sentenced to
leath to Berlin's Moabit and Lehrterstrasse prisons, while those who had received
entences of imprisonment with hard labour were transported to the Potsdamer
tation, where they boarded a train bound for the notorious Mauthausen
oncentration camp situated near Linz in Austria.

Their arrival has been described in simple, undramatic terms by Robert
hristen, the Belgian nightclub owner who had been persuaded to become a
hareholder in Simexco by 'Kent'. Mauthausen first appeared as a long, walled
ortress on the horizon, then they passed an immense, deep quarry swarming with
housands of human ants in striped uniforms. It was like a lunar landscape. 'Who
an they be, working there?' the new arrivals asked one another. 'Where are we?'
That evening they saw for the first time a man murdered before their eyes. The
*Kapo*s (inmates appointed by the camp authorities as overseers) had pounced on
im and beaten him almost to death; he lay there, unconscious but still living. The
*Kapo*s called for the camp executioner to give the *coup de grâce*, and the unfortunate's
ame rang through the camp from one hut to the next. The terrified members
f the Dutch, Belgian and French *apparat*s did not sleep that night, wondering what
would happen to them next.[411]

Only nine of the 68 who had been transported to Germany survived to see
he end of the war. Those in Mauthausen died slowly and painfully of
exhaustion, starvation, disease and brutality. The majority of those condemned to death were executed in Plötzensee on 28 July 1943. Amongst them
was Alfred Corbin, who wrote a letter to his wife Marie which broke off abruptly

on the morning he was hanged by the men in top hats, white gloves and tailcoats:

> When I was arrested on 19 November 1942 I was subjected to two short interrogations by the policemen who arrested me. They hit me a few times, but nothing really serious. On 30 November they brought me together with you and Denise [his daughter] and this marked the beginning of an odious psychological blackmail – 'Your wife and daughter will be shot as hostages, unless . . .' On 3 December they came for me at 6.30 in the evening and took me to the Ministry of the Interior [in Paris], to what they called the Tribunal, and there I was tortured by a specialist and left half dead. I was hit with a club on the soles of the feet, the thighs and the buttocks, and kicked – in short a thorough job! This went on for three hours.
>
> [He was interrogated on four further occasions between 7 December and 27 February.] On 27 February a final interrogation concerning you [Marie]. This time I got angry because they tried to make me say that you were aware of the activities of people you had never heard of, nor I either for that matter.
>
> Finally on 8 March this farce of a trial and a death sentence for almost everyone! This, without any possibility of appeal. Moreover, throughout our stay in Fresnes prison I was kept in solitary confinement and handcuffed night and day; I still have the scars!
>
> . . . Well, my dear love, that is a brief account of the last five months. I cannot forgive myself for being the cause of your arrest and Denise's, for in the course of the interrogations I said that I loved you more than anything in the world and that nothing else mattered to me, but since then I have realized . . .[412]

His wife Marie was one of those sent to Mauthausen, from where she was later transferred to Ravensbrück concentration camp; she did not survive the barbarous conditions and maltreatment. Marie Corbin was in fact entirely innocent of any knowledge of the Red Orchestra and its activities, as were one quarter of the 68 people transported to Germany in April 1943. Guilty and innocent alike paid a terrible price for their witting or unwitting connection with the Red Orchestra.

33. The Great Game

In comparison to his doomed army of agents, couriers and informers, the *Grand Chef* was afforded a life of relative comfort by the *Sonderkommando*. On 23 February 1943 Trepper was moved from his cell in the Rue des Saussaies to a private house on the corner of the Boulevard Victor Hugo and the Rue du Rouvray in the suburb of Neuilly, to the north-west of the centre of Paris. He was joined by Hillel Katz (who the *Gestapo* believed would be able to give them leads into the French Communist Party) and 'Kent' along with the latter's Czech mistress Margarete Barcza.

The house in Neuilly was an imposing place, surrounded by a large garden, with a façade of white columns that gave it the air of a Greek temple. It was guarded by a dozen Slovak volunteers. Conditions for the inmates were by no means rigorous. Each had a comfortable room with plenty of books, and the food, which was brought in from nearby restaurants, was excellent. Although the four prisoners were kept locked in their rooms, they only had to knock for a guard to appear, ready to accede to any reasonable request. Two maids did the cleaning and changed their bedding, and daily exercise was provided by walks around the spacious, well-tended garden: the iron grill-work fence surrounding the property and the abundant foliage concealed them from the eyes of passers-by. They were also treated to occasional visits to a cinema in a small town on the outskirts of Paris.[413]

The reason why the *Sonderkommando* went to these lengths to make their selected 'guests' as comfortable as possible was that they needed their co-operation in mounting a *Funkspiel* (radio play-back) with Moscow. For out of the ashes of the *Grand Chef*'s circuit a new Red Orchestra arose – but this time it was the *Gestapo* who conducted the pianists.[414] Trepper in his self-effacing autobiography *Le Grand Jeu* and Gilles Perrault in his book *L'Orchestre Rouge* both maintain that the Gestapo's *Funkspiel* concealed some high-level political motivation: that it was an attempt on the part of the Germans to enter into political discussions with the Russians, in the hope that a compromise peace agreement could be arrived at. There is no evidence whatsoever to support this claim, and the fact of the matter is that *Kriminalkommissar* Thomas Ampletzer, the *Gestapo* expert in *Funkspiel*, had a much more prosaic objective in mind – to confuse the 'Centre' and lure the Director into giving away his own secrets.[415]

Ampletzer had been supervising a radio play-back to Moscow since September 1941 with Johann Wenzel until his dramatic escape in January 1943 (see Chapter 9) and thereafter with Konstantin Yefremov and Anton Winterinck, both of whom were lodged in an apartment on the Rue l'Aurore, Brussels. Ampletzer's aim was to convince Moscow that although the Dutch and Belgian circuits had been ravaged by the German counter-espionage agencies, remnants were still operating effectively, as shown by Yefremov's and Winterinck's continuing transmissions of information. With Trepper, 'Kent' and Katz ensconced in the house in Neuilly, the *Gestapo* now hoped to dupe Moscow into believing that the Paris *apparat* was also still functioning.

For the last two months of the French *apparat*'s existence all messages to Moscow had been relayed over the short-wave transmitters of the French Communist Party. As this avenue of communication was now severed, the *Gestapo* instructed Yefremov to inform Moscow that henceforth, on account of communication difficulties experienced in Paris, he and Winterinck would be handling the French *apparat*'s messages. Moscow, it seemed, accepted the story, and from the end of February 1943 radio traffic began flowing betwee Moscow and the *Grand Chef* as smoothly as if it had never been interrupted.[4]

This, however, gave rise to a major dilemma. The 'Centre' constantl requested sensitive military information, and as it was necessary to provid a certain amount of accurate information to preserve the fiction that the Re Orchestra was still functioning a complex procedure of obtaining approval t transmit factual information was inaugurated. When the 'Centre' requeste military information the *Sonderkommando* had to ask the *Abwehr*'s French Office located in the Hotel Lutetia in Paris, to release the necessary information. Th *Abwehr*, in turn, had to apply for approval to Field Marshal Gerd vo Runstedt, the Commander-in-Chief of the German forces in the West, an only with his sanction could the *Abwehr* compile the necessary material. The the *Sonderkommando*, with the assistance of Trepper, could draft the radi message in the proper form for transmission to Moscow. The enciphering c the messages was done by 'Kent', after which the *Sonderkommando* had to pas the message on to the *Funkabwehr* office in the Boulevard Suchet for the tex to be checked. Finally the message was passed on to *Gestapo* Headquarters o the Prinz-Albrecht-Strasse in Berlin, where it was checked to ensure that i fitted into the overall picture of the *Funkspiel* with Moscow.[417]

In spite of these bureaucratic obstacles, however, Ampletzer contrived to giv the 'Centre' a prompt service and the traffic between the *Gestapo* and Moscov increased week by week, as the Director's questions became increasingly mor urgent and precise. On 19 February 1943 the 'Centre' radioed: 'Try to establisl the numerals of units being transported to the Spanish frontier and the types o guns and tanks.'[418] On 21 February came an order: 'Get the Manufacture [Raichmann] to observe transport and equipment of German troops, primaril those moving from France to Germany en route for Russian Front, but als movement back to France.'[419] The next day the 'Centre' wished to know: 'Wha German divisions are being held in reserve in France and where? This questio is of particular importance to us.'[420] On 9 March the request was made: 'Infor us what German troops are located in Paris and Lyon. Numerals, arm of service ration strength and equipment.'[421]

Questions of this sort threw the *Sonderkommando* into profound confusion It was impossible for them not to answer, but to answer with false informatio would risk blowing the *Funkspiel*; for careful examination of the 'Centre'' questions led Ampletzer to conclude that Moscow was trying not so much t obtain information as to verify information already in their possession, whic they had received from the French Communist Party. This suspicion seeme to be confirmed by a query from the 'Centre' dated 18 March: 'Check an inform us forthwith whether 462 Infantry Division is in Nancy, 465 Infantr Division in Épinal and 467 Infantry Division in France – we do not know th exact location;'[422] and by another received ten days later: 'What divisions are located in Châlons-sur-Marne and Angoulême? We have information that 9 Infantry Division is at Châlons-sur-Marne and 10 Panzer Division at Angoulême. *Confirm truth of this intelligence* [author's italics].'[423]

Almost every day very precise requests for information arrived from the 'Centre', to which the *Sonderkommando* had no choice but to reply in just as much detail. For example, they reported to Moscow:

> Reliable source informs us that in the closing weeks of December the Germans initiated extraordinarily extensive troop movements towards the Spanish frontier, particularly in the area Bordeaux–Angoulême–Hendaye. Between 10 and 20 December troop transport traffic was so dense that on many days up to eight troop trains were observed on the vital stretch of railway between Poitiers and Angoulême.[424]

On 16 March they reported:

> Numerous troops from Antwerp and the vicinity moving in the direction of southern France, comprising 26 troop trains, 18 of more than 50 carriages and 8 of about 40 carriages primarily infantry.[425]

On the 2 April the 'Centre' was told that

> The new SS division in Angoulême has no number but the soldiers wear a grey uniform with black epaulettes and the insignia of the SS. Equipment – an extraordinarily large number of motorized vehicles.[426]

On 4 April further information was provided about this SS division:

> Artillery, medium and heavy howitzers and heavy long-barrelled guns, all motorized. In addition extraordinarily numerous anti-tank guns of modern type and numerous anti-aircraft guns. The division has a number of medium-heavy armoured cars. Strength of the division about 16,000 men.[427]

The substance of the information passed to Moscow was entirely accurate – the price the *Gestapo* had to pay in the attempt to make the Director reveal his network of informers still working in the West. For although the *Sonderkommando* was reasonably certain that the entire Red Orchestra *apparat* in Germany, France, Belgium and Holland had been swept up, they knew that the Comintern network and the underground circuit of the French Communist Party were also involved in spying for the Russians. Indeed, the main *raison d'être* of the *Funkspiel* was to provide the means of tracking down these circuits.

This hunt, however, would not be led by Karl Giering. By the spring of 1943 Giering had become so ill from cancer that he was no longer able to continue his duties. Admitted to the Landsberg hospital in Germany, he died in the autumn, with the consolation of having won his race against time: he had lived long enough to see the Red Orchestra destroyed and the *Grand Chef* and *Petit Chef* reduced to his obedient servants. Giering had shown himself to be cruel and violent but also cunning and intelligent. He had inflicted torture without flinching and had borne the torture of cancer without flinching, but it is doubtful that he was prepared to meet his Maker without flinching!

Giering's post as head of the *Sonderkommando* was filled by *SS-Hauptsturmführer* and *Kriminalrat* Heinz Pannwitz, whom Trepper described as 'young, fat elegantly dressed, with a round pink face and keen eyes hidden behind thick glasses'. Born in Berlin in 1911, Pannwitz had been a practising Christian since his early years, and when Hitler came to power in 1933 he was studying to become a pastor, but he did not complete his theological studies and joined the *Gestapo* instead! However, even after joining the *Gestapo* he remained a member of the Confessional Church. In 1941 he became a member of Reinhard Heydrich's immediate entourage in Prague (Heydrich had been appointed Protector of Bohemia and Moravia), and when Heydrich was assassinated in the summer of 1942 Pannwitz was placed in charge of the investigation. It was he who directed the assault of a whole SS battalion on the crypt of the Karl Borromaeus Church in Prague, where the Czech assassins had taken refuge. During the process of tracking down Heydrich's assassins he became convinced that nothing could be achieved by the mere brutal persecution of anti-Nazi resisters. He expounded these views to Heinrich Müller, the head of the *Gestapo*, arguing that the *Gestapo* must abandon the pure persecution of espionage and resistance groups and play along with them, because 'if a group were totally destroyed a hundred others would spring up after it, and that had to be prevented'.[428] Müller was not particularly impressed by this line of reasoning, but when Giering's post fell vacant Pannwitz seemed the ideal candidate. Müller exhorted him 'to do what he had proposed [play along with an espionage group] and play for any stakes he liked'.[429]

When Pannwitz arrived in Neuilly at the beginning of July 1943, he began the task of attempting to cause the Director to reveal the whereabouts of Comintern and Communist Party agents in France. His opening gambit was to relay a message from the *Grand Chef*, via the 'converted' pianists in Brussels, asking the 'Centre' to put Trepper in touch with a radio technician from the French Communist Party. Moscow's reply – giving the time and place of a rendezvous – resulted in the arrest of Comrade 'Jojo'. His parents kept a café in the St Denis quarter of Paris, at the back of which was a workshop where 'Jojo' built and repaired radio transmitters for the Communist Party. Under interrogation at the Rue des Saussaies 'Jojo', who could no longer bear the pain inflicted by the *Gestapo*, betrayed a whole chain of Communist agents and informers, amongst them Fernand Pauriol (who had rigged up a transmitter for Trepper after the Rue des Atrébates raid).[430] Pauriol was arrested on 13 August 1943, at Pierrefitte, north of Paris, and taken to the Rue des Saussaies where he was atrociously tortured. Despite the *Gestapo*'s brutality, Pauriol refused to betray any of his comrades and he was executed in Fresnes on 12 August 1944, shortly before the Allies liberated Paris.[431] In a letter to Trepper dated March 1974, Pauriol's wife Hélène described her last meeting with Fernand and how she found out about his fate:

In early January 1944 I received a letter with the address in my husband's handwriting. The letter was addressed to *Madame* Hélène Pauriol, in care of *Madame* Prunier, 19 Avenue de la Grande-Pelouse, Le Vésinet. Inside were a few lines asking me to go to the *Gestapo* headquarters on the Rue des Saussaies on the 19th – perhaps I would be able to see him – and to bring him a suit. So on 19 January I went to the Rue des Saussaies, taking the letter with me. I took my little girl along. It wasn't until I was inside the building that I said to myself, 'I'm crazy – I shouldn't have brought the child with me.' I hadn't realized at first how much I longed to see whether he was alive, to see if it was really him. I didn't realize that it was madness to bring a child, because they could just as easily have taken the girl, and besides I didn't know how I was going to react.

I was taken upstairs to the fourth floor. I waited in a room, sat on a sofa, with my little girl, and after about five minutes two Germans came in, and behind them was my husband. He sat down beside me. He had on the same suit he had been wearing the day he was arrested. There were bloodstains on it. He took the suitcase that I had brought his clean suit in. We were allowed fifteen minutes together and then I was told to leave. I waited outside and I saw him leave in a *Gestapo* car. And that was the last time I saw him.

After that I heard nothing . . . until after the liberation of Paris by the Allies. I went to the newspaper *L'Humanité* because they had lists there of the fates of people who had been arrested by the Germans during the occupation. They told me they had no information regarding Fernand, but that I was not to give up hope.

On the first Sunday in October 1944 a young girl called at my home . . . and handed me a letter from my husband . . . which turned out to be my husband's last letter and his wedding rings . . . I couldn't rest until I had identified his body. I was able to do this on 14 November 1944. At the cemetery in Bagneux were buried two unknown persons, a Belgian woman and a Frenchman, who had both been executed on 12 August 1944. When they exhumed the coffin and opened the lid I knew it was Fernand because he was wearing the grey flannel suit I had delivered to him at the Rue des Saussaies.[432]

Pannwitz was equally successful with a second ploy, which resulted in an entire Communist espionage organization working for the *Gestapo* without realizing it. In 1940 a Latvian Comintern functionary named Waldemar Ozols (code-name 'Solja') had formed a small espionage circuit on the orders of the Soviet Military Attaché in Vichy. The Director, however, found the work of the Ozols group unsatisfactory, and when two of its informers were arrested by the *Gestapo* in 1942 he decided to merge the remainder of the Ozols circuit into the Red Orchestra. In the summer of 1943 'Kent' received a message from the 'Centre' instructing him to use Ozols' group for informer work within his own organization.[433] Of course 'Kent' was, at this time, enjoying the *Gestapo*'s hospitality in Neuilly, which indicated to Pannwitz that the 'Centre' had not seen through the game the *Sonderkommando* were playing.

The 'Centre' obligingly included the address of Ozols' hide-out in Paris – 24 Villa Molitor – and 'Kent' sent him a message arranging a meeting at the Café Dupont in the Place des Ternes on 1 August. Ozols kept the appointment and the results were disastrous. 'Kent' persuaded Ozols to introduce him to Captain Paul Legendre, head of the 'Mithridates' resistance network, who agreed to furnish him with information which could be passed to Moscow. Neither Ozols nor Legendre realized that the information they provided was actually benefiting the *Gestapo*.[434]

Through the Ozols and Legendre groups the *Gestapo* were able to keep under surveillance wider and wider sectors of the French underground. Captain Karl von Wedel of the *Funkabwehr* maintains that the Ozols–Legendre circuits

> ... provided valuable pointers as to the weak points in our own security system and in some cases served to keep Moscow confident. In this way we succeeded in penetrating further into the organization of the French Communist Party and learning more about the kind of messages in which Moscow was more interested.[435]

Despite this advantage the *Sonderkommando* began to find it increasingly difficult to maintain the credibility of the *Funkspiel* with Moscow. The 'Centre' was demanding detailed reports on increasingly sensitive issues, and Field Marshal von Runstedt was becoming increasingly reluctant to release secret military information. Matters came to a head when the Director demanded the following information:

> Order the Manufacturer to discover whether the army of occupation is preparing to use poison gas. Is gas moved in its pure state without adulteration? Other secret consignments or movements will, of course, also be carefully camouflaged. Are there stocks of gas bombs on airfields and if so which? What is their quantity and size? What gas do they contain and what is the effect of this gas? Are experiments on the effects of the various poison gases being undertaken? Have you heard anything about a new gas named 'Gay-Hale'? The same questions are applicable to Gastronomy [the code-name for France]. Pass all intelligence about gases and poisons as quickly as possible. Director.[436]

When the *Sonderkommando* informed the *Abwehr* that they needed a compilation of information on this subject to relay to Moscow, they in turn passed the request on to the C-in-C West, but Runstedt was adamant that an answer to this enquiry was unthinkable.[437] Moreover, the *Abwehr* reported to Berlin that

> The position of C-in-C West is that for some time the master station in Moscow has been putting such precise questions of a military nature that continuation of the *Funkspiel* is only possible if these precise questions can be answered with equal precision; otherwise the Moscow master station will see through the game. For military reasons, however, he finds it impossible to provide the material to answer

questions by Moscow, which continually include details of divisional and regimental numbers, names of commanders, etc . . . C-in-C West adheres to his opinion that in the present military situation in the West, no further interest attaches to deception of the Moscow master station, and sees no virtue in continuing the *Funkspiel*.[438]

By this time the *Gestapo* too had begun wondering whether Moscow had seen through the *Funkspiel*, and whether the matter should be brought to an end. As it transpired, it was the *Grand Chef* who made the decision for them. Shortly after Trepper was moved from the Rue des Saussaies to the house in Neuilly he managed to convince Giering that he was constantly shadowed by agents of the NKVD (renamed the KGB in 1954), and that if these agents did not see him turn up at places he habitually frequented in Paris – cafés, barbers' shops, restaurants, tailors' and other shops – they would report that he had been arrested and the *Funkspiel* would be blown.[439] As a result Trepper was taken on short outings around the city. On the first few occasions two *Gestapo* cars flanked the vehicle he was in, but as time wore on the *Sonderkommando* gradually relaxed their guard and he was accompanied only by Willy Berg and a driver. In this way he went to a barber on the Rue Fortuny, a tailor's shop in Montparnasse, a haberdasher on the Boulevard Haussmann and cafés and restaurants in the various *arrondissements* and suburbs of Paris.[440]

Kriminalobersekretär Willy Berg was an unhappy man. Two of his young children had died of diphtheria and his third daughter had been killed in an air raid. His wife, unable to endure this series of blows, tried to commit suicide and was confined to a mental hospital. To cope with all this Berg indulged in heavy drinking and regularly suffered from monumental hangovers. On Monday 13 September 1943 he arrived at the house in Neuilly suffering from a particularly severe hangover and Trepper suggested they take a trip to the Pharmacie Bailly on the Rue de Rome, which reputedly sold an effective remedy for such a condition. By the time the car pulled up outside the pharmacy Berg was prostrate with nausea and a violent headache and he sent Trepper to buy the remedy unsupervised. After some ten minutes had passed Berg grew apprehensive and, more dead than alive, he went into the pharmacy, only to find to his horror that the *Grand Chef* had fled through a door at the back of the shop which led on to the Rue du Rocher. The Great Game had come to a sudden end.

34. The Hungarian Mapmaker

The Red Orchestra circuits in the Reich and German-occupied Europe were dead, but this was not the end of the story. During the latter half of 1942 the German long-range radio monitoring stations in Dresden and Prague reported heavy radio traffic from three short-wave transmitters operating in neutral Switzerland. Through cross-bearings two were tracked down to Geneva, close to the Franco-Swiss border, and the third to Lausanne on the northern shore of Lake Geneva. When the intercepts of these transmissions were sent to the radio traffic analysts in the *Funkabwehr* offices on the Matthäikirchplatz they concluded that the cipher employed by the Swiss operators was of an identical format to the one-time pad that had been used by the *Grand Chef*'s pianists.

The existence of a Swiss *apparat* of the Red Orchestra was confirmed by Raichmann's Czech mistress, Malvina Gruber, who after her arrest in September 1942 revealed that she had crossed the Franco-Swiss frontier as a courier on many occasions, carrying messages to and from 'cut-outs' operating for a GRU *apparat* in Switzerland. 'Kent' also confirmed its existence, informing the *Gestapo* that he had gone to Geneva on two occasions, in March and December 1940, to deliver details of the cipher and radio schedules that were to be employed by the Swiss *apparat* in liaison with the 'Centre' in Moscow. Finally there was the matter of the passports found in the hotel room of the Comintern agent Henry Robinson, which showed that he too had made frequent trips to Switzerland.

The Germans named this *apparat Die Rote Drei* (The Red Three) on account of their being three pianists, which was in fact all that they knew about the extent and structure of the network. For, unlike the Red Orchestra circuits in Germany, Holland, Belgium and France, the Swiss frontier acted as an effective safety curtain, providing *Die Rote Drei* with reasonable security from the *Abwehr* and the *Gestapo*. Force was out of the question, and the only hope that the German security agencies had of silencing the transmitters was to resort to guile by attempting to infiltrate the Swiss *apparat*, discover its sources of information and destroy it from within. But the Germans were never to discover the full extent of the Swiss circuit nor its sources of information, which were situated in the very centre of the German High Command.

The head of *Die Rote Drei* was an Hungarian *émigré* called Sándor Radó. He was born in Ujpest, an industrial suburb of Budapest, in 1899. He came from a prosperous middle-class family and he was well educated, excelling in languages and geography, the latter being his lifelong passion.[441] In 1916, at the age of seventeen, Radó was called to the Austro-Hungarian colours and he served as an officer on the general staff of the artillery in Budapest, being spared active service at the front. At the end of the First World War, which resulted in the dissolution of the Austro-Hungarian Empire, he entered Budapest University to read law and politics. There he first became aware of the works of Karl Marx and Friedrich Engles, which, coupled with reports of the revolution and the new social order in Russia brought back by returning Hungarian prisoners of war, quickly led him to become a Communist disciple.[442]

On 16 November 1918 Hungary broke away from Austria and the Prime Minister, Karolyi, proclaimed the country to be an independent republic. But Serb, Czech and Romanian troops quickly installed themselves in two-thirds of the helpless country, and in the confusion Karolyi's government was overthrown by Bela Kun, who declared Hungary to be a soviet republic. Radó joined the newly formed Hungarian 'Red Army' and, although only nineteen years of age, was appointed a political commissar. But the Communist revolution in Hungary collapsed within a year and Radó was forced to flee for his life to Austria when the 'White Terror', instituted by Admiral Horthy and his counter-revolutionary forces, took control of the country.[443]

Making his way to Vienna, Radó enrolled in the university, where he read geography. Penniless, he was forced to support himself by carrying out part-time work loading barges on the Danube for a Transylvanian merchant. He still found time, however, to edit a German-language periodical called *Kommunismus*, which he founded with a group of other students from the university and which he described as the 'first scientifically edited Communist review outside Russia'.[444] In addition he discovered that the Austrian Government's wireless telegraphy office was picking up daily radio transmissions from Moscow, giving news of events in the Soviet Union. Cut off from the rest of the world by the civil war raging between the Bolshevik and White Russian forces, the Soviets' only method of communicating what was happening was by means of radio broadcasts. Little of this was available to Western newspapers, and Radó hit upon the idea of setting up a unique news agency dealing exclusively with Russian internal matters, his source being copies of the Soviet radio messages, which he obtained by bribing the director of the Austrian wireless telegraphy office.[445]

Radó set up his news agency, which he called the Rosta-Wien, in July 1920. He staffed it with Hungarian communist *émigrés*, who prepared a daily bulletin in German, French and English which Radó sold to newspapers and left-wing organizations throughout Europe. As the business flourished, Radó abandoned his studies and was able to extend his activities by setting up the telegraphic agency Intel, which gathered news from left-wing sources outside the Soviet Union, which were then broadcast to Moscow.[446]

Radó was still only twenty-two years of age, but through his news agencies he had already established himself as a person of some importance in international Communism. As a mark of Moscow's recognition he was invited to the 'Third International' in the Russian capital in May 1921, and again in October 1921, to attend a conference on the co-ordination and extension of Communist information services. However, his career in the news agency business proved to be short-lived: early in 1922 the Soviet Union established diplomatic relations with Austria, which meant that information from and to Russia was thereafter distributed and controlled on an official basis through the Russian and Austrian embassies, rendering both Rosta-Wien and Intel defunct.[447]

Deprived of his income, Radó appealed to the Russians for help, and they provided him with a modest grant so that he could pursue his geography studies. But, rather than remain in Vienna, Radó obtained a place in Leipzig University, where he met and married Hélène Jansen, a Communist activist known to her friends and family as Lène.[448]

By 1924 Radó had not only completed his studies at Leipzig University but had also completed and published a political atlas of the USSR, which instantly established him as an expert on that country. He then began work on the world's first aerial maps, which involved flying all over Europe, Asia and Africa. This served to build up his reputation as a geographer of some distinction, becoming a corresponding member of the prestigious Royal Geographical Society in London. Radó then went on to write the first guidebook of the USSR, and the first political atlas of the workers' movements, the *Arbeiter-Atlas*, which was published in many countries including Britain, where it appeared under the title *Atlas of Today and Tomorrow*. He also claimed to have been the first person to coin the term 'Soviet Union' as acceptable shorthand for the Union of Soviet Socialist Republics.[449]

While all this was going on Radó also created the world's first press agency dealing in maps and geographical diagrams, which he called Pressegéographie. This agency quickly proved successful and Radó, who was supporting his wife, two sons and mother-in-law, was able to purchase a small house on the outskirts of Berlin. But they were unable to live there for long because in February 1933, shortly after the Nazis seized power, Radó and Lène, being Communists, were forced to flee to Vienna with the rest of the family.

While settling in the Austrian capital Radó made the acquaintance of Kurt Rosenfeld, a Communist lawyer, and between them Radó and Rosenfeld set up a news agency with the sole aim of distributing uncensored news and information about Nazi Germany, untainted by Joseph Goebbels' Propaganda Ministry. To avoid confrontation with Nazi groups in Austria, it was decided that Paris would be a better base for the agency, and so in May 1933 Radó and his family moved into a cottage at Bellevue on the outskirts of the French capital, which soon became a meeting place for left-wing *émigrés*. The new agency, Inpress (Agence de Presse Indépendante), was originally situated in a small office in the Rue Mondetour, near Les Halles, the Paris market place, but the success of the enterprise allowed Radó and Rosenfeld to acquire more salubrious premises in the Élysée Building in the Faubourg St Honore, opposite the British Embassy.[450]

Once more, however, political events put paid to one of Radó's enterprises. In 1935 the right-wing politician Pierre Laval became premier of France, which doomed the left-wing Inpress, and again Radó was forced to rely for his living on his geographical activities, which he kept alive by writing articles for magazines, preparing maps for the French press and editing the volume on foreign countries for the *Great Soviet World Atlas*. Work on the Soviet atlas required Radó to make a trip to Moscow in October 1935, to discuss his contribution to the work with the publishers. While there he was approached by a GRU recruiting agent, who put a proposition to him which was to place him at the forefront of the struggle against fascism.[451]

35. Pakbo

Through the GRU recruiting agent, who approached him while he was in Moscow, Sándor Radó was introduced to the Director of Soviet Military Intelligence. Offered an income that would solve his precarious financial difficulties, and the opportunity to work more effectively against fascism, Radó readily agreed to become a GRU agent. According to Radó's account, the Director then said:

> I know that you are no novice in secret work, but secrecy is not the only thing for an intelligence service. You must be able to assess speedily changing political situations, because the work of an intelligence agent lies in the political field. We must first define those who will be our enemies in the future, so that our intelligence operations can be directed against them. You know that the Soviet Union has several potential enemies in Europe, the most threatening being Germany and Italy.[452]

Thus briefed, Radó, who was given the code-name 'Dora' (an anagram of Radó), was dispatched to Switzerland with enough funds to set up a mapmaking agency as a cover, from where he was to collect intelligence on Germany and Italy. He arrived in Geneva at the beginning of 1936, moving his family into a fifth-floor apartment of a large, six-storey block at 113 Rue de Lausanne, in the Secheron district of the city, and set about establishing the Geopress mapmaking agency.

During the summer of 1936, the Spanish Civil War broke out and Radó was inundated with requests from many quarters for maps illustrating the progress of the fighting. Geopress was soon supplying maps to newspapers and journals throughout Western Europe as well as to libraries, academic institutions, embassies, consulates, ministries, military establishments and even private individuals with an interest in international affairs, including the deposed German *Kaiser*. Most of the work was done by Radó himself, assisted by a draughtsman who did the finished artwork and Lène who ran the administrative side of the business.[453]

With Geopress well established, Radó gained accreditation to the League of Nations Press Office, which was situated literally round the corner from the Radó family home. The accreditation gave Radó access to the League of Nations library and other facilities, where he made the acquaintance of many highly placed and useful contacts. From these contacts Radó gleaned highly sensitive political information, which he passed to the 'Centre' via Henry Robinson's Comintern *apparat* in Paris, which had instituted a courier line between Geneva and the French capital. Radó also prepared a detailed map for the 'Centre' showing the locations of all the munitions and armaments factories in Germany and Italy.[454]

In April 1938 Radó's one-man *apparat* expanded when the 'Centre' put him in touch with Otto Pünter. A native of Switzerland (he was born in Berne in 1900), Pünter founded a small press agency in 1927 which he called INSA (International Socialist Agency). The *raison d'être* of INSA was to provide the Swiss newspapers with uncensored reports of developments in Italy after Mussolini and his fascist party came to power. Through the work of his agency Pünter came into contact with Randolfo Pacciardi, an Italian exile in Switzerland and leader of the Italian anti-fascist organization *Giustizia e Libertà* (Justice and Liberty). This organization had members spread throughout Italy, including men who held positions in the highest echelons of industry, commerce, politics, law, the universities and the military. From these varied sources Pacciardi received a continual flow of information which he passed on to Pünter's INSA for distribution to the press.[455]

In 1933, when Hitler came to power, Pünter added Germany to his list of targets and he quickly established important contacts there. Shortly after the Nazis seized power, Goebbels, the Reich Propaganda Minister, began swamping Switzerland with Nazi propaganda designed to exploit the Swiss fear of Communism. The Swiss believed with fervour in the sanctity of capitalism and consequently their news reports tended to be written from a right-wing point of view, but under fascist influence the slant became a perilously steep slope on which the truth was in danger of being swept away in an avalanche of lies propagated in fascist magazines and newspapers, funded by Berlin, which mushroomed on the Swiss market.[456]

Aware of the pressures being applied by the fascists, and of their methods, Pünter complained to the BUPO (*Bundespolizei*, the Swiss equivalent of the FBI), which was responsible for dealing with subversive activities and crimes affecting the security of the state. Although BUPO was aware of the influx of Nazi propaganda, they had not realized the scale of it nor the methods used to spread it, and Pünter was able to give them the names of the Swiss journalists and newspaper editors, and of the publishing firms and press agencies, being used as fronts for Goebbels' propaganda onslaught. Impressed by Pünter's list of contacts in Germany and Italy, and the information he was able to provide, BUPO enrolled him as an unofficial agent, offering their protection in return.[457]

When the Spanish Civil war broke out in 1936 Pünter founded the Swiss-Spanish Society, the purpose of which was to inform the Swiss public of events in Spain through films, lectures, articles and pamphlets. To obtain first-hand information for the society, Pünter paid a visit to Valencia and Barcelona, where he made the acquaintance of a GRU recruiting agent working under the code-name 'Carlo', who persuaded him to begin passing information to Moscow. Working under the code-name 'Pakbo' (composed from the initial letters of the principal meeting places where Pünter met his informants – Pontresino/Poschiavo, Arth-Goldau, Kreuzlingen, Berne/Basle and Orselina), Pünter became one of the 'Centre''s most important sources of information.

The flow of material from 'Pakbo''s vast network of informers was passed to Radó, whom the 'Centre' had appointed the Resident Director of all Soviet agents at large in Switzerland. 'Dora' and 'Pakbo' were brought together for the first time at the end of 1936, at a rendezvous in a Berne restaurant arranged by the 'Centre'; and from then on Radó was provided with a steady flow of information from Pünter's sources.[458] Both agents agreed that they should not only make use of their existing sources but also do everything they could to expand their contacts in Germany and Italy, the perceived enemies in any future war with the Soviet Union. Up to the outbreak of war in September 1939 the flow of information on the German and Italian military build-up, and the economics and political machinations of the two countries, increased month by month in quantity and detail. The network was still expanding when Britain and France declared war on Germany, and Switzerland reacted by closing her frontiers, temporarily severing Radó's means of communicating with the 'Centre' by way of the courier lines to Paris – a breakdown that was not rectified until December 1939, when Radó received a visit from a slim, attractive woman who introduced herself as Sonia.

36. Geneva Calling Moscow

'Sonia' was the code-name of Ruth Kuczynski, a German by birth, who had been recruited into the GRU by the Soviet agent Richard Sorge while she was living in Shanghai with her husband in the early 1930s. Sorge arranged for her to go to Moscow for training, after which she operated in China and later in Poland. With the intention of infiltrating 'Sonia' into Britain the 'Centre' sent her to Switzerland at the end of the Spanish Civil War with the object of recruiting British veterans of the International Brigades who had gone to

Switzerland and with instructions to marry one of them as a way of obtaining unobtrusive entry into Britain. She eventually recruited and married Len Brewer, and she left Switzerland for London, travelling via Spain and Lisbon, on 18 December 1940. In England she operated for a time as a channel for the atomic bomb secrets passed to Moscow by the scientist Klaus Fuchs, escaping to East Germany after the war.[459]

In the years leading up to her departure for London 'Sonia' recruited a small network in Switzerland which included the Englishman Allan Foote, code-name 'Jim' (born in Liverpool in 1905); Jules Humbert-Droz of the Swiss Workers' Party, who had many useful contacts with Germany through workmen who daily crossed the border between Switzerland and Germany; Max Habijanic, a police official in Basle who had access to blank Swiss passports which he supplied to the 'Centre'; and Anna Müller, who worked as 'Sonia''s courier, regularly travelling to Germany under the cover of running a private employment agency.[460]

'Sonia' had a radio transmitter with which she kept in contact with Moscow, and in December 1939 she received a message instructing her to make contact with agent 'Dora' (Sándor Radó) at his apartment in Geneva. She was also instructed to relay 'Dora''s messages on her transmitter until she could find some way of equipping him with his own short-wave radios.[461]

As Radó's sources were still expanding, particularly those in the 'Pakbo' ring, and the amount of information awaiting transmission to Moscow was building into a mountain, the need for transmitters and pianists to work them had become acute by the time 'Sonia' turned up on Radó's front door. To overcome the problem she turned to Léon Nicole, the leader of the Swiss Communist Party. Nicole found the answer in Edmond Hamel, who ran a radio sales and repair shop at 26 Rue de Carouge in Geneva, which was conveniently situated within easy walking distance of Radó's Geopress office.[462]

Although Hamel and his wife Olga were not Communists, they were virulently anti-fascist, and when they were cautiously sounded out by 'Sonia' the Hamels not only agreed to build transmitters but also offered to operate them. Training in Morse code and other techniques was provided by Allan Foote, who also lived in Geneva, while the nature of the cipher they were to employ, along with a list of call-signs and radio schedules, was provided by 'Kent' – the *Petit Chef* – who travelled to Geneva from Brussels in March 1940.

The Hamels also constructed a transmitter for Foote – agent 'Jim' – who moved to Lausanne from Geneva, installing himself and his set in Flat 45, on the fifth floor of a six-storey block of apartments at 2 Chemin de Longeraie. The cipher that the *Petit Chef* provided for Foote and the Hamels was a variant of that used by the *Grand Chef*'s pianists in France, Holland and Belgium, which was based on a chequerboard system. If, for example, the Swiss pianists used the word 'finger' as their key-word, they set up a chequerboard in which each letter was represented by figures, with the letters of the alphabet not represented in the key-word written in alphabetical order in horizontal lines under the key-word, thus:

00	3	6	40	8	9
F	I	N	G	E	R
1	03	06	41	44	47
A	B	C	D	H	J
01	04	07	7	45	48
K	L	M	O	P	Q
2	5	08	42	46	49
S	T	U	V	W	X
02	05	09	43		
Y	Z	Signal	.		

The chequerboard figure '09', standing for 'signal', indicated a change in the text of the message from letters to figures, while the number '43' stood for a full stop.

Using this system, the word 'Germany' would be enciphered as 4089071602, which was then rearranged into a five figure grouping, 40890 71602. To refine this simple cipher into a more secure form of encipherment, statistics from the 1938 edition of the *Statistical Handbook of Foreign Trade* were used to provide key-figures. Numbers from the third column of statistics on a given page of the *Handbook* were added, in non-carrying addition, to the chequerboard figures: if, for instance, the statistics in the third column of a given page were 94320, then the original encipherment of 'Germany' would become 40890 65922.

In order for the message to be deciphered in Moscow an 'indicator group' was added. If, for example, the statistics were taken from page 68, column 3, line 2 of the *Handbook*, the indicator would read 68302. To secure the all-important 'indicator group' a five-figure constant, 73737, was added, by non-carrying addition, which would change the indicator example 68302 to 31039. In a final refinement, the fifth cipher text group from the beginning of the message (say 90636) and the sum of the fifth cipher text group from the end of the message (say 19362) were also added by non-carrying addition, thus:

$$
\begin{array}{r}
31039 \\
90636 \\
\underline{19362} \\
30927
\end{array}
$$

This cipher, like the one used by the pianists in the *Grand Chef*'s circuits, proved to be unbreakable by the deductive methods employed by the *Funkabwehr* cryptanalysts in Berlin.

Thus armed, the Hamels and Foote began transmitting 'Dora''s enciphered messages to the 'Centre'. Foote was the first, making his initial broadcast on the night of 12/13 March 1941. Tapping out his call-sign, 'NDA from FRX . . . NDA from FRX . . . NDA from FRX', he received the reply 'FRX from NDA . . . 0 . . . QRK5', Moscow's acknowledgement that the 'Centre' was receiving him loud and clear.[463] The Hamels joined in at the end of March, taking it in turns to operate their set from the flat above their radio shop. Foote and the Hamels were later joined by a third pianist, which gave rise to the Germans' referring to the Swiss *apparat* as *Die Rote Drei* when the long-range radio monitoring stations in Prague and Dresden intercepted the Swiss-based transmissions in the latter part of 1942 – some eighteen months after Foote first began playing his Morse key.

37. Code-Name 'Lucy'

At the beginning of May 1941 Radó received a message from the 'Centre' instructing him to rendezvous with a GRU agent operating under the code-name 'Sissy', with the intention of absorbing her small network, which had been operating in Geneva unknown to Radó, into his *apparat*.[464] 'Sissy' turned out to be a plump Polish Jewess called Rachel Dübendorfer (*née* Gaspary), who worked as a secretary in the ILO (International Labour Office), a semi-autonomous organization within the League of Nations. 'Sissy' had recruited a small number of officials within the ILO into her network, all of whom had diplomatic status, which allowed them to move freely between countries without custom checks. These provided 'Sissy' with vital information about the German and Italian economic situations which, up until the outbreak of war in September 1939, she had passed on to Moscow via the Soviet Embassy in Paris. But, like Radó's, her lines of communication were severed when the Swiss closed their frontiers. Hence the 'Centre''s decision to employ Radó's pianists to transmit the ILO ring's information.[465]

It was through 'Sissy''s network that the most important source – which was to outweigh the sum total of all the other sources in the Swiss *apparat* – was to be recruited. Amongst 'Sissy''s informers was a short, gloomy-faced, unimposing man with a rather sour disposition called Christian Schneider (code-name 'Taylor') who worked as a translator in the ILO. Up until the spring of 1941 the information 'Taylor' passed to 'Sissy' had been of a purely political nature.

Then, suddenly, he began providing detailed reports of German military strength and planning. Puzzled, 'Sissy' enquired where he was getting this information and was told that he had found a completely reliable source, who would continue to supply high-grade intelligence provided that no one but he, Schneider, knew his identity. This source, of which no one in the Swiss *apparat* or Moscow discovered the identity until long after the war had ended, was in fact a German refugee publisher living in Lucerne by the name of Rudolf Rössler, whom Radó – in the absence of any knowledge as to who he was, other than that he lived in Lucerne – code-named 'Lucy'.

Rössler was born at Kaufbeuren, some fifty miles to the south-west of Munich, on 22 November 1897. Kaufbeuren, a former imperial free city, medieval in atmosphere, was at the turn of the century one of Bavaria's industrial centres with a population of 23,000. Rössler's father, a local dignitary and a senior civil servant in the Ministry of Waters and Forests, brought his children up in the Protestant faith. Rudolf was educated at the *Realgymnasium* in Augsburg, to the north of Kaufbeuren. He matriculated in 1914, and shortly after the outbreak of the First World War in August that year he volunteered to join the Army. He emerged unscathed from the conflict in November 1918 with the rank of Corporal and a profound horror of war which turned him into a pacifist for the rest of his life.[466]

On his return to civilian life the 21-year-old Rössler turned his hand to journalism, working for the provincial Augsburg *Post Zeitung* and later, in 1925, becoming the editor of the conservative magazine *Form und Sinn* (Form and Meaning). After three years Rössler moved to Berlin, where he became the manager of an organization called the *Bühnenvolksbund* (Popular Association of the Theatre), devoted to the advancement of the theatre in a 'national and Christian spirit'. In the *Bühnenvolksbund* Rössler combined the roles of producer, agent, publisher and ticket agent, and at one time he had five theatre companies touring all over Germany. Through his work he made connections with clerical, liberal and conservative organizations, numbering many of Germany's leading literary and intellectual figures of the day among his friends, including the author Thomas Mann. He was also invited to become a member of the prestigious *Herren Klub* on Berlin's Vosstrasse, where he was to deliver no fewer than two thousand lectures.[467]

The *Herren Klub* was patronized by prominent German industrialists, aristocrats, bureaucrats and high-ranking officers from all three branches of the armed forces. This was the club that Arvid Harnack of the Berlin *apparat* joined in 1937, and where he made contact with many valuable sources of intelligence (see Chapter 18). It was in the *Herren Klub* that Rössler too, seven years before Harnack joined the club, made contacts that were to become his chief sources of information.

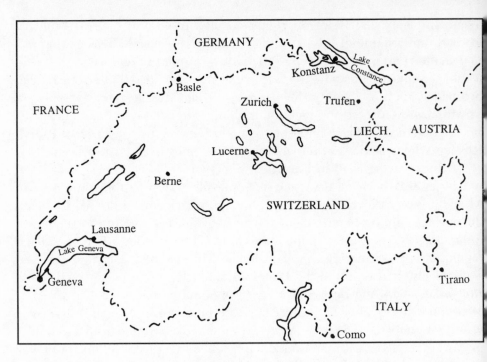

The Swiss Sector

In 1933, shortly after the Nazis came to power, Rössler's career as the manager of the *Bühnenvolksbund*, which by then had an annual turnover of more than 13,000,000 marks, came to a sudden and ignominious end. Alfred Rosenberg, the Nazi Party 'philosopher' and a notorious anti-Semite, had long coveted control of the *Bühnenvolksbund*, and he ousted Rössler from his position and took over control of his profitable organization. Deprived of his income and what he regarded as his life's work in one foul stroke, Rössler was transformed into a fervent anti-fascist discovering a cause he was prepared to die for – the overthrow of the Nazis.

Bitter and at a loose end, Rössler was persuaded to emigrate to Switzerland by Xaver Schnieper, whom Rössler had befriended while the young Swiss was studying at Berlin University. Schnieper was, in 1934, working as a cantonal librarian, and with his help Rössler moved into a small flat with his wife Olga in Wesemlin, a suburb of Lucerne. Schnieper also helped Rössler to set up an anti-fascist publishing house called Vita Nova at 36 Fluhmattstrasse, in the winding streets of the old quarter of Lucerne. The Vita Nova Verlag published works of philosophy and theology by essentially anti-fascist authors, especially those whose works had been banned in Hitler's Reich. It quickly flourished, and in 1936 Rössler expanded his commercial activities by publishing a magazine called *Die Entscheidung* (The Decision) for a group of young Swiss Catholics of iberal or 'leftish' persuasion which included Xaver Schnieper. The main thrust of the magazine was to convince German expatriates to stop regarding Nazism as an alien affliction forcibly imposed on an otherwise ordered and piritually healthy German nation but rather to recognize it as the most recent manifestation of a fundamental flaw in the German character, and to deprecate the belief that ideas are more important than people and that the latter are there to be sacrificed to the former.[468]

Publishing anti-fascist literature would have been Rössler's only method of ighting the Nazis had it not been for a visit paid to his home in Lucerne by wo Germans who had been acquaintances of his during his years as a member of the *Herren Klub*. In their account of the meeting Pierre Accoce and Pierre Quet identify the two Germans cryptically as 'General Fritz T' and 'Rudolf G', members of a group of German officers who were conspiring to assassinate Hitler and overthrow the Nazi regime.[469] They were in fact Lieutenant-General Fritz Thiele, second-in-command of the German High Command's communications branch, and Baron Colonel Rudolf von Gersdorff, who was eventually to become chief of intelligence on the staff of Army Group Centre on the Eastern Front.

These two officers travelled to Lucerne incognito in civilian clothes, carrying with them one of the *Wehrmacht*'s latest models of short-wave transmitter/receiver, housed in a suitcase, and a highly secret 'Enigma' automatic cipher machine. Light, portable and very simple to operate, the Enigma machine looked like a compact typewriter but it was capable of producing the most incredibly complex ciphers. Messages typed on its keyboard, which was similar to that of a conventional typewriter (29 letters – A to Z and the 'ä', 'ö' and 'ü' German vowel variations), were automatically enciphered by ever-changing electrical contacts on a series of revolving cylinders. As each letter was typed, it appeared as a different letter in an illuminated display panel carrying an arrangement of 29 letters above the keyboard, and every time an individual key was depressed the replacement letter would be different as the revolving cylinders activated different contacts. Additional variation could be achieved by changing the cylinders around or replacing them with different ones. Once a message had been enciphered it was sent to the recipient by short-wave radio and deciphered on an Enigma machine by an operator using the same pre-arranged setting of the cylinders. If four cylinders were used the number of cipher permutations the Enigma machine could produce was four thousand million million million!

By way of the transmitter General Thiele intended to arrange for the relay of highly sensitive military information to Rössler which would be enciphered on an Enigma machine and which Rössler would be able to decipher on his machine. To do this Thiele provided him with a list of Enigma keys, an instruction manual and a list of wavelengths and schedules on which the messages would be transmitted. In fact the messages to Rössler were to be transmitted from inside the broadcasting centre in the Defence Ministry building on Berlin's Bendlerstrasse, where the German High Command was situated. Inside the Bendlerblock, as the Defence Ministry was known, were two huge halls that buzzed permanently, night and day, with noise from about a hundred transmitters. On one side was a long row of small offices housing the cipher technicians enciphering and deciphering messages on their Enigma machines; on the other were the radio telegraphists who transmitted uncomprehendingly, on their Morse keys the long series of cabalistic letters produced by the Enigma machines, taking note of the time and wavelengths indicated in the margin of every message. In the same way they wrote down without the slightest idea of their meaning, the floods of mysterious dots and dashes they received.[470]

General Thiele, as second-in-command of the communications department of the German High Command, was ideally placed to carry out this task for he controlled the communications department in the Bendlerblock and his immediate superior, General Erich Fellgiebel, was also part of the conspiracy to overthrow Hitler. In addition Thiele took a number of trustworthy cipher technicians and wireless telegraphists into his confidence although they enciphered and transmitted the messages to Rössler – who was given the call-sign RAHS – without knowing in the least what or to whom they were communicating.[471]

By this method Thiele intended to send regular messages to Rössler containing information of great importance, which Rössler was to use as he thought fit preferably finding a way of passing it on to the staunchest enemies of Nazism. Only one outstanding point remained to be settled – how and to whom was Rössler to pass the information he received from the conspirators? The answer was provided in the first instance, by Xaver Schnieper, who had been called up into the Swiss Army as the war clouds gathered over Europe. Schnieper was earmarked for service with Swiss Military Intelligence, and was attached to a strange organization called the Bureau Ha. This was a private intelligence agency created and run by Hans Hausamann, a dealer in photographic and optical equipment such as binoculars and telescopes in Teufen in the Swiss canton of Appenzall. The name of the bureau was simply a play on Hausamann's initial, 'Ha' being the German pronunciation for the letter 'H'.

The *raison d'être* of the bureau was that Roger Masson, the head of Swiss Military Intelligence, was in a quandary. He needed information about Germany's intentions but feared antagonizing Hitler by mounting clandestine operations in the Reich with his own agents in case they were discovered Hausamann's unofficial intelligence bureau was based in the Villa Stutz situated on a promontory jutting out into the lake near Lucerne. Through a small but efficient network of agents he quickly established contact with informants in Germany, Austria and Italy, particularly amongst the military. All the information gathered by the Bureau Ha was passed to Masson who, although relying heavily on Hausamann's network, was in a position to disown it should the counter-intelligence agencies in Switzerland's powerful neighbours unmask any of the Bureau Ha's agents or informers.[472]

Through Xaver Schnieper, who acted as a 'cut-out', Rössler was persuaded to begin passing the highly classified intelligence he was receiving from Thiele to the Bureau Ha, who in turn passed it on to Roger Masson in Swiss Military Intelligence. But the flow did not stop there, for Masson summarized the information and passed it on to British secret service agents in Switzerland, who then relayed it to Secret Intelligence Service headquarters in London.[473]

The final link in this complex tangle of intertwined threads was forged in September 1939. During that month Rudolf Rössler advertised in the newspapers for someone to read galley proofs and do part-time editorial work for his Vita Nova publishing house. By sheer chance – and it was nothing more than chance – the advertisement was answered by Christian Schneider ('Taylor'), one of 'Sissy''s ILO ring. He was given the job by Rössler, and, working from home, 'Taylor' began travelling regularly between Geneva and Lucerne to collect and then return the corrected proofs and other copy. This went on for eighteen months, without 'Taylor''s realizing that Rössler was playing a game other than publishing. The two men frequently discussed politics and the international situation, and in one of their conversations Rössler let slip the fact that he was regularly receiving information from contacts inside the Reich. He also complained that, although he was passing on this information to the Bureau Ha, it was not being used actively against Nazi Germany because Switzerland was neutral: Rössler was unaware that the bureau was passing on the information to Roger Masson who in turn was passing it on to London.

The upshot was that 'Taylor' revealed that he was in a position to pass on Rössler's information to GRU agents operating in Switzerland. This was in the spring of 1941, when Rössler began receiving messages from Thiele that Hitler was planning to invade the Soviet Union in the near future. Although Rössler was not a Communist sympathizer – in fact he was a right-wing conservative – he decided that the Soviets would be able to make effective and active use of his material and so he agreed to pass on the intelligence via Schneider provided that he did not, on any account, reveal his identity to the GRU *apparat* in Switzerland or to Moscow.[474]

Thereafter 'Taylor' made regular trips from Geneva to Lucerne to collect the sheaves of proofs and manuscripts which Rössler gave him to correct, amongst which were copies of the messages Rössler had received from Germany and which he had deciphered on his Enigma machine. 'Taylor' then passed these on to 'Sissy', who in turn passed them on to Radó, who enciphered them ready for relay by couriers to Foote or the Hamels for transmission to Moscow. The final links had been forged.

38. The Priceless Source

'Lucy', as Rössler was code-named by Sándor Radó, began passing his high-grade intelligence to the Swiss GRU *apparat* at the right time; in fact the timing could not have been more fortuitous. In April 1941 he passed on the information received from the Bendlerstrasse that Hitler intended to invade the Soviet Union on 15 May. This date was amended at the beginning of May: 'General attack on territories occupied by Russians dawn Sunday 22 June, 3.15 a.m.' Then, during the night of 17/18 June 1941, Radó instructed Foote to transmit the following message on the strength of information originating from agent 'Lucy':

> Director. About 100 infantry divisions are now positioned on the German-Soviet frontier. One-third are motorized. Of the remainder, at least ten divisions are panzer. In Romania German troops are concentrated at Galatz. Elite divisions with a special mission have been mobilized. The 5th and 10th Panzer Divisions which are stationed in the General Government [as German-occupied Poland was called] are taking part. Dora.[475]

'Lucy' also reported that the Skoda arms factory in Czechoslovakia had been ordered by Berlin to cease delivering orders to the Soviet Union. A few days later, literally on the eve of the German attack, Rössler passed on more precise information which revised the strength of the German forces amassed on the frontier to 148 divisions, which included nineteen panzer and fifteen motorized. He also provided an accurate outline of the German plan, which was designed to destroy the mass of the Red Army to the west of the Dvina and Dnieper rivers. To achieve this Army Group North was to cross the Niemen river, wipe out the Russian troops in the Baltic States and advance on Leningrad; Army Group Centre had the first objective of capturing Smolensk; and Army Group South was to break through the Pripet Marshes to invade the Ukraine and advance on Kiev. This assessment was entirely accurate, but Radó refused to believe that Germany had any firm intention of invading Russia:

> . . . like most devout Communists at that time, Radó chose to follow Stalin's line: that German military activity on the frontier with the USSR was part of a war of nerves designed to extract greater concessions from Russia by way of trade and strategic supplies.[476]

Radó was also sceptical about the source of the material: it was so detailed that it seemed too good to be true. Being unknown to everyone in the *apparat* except Christian Schneider, 'Lucy' might well be a German *Abwehr* plant, intended either to penetrate the *apparat* or to lull the 'Centre' into a false sense of security by furnishing a certain amount of accurate, high-grade intelligence and then, at a crucial moment, misleading the Soviet High Command with the intention of administering a decisive blow against the Red Army.[477] The 'Centre' was also sceptical but instructed Radó to go on receiving information from 'Taylor''s source but to exercise the utmost caution.[478]

Taken in conjunction with the warnings provided by the *Grand Chef* in France, the Berlin *apparat* and Richard Sorge, the GRU agent in Japan, the Soviets should have been well prepared to meet the invasion. But Stalin preferred to believe the screen of false reports put out by the Germans presenting the build-up of the German forces in the east as a major deception exercise designed to divert attention from Hitler's real intention, which was to invade England.[479]

More effective than the screen of disinformation put out by the Germans, however, was the method of processing all reports received from agents abroad in the 'Centre', which were sent on to Stalin under the headings 'Reliable Sources' and 'Doubtful Sources', 'Lucy''s information being classified under the latter. Gnedich, the man responsible for delivering the reports to Stalin, testified that Stalin did not fail to read those which did not fit in with his picture of Hitler's intentions but deliberately chose to ignore them.[480]

Stalin convinced himself that no one in his right mind would think of attempting to conquer the huge spaces of Russia and that the German build-up was intended to apply pressure to extort more supplies from the USSR. This was also the view of the British Joint Intelligence Committee up to late May 1941. Alternatively, Stalin believed that the British were attempting to involve Germany and Russia in a war, and the warnings which the GRU agents were sending in were 'planted' by the British with the intention of causing Russia to mobilize, thus provoking Hitler to attack.[481]

Stalin did not allow Zhukov, the Chief of the Soviet General Staff, or Timoshenko, the Commissar for Defence, to see any of the intelligence data. Neither would he allow the commanders of the ground forces in the forward regions to bring their forces up to full strength and put them on a war footing – which would amount to mobilization – because of the danger of provoking the war with Germany which Stalin wanted to avoid at all costs.[482] Stalin's delusion was rent apart at 3.15 a.m. in the morning of Sunday 22 June 1941, precisely when 'Lucy' had predicted, when, after a huge artillery bombardment, 3,000,000 German troops and 3,350 tanks, supported by 2,770 aircraft, poured over the Bug and Niemen rivers and smashed through the unprepared forward Russian defences. At 1.00 a.m. the following morning Foote received a message from the 'Centre':

> Calling all networks . . . calling all networks. Fascist beasts have invaded the motherland of the working classes. You are called upon to carry out your tasks against Germany to the best of your ability. Director.[483]

In response Radó drafted a reply which Foote transmitted during the night of 23/24 June:

> Always faithful at our post and conscious of our position in the front line, we will fight with redoubled energy from this historic hour. Dora.[484]

A few days later Foote received a reply:

> The Centre has decided that from now on messages will be divided into three categories. MSG will designate routine communications; RDO urgent messages; and VYRDO will preface messages of the greatest importance. From today all information communicated by Lucy will be classified as VYRDO and be sent immediately. The Centre will be available to receive communications twenty-four hours a day. NDA [Foote] will transmit Lucy's communications.[485]

Moscow had finally woken up to the fact that 'Lucy' was a priceless source of information, for which the Director decided to pay their unidentified source 7,000 Swiss francs a month – which by 1941 standards was something of a small fortune.[486]

But money did nothing to change Rössler's habits. He rose each morning at 6.30 a.m., ate a frugal breakfast of coffee and toast and left home at 7.30 a.m. to catch a tram to his Vita Nova publishing offices in Lucerne's Fluhmattstrasse. Devoting the morning to correspondence and the day-to-day affairs of the publishing house, he went home at noon for a light lunch. His tastes in food were extremely simple, not to say ascetic. His clothes were few – a dark, ready-made suit, a long black overcoat for winter and an equally long mackintosh for other seasons, and a soft felt hat that he wore pulled down to his ears. He spent the afternoons deciphering and evaluating the messages he had received from the Bendlerstrasse, which he passed on to Schnieper, who, in turn, passed them on to the Bureau Ha, which relayed them to Masson in Swiss Military Intelligence, who then passed them on to London via British SIS agents in Switzerland; other copies, in 'clear', Rössler passed to Radó via 'Taylor', who had found it necessary to give up his job in the ILO so that he could make daily contact with 'Lucy'. After his evening meal Rössler prepared to receive further transmissions from Berlin, often working until three in the morning receiving messages and deciphering them on the Enigma machine and writing up evaluations.

Rössler's performance was, in fact, magnificent. No sooner had the Germans invaded the Soviet Union then he began supplying on a daily basis accurate data of extreme importance on Hitler's strategic plans, on the strength and composition of the German forces and on the nature of German weaponry – even information in the possession of German intelligence relating to Soviet plans.[487] According to Allan Foote, 'Lucy''s information,

> . . . at least all that which passed over my transmitter, had a suffix [VYRDO] of one code group meaning 'Urgent decipher at once'. In fact, in the end Moscow very largely fought the war on 'Lucy''s messages – as indeed any high command would who had access to genuine information emanating in a steady flow from the high command of their enemies . . . In effect, as far as the Kremlin was concerned, the possession of 'Lucy' as a source meant that they had the equivalent of well-placed agents in the three British service intelligence staffs plus the Imperial General Staff plus the War Cabinet Offices . . .
>
> 'Lucy' provided Moscow with an up-to-date and day-to-day order of battle of the German forces in the East. This information could only come from the *Oberkommando der Wehrmacht* [German High Command] itself. In no other offices in the whole of Germany was there available the information that 'Lucy' provided daily. Not only did he provide information on the troop dispositions, information which could only have come from the *Oberkommando der Wehrmacht* in the Bendlerstrasse, but he also produced equally good information emanating from the headquarters of the *Luftwaffe* . . .
>
> One would normally think that a source producing information of this quality would take time to obtain it. No such delay occurred in the receipt of 'Lucy''s information. On most occasions it was received within twenty-four hours of its being known at the appropriate headquarters in Berlin – in fact, barely enough time to encipher and decipher the messages concerned. There was no question of any courier or safe hand route.[488]

Foote, of course, was unaware of the identity of 'Lucy' and had no way of knowing that his source was in fact in the Bendlerblock (although he guessed as much).

Despite the flow of information to the 'Centre', the *Wehrmacht* continued its relentless advance ever deeper into the Russian interior. By the beginning of November the Germans were within fifty miles of Moscow, but the conquests had been bought at a terrible price. The extremes of cold, the infinite horizons of the hostile terrain and the toughness and indomitable tenacity of the Russian soldiers had ground Hitler's war machine to a standstill. Two pieces of information, one from Richard Sorge in Japan and the other from one of Otto Pünter's agents, now served to allow the Russians to launch a massive counter-offensive that was to throw the German front line back some 200 miles – a retreat that almost degenerated into a rout.

Stalin had been compelled to retain large forces in the far east of the country to guard against a possible attack on Russia by Japan. Fortunately, both Sorge's and Pünter's agents were able to allay such fears. As early as 7 August 1941 Radó was able to send the following message, based on information gathered by Pünter:

Director. The Japanese ambassador in Berne has declared that there can be no possible question of a Japanese attack against the Soviet Union, until Germany wins a decisive victory on the Eastern Front. Dora.[489]

This assurance allowed Stalin to move substantial forces from the Far East to the Moscow front, which resulted in the massive Russian counter-offensive launched on 5 December 1941. During the following spring, after the German front has stabilized and Hitler began preparing for a summer offensive, 'Lucy' began receiving detailed information from Berlin of Hitler's planning for an advance on Stalingrad and the oilfields of the Caucasus. From the Bendlerblock Lieutenant-General Thiele arranged for the whole ten pages of Hitler's 'Directive No 41', which set out in detail the strategic planning of the summer offensive, code-named *'Fall Blau'* ('Case Blue'), to be transmitted to Rössler. In this document was spelled out Hitler's plan to launch three consecutively launched parallel thrusts on the southern wing of the Eastern Front. The first and most northerly thrust, involving the German 4th Panzer Army and 2nd Army along with the 2nd Hungarian Army and four Romanian divisions, was to capture Voronezh, some 300 miles north-west of Stalingrad; and while the infantry consolidated the north-eastern flank the panzers were to wheel south-eastwards to move rapidly down the west bank of the Don river, rolling up the enemy from north to south, to link up with the spearhead of the second (central) parallel thrust, consisting of the German 6th Army (eighteen divisions strong), in the area of Millerovo (200 miles west of Stalingrad). The two united thrusts were then to strike out eastwards along the banks of the upper Don to approach Stalingrad from the north-west, to link up with the panzer spearhead of the third and southernmost parallel thrust, consisting of the German 1st Panzer Army and 17th Army, supported by the 8th Italian Army and four Romanian divisions, which was to approach Stalingrad from the south-west. Once Stalingrad had been captured the bulk of these forces were then to wheel south into the Caucasus to capture the oilfields.

The receipt of such detailed intelligence of German intentions enabled Stalin to develop a strategy whereby he was able to draw the Germans into the jaws of an enormous steel trap, which was to cost the Germans 269,000 casualties at Stalingrad and break the back of the *Wehrmacht* when the Russians launched a massive counter-offensive on the southern wing of the Eastern Front (see Chapter 14).

During July 1942, the first month of the German summer offensive, which was to end so disastrously at Stalingrad, scarcely ten hours elapsed between the taking of a decision in the German High Command and the receipt of this decision in Moscow, via Thiele in Berlin, Rössler in Lucerne, Radó in Geneva and finally Allan Foote in Lausanne. On one occasion the interval was reduced to only six hours. Rössler had calculated rightly that only speed in the transmission of this news would enable the Kremlin to develop a strategy which, in the course of the decisive battle of Stalingrad, would turn the war in Russia's favour.[490]

'Lucy', although the most important source, was only one of a hundred agents and informers who were feeding information to Sándor Radó. For example, Otto Pünter was receiving information from what was called 'the Catholic lines' from Germany, one of which extended to Switzerland from a Catholic monastery near Freiburg. From this source Pünter obtained, in September 1942, a long document originating from a German officer and containing detailed data on the German order of battle along the Stalingrad axis. Another 'Catholic line' from Germany, called 'Lilly of the Vatican', led to Italy, and 'Pakbo', the neutral Swiss citizen, made risky trips to Rome to receive information from this source.[491] In August 1942, during the German drive on Stalingrad, Pünter, on the strength of information received over the 'Catholic lines', passed on the following message to Radó for transmission to Moscow:

Director. Through 'Pakbo' from Berlin. Serious divergencies within the OKW regarding operations on the southern part of the Eastern Front. Prevailing opinion that offensive in direction of Stalingrad is useless and the success of the Caucasus operation is doubtful. Hitler insists on continuation of Stalingrad offensive and is supported by Göring. Dora.[492]

Moscow replied:

Dora. 'Pakbo''s report on divergencies within the General Staff regarding the operations on the German Eastern Front is interesting. He should give detailed information since when [relations] deteriorated and who belongs to the different groups. From what does he infer that an open conflict is possible? Director.[493]

These are examples of the literally hundreds of messages that Foote and the two Hamels transmitted to and received from Moscow every month.

The workload was such that Radó and his wife Lène, who did the enciphering, and the three pianists were stretched almost beyond endurance. Such was the flood of information pouring in from all sources that Radó was forced to seek help. First he turned to Otto Pünter, who readily agreed to help with the enciphering, but he quickly discovered that the amount of material involved was so enormous that it began to interfere with his other activities, preventing him from carrying on his profession as a working journalist running his INSA press agency.

To speed up the laborious task of encipherment 'Pakbo', taking his key-words from Sven Hedin's book *From Pole to Pole*, developed a system whereby he was able to encipher the plaintext of a message into numerals by way of a board which he invented with electrical contacts. The board was connected to an adapted typewriter in such a way that when Punter typed the plaintext the equivalent enciphered numerals lit up on the board. While 'Pakbo' typed his messages on what was to all intents and purposes a simple but ingenious form of the German Enigma machine, his wife sat on the other side of the table with another typewriter copying down the cipher numerals which were illuminated on the board.[494]

However, even with Pünter and his wife, Radó and Lène, Edmond and Olga Hamel and Allan Foote all working flat out, it was still extremely difficult to cope with the quantity of material being handled. Consequently Radó decided to turn to Léon Nicole, the leader of the Swiss Communist Party, for help. Nicole recommended Margrit Bolli, an attractive, dark-haired, 22-year-old who lived with her parents on the outskirts of Basle. When she was approached Margrit readily agreed to work for the *apparat* as a way of fighting fascism. Radó put her under the tutelage of Allan Foote, who taught her the rules of clandestine operations as well as Morse and how to operate a short-wave radio transmitter. Once trained, 'Rosie', as Margrit was code-named, was set up in a flat in a block at No 8 Rue Henri Mussard in Geneva, where she operated the third transmitter, constructed by Edmond Hamel, of *Die Rote Drei*. Foote taught her to use the following transmission schedule, which was radioed to him by the 'Centre':

Day	Call-sign	Start time
Monday	DVS	00.40
Tuesday	FSY	12.00
Wednesday	INK	00.20
Thursday	FBT	00.40
Friday	DPW	00.20
Saturday	IKW	12.00
Sunday	FW	00.20

As a subterfuge 'Rosie' was also instructed to change her wavelengths at given times:

Time	12.00	00.30	01.00	01.30	02.00	02.30
Wavelength	37m	37.5m	39m	40m	42m	43m

Time	03.00	03.30	04.00	04.30	05.00	05.30
Wavelength	45m	46m	47.5m	49m	50m	51m

Even with 'Rosie' joining in the Swiss *apparat*'s Morse concerts, the pianists were still hard pressed to keep up with the mass of information that had to be transmitted to Moscow – an effort that did not go unrecognized, for on 4 November 1942 the Director sent his congratulations to all the members of the Swiss *apparat*:

Dora.

1. Congratulate you, Jim, Sissy, Pakbo and all other friends, on the forthcoming great holiday [the twenty-fifth anniversary of the Russian Revolution] and wish all of you great success in the struggle against our common enemy.

2. Maude and Edward [the code-names of Olga and Edmond Hamel] have been awarded Government decorations for their tireless work. We have applied for a decoration for Sissy [Rachel Dubendorfer].

3. To you and Jim we express gratitude for your excellent work. Your decoration [the Order of Lenin] is waiting for you and we are certain many will follow.

Best regards to all. Director.[495]

No award for Foote is mentioned in this message, but he was decorated no fewer than four times during the war and was given the rank of Major in the Red Army.[496] The Swiss *apparat* had earned its laurels, but its greatest service was yet to come

39. The Ultra Myth

At the end of 1942 the German long-range monitoring stations in Dresden and Prague intercepted transmissions from the Swiss *apparat*'s three short-wave radios. At the beginning of 1943, with the aid of 'Kent', who was then in *Gestapo* custody, the *Funkabwehr* cryptanalysts on Berlin's Matthäikirchplatz managed to decipher a few of the intercepted messages, all of which referred to military information being provided by someone called Werther. As the highly secret military information contained in the messages could only have originated from a high-ranking German officer or officers, the counter-intelligence agencies set about trying to identify the offender or offenders.

In fact 'Werther' was simply a code-word which Lieutenant-General Thiele used to prefix every message which contained information concerning the German Army, while 'Olga' prefixed every message communicating information concerning the *Luftwaffe*.[497] To Radó and the 'Centre' the code-words 'Werther' and 'Olga' came to be used as references to 'Lucy''s sources, and when the Germans deciphered messages prefixed 'Werther' they in turn referred to the traitor or traitors in their midst as having that name.

In their book *Operation Lucy*, Anthony Read and David Fisher argue that there never was a 'Werther', in the sense of a single German officer or a group of officers passing information to Rössler, and they have concocted a complex conspiracy theory which is not only fantastic but totally untrue. Winston Churchill, Read and Fisher's story goes, wanted Stalin to have the benefit of German Enigma decrypts which the cryptanalysts at the Government Codes and Cipher School (GC&CS) at Bletchley Park were reading with varying degrees of success and regularity. They would also have us believe that Sir Claude Dansey, the Assistant Chief of the British Secret Intelligence Service (SIS), took it upon himself to make certain that the Russians received the information gleaned from the Enigma decrypts but, it is alleged, had to do it in a way that protected the source – the breaking of the German Enigma ciphers being the most sensitive secret of the war – and yet, at the same time, impress upon Stalin the importance and reliability of the information. Dansey achieved this, Read and Fisher maintain, by feeding 'Ultra' (the information gained from the intercepted Enigma messages) to 'Lucy' via Allan Foote and Rachel Dübendorfer ('Sissy'), who, they (erroneously) maintain, were British double-agents who had been infiltrated into Radó's *apparat*. In this way the 'Ultra' material was disguised and Stalin would be more inclined to accept its reliability because it came from his own agents.

Thus Read and Fisher credit the British SIS with a major part in the espionage *coup* that virtually won the war on the Russian Front. There is, of course, no truth in this nonsense. The assertion had also been emphatically denied by Professor F. H. Hinsley, the official historian of the monolithic four-volume work *British Intelligence in the Second World War*, who states that

> There is no truth in the much-publicised claim that the British authorities made use of the 'Lucy' ring, a Soviet espionage organization which operated in Switzerland, to forward intelligence to Moscow.[498]

Moreover, as Philip Knightley points out, Dansey had no access to 'Ultra' material about the Russian Front. Of course, there can be no absolute certainty that, contrary to all the rules regarding 'Ultra', Dansey did not get to see this material from time to time; but he certainly did not have access to it on such a regular basis that he could conceivably have been 'Lucy''s source.[499]

The main proof that 'Lucy' did not receive 'Ultra' material is, however, very straightforward: it could not possibly have reached him with the speed that he was receiving his information. Eastern Front 'Ultra' was always something of a problem for the cryptanalysts at Bletchley Park. The Germans used a lot of teleprinter landlines in the East, so not everything was transmitted by wireless (the only medium through which the British could intercept Enigma traffic), and, where wireless was used, the distance and other factors frequently made for very poor reception in Britain. This resulted in garbled messages with missing words and a corrupt text – the first cause of delay.[500] There was a further delay because Russian Front Enigma did not have a very high priority. GC&CS naturally preferred to work on material that was of immediate operational value to London and the British Commands. So, at best, GC&CS's interception of Russian Front Enigma was able to furnish little more than a guide to the scale, objectives and progress of the German offensive – and that only after a delay of two to three days and sometimes longer. If Read and Fisher are to be believed, this two-day-old material then made its way from Bletchley Park to London, from where Dansey found ways of sending it to Switzerland.[501] But we know that during July 1942, when the GC&CS had lost the ability to read the German Army Enigma keys on the Eastern Front, 'Lucy' was receiving highly detailed information within hours of decisions being made in the German High Command.

The final nail in the coffin of Read and Fisher's hypothesis is provided by Professor Hinsley, who points out that the British authorities at no time contemplated that the British success in breaking the German Enigma ciphers should be revealed to the Russians.[502] However, the Chiefs of Staff accepted early in July 1941 the risk of allowing the Russians to receive the more important Enigma intelligence on a regular basis in camouflaged form. In doing so they gave way to pressure from Winston Churchill. On 24 June 1941, in reply to his request that some unspecified item of intelligence should be sent to the Russians, Stewart Menzies, the Chief of the SIS, advised against divulging Enigma intelligence to the Russians, but Churchill instructed him to proceed provided no risks were run in allowing the enemy to discover that their Enigma ciphers had been compromised.[503] The method adopted for passing 'Ultra' intelligence to the Russians was by way of the British Military Mission (BMM) in Moscow. Formulae such as 'a well-placed source in Berlin' and 'a most reliable source' provided the cover, but care was taken to withhold details like unit identification that could only have been obtained from Enigma decrypts, and the BMM was instructed to take the further precaution of asking the Russians not to disclose by wireless that they were receiving intelligence from British sources.[504]

A good deal of operational intelligence derived from Enigma decrypts was sent through the BMM up to the summer of 1942. By the spring of that year, however, the BMM and the British Embassy in Moscow had become frustrated by the cumbersome liaison protocol which the Russians had insisted on applying to most of their contacts, and, though constantly bombarded by Soviet requests for further information about German strengths, dispositions and intentions, they had failed to elicit either a regular intelligence bulletin from the Russians or even answers to specific enquiries from the United Kingdom about, for example, unidentified *Luftwaffe* units and aircraft that were known to have fallen into Russian hands. At the same time, the service intelligence branches had encountered a wall of resistance to their efforts to exchange intelligence via the Soviet Military Mission in London.[505] In these circumstances it was decided that the supply of high-grade intelligence via the BMM must cease, or at least be greatly reduced. Consequently, from the end of June 1942, when Hitler launched his summer offensive designed to capture Stalingrad and the Caucasus oilfields, the flow of information dwindled to a trickle, and from the middle of 1942 items bearing on the Russian Front were commonly not forwarded to Moscow.[506]

So much for Read and Fisher's 'Ultra' myth. The truth is, of course, that 'Lucy''s source of information lay in the Bendlerblock in Berlin, home to the German High Command. Apart from Lieutenant-General Fritz Thiele, General Erich Fellgiebel and Colonel Rudolf Gersdorff, who have already been identified, seven others were involved in the conspiracy to provide Rudolf Rössler with high-grade intelligence. Though none of these have been identified with certainty, a CIA study has concluded that amongst them were probably Major-General Hans Oster, Chief of Staff to the head of the *Abwehr*, Hans Bernd Gisevius, another *Abwehr* officer, who also served as German Vice-Consul in Zürich; Carl Goerdeler, an ex-mayor of Leipzig and civilian leader of the conservative opposition to Hitler; and Colonel Fritz Boetzel, Commanding Officer of the Intelligence Evaluation Office of the South-East Army Group in Athens.[507] Of the seven officers identified, all bar Gisevius and Boetzel were hanged for their part in the unsuccessful 'Bomb Plot' to kill Hitler in July 1944. This still leaves three of 'Lucy''s sources unaccounted for, but it is believed that they were high-ranking officers in the *Luftwaffe* who were not connected with the Schulze-Boysen/Harnack group. It was these nine officers and one prominent civilian who collectively made up 'Werther' and 'Olga' – 'Lucy''s sources which were to cost the Germans the war on the Eastern Front.

40. *Zitadelle*

Allan Foote's capacity for work was astounding. During his most active period as a pianist of the Swiss *apparat*, from June 1941 to October 1943, he transmitted and received more than six thousand messages to and from Moscow. He handled a workload that would ordinarily require a whole team of pianists.[508] Unlike the majority of GRU agents recruited in the 1930s, who had embraced Communism in their youth, Foote's early political sympathies had lain with the conservatives. He had worked first as an automobile mechanic and then for a time as a motorcycle salesman. During the early 1930s, through the influence of friends, his political sympathies began to veer to the left and he attended meetings at which Harold Laski and other leaders of the left wing of the Labour Party discussed political affairs and attacked the British Government for its anti-Soviet attitude. In 1933 he veered even further to the left when he made the acquaintance of newly arrived German *émigré* Communists who had fled from the Nazis.[509]

Foote did not occupy himself with theoretical problems of Communism but developed into a 'practician' – a man with sound common sense about political and underground work, a sound understanding of the precepts of *konspiratsia* and a strong personal taste for taking chances, evinced by his decision to join the International Brigade in Spain during 1936. On his return to Britain in 1938, at the age of thirty-three, he was recruited, on the recommendation of the British Communist Party, into the GRU and was sent to Switzerland to be trained by 'Sonia' (Ruth Kuczynski). She gave him a thorough grounding in ciphers, radio transmission, false passports and other clandestine matters. Well satisfied with her pupil, 'Sonia' ordered Foote to go to Munich posing as a tourist, with instructions to learn to speak German and make contacts; he was given 2,000 Swiss francs to cover his expenses.[510]

Returning to Switzerland in August 1939, Foote settled in Geneva for a while before moving to Lausanne, where he installed himself and a transmitter made by Edmond Hamel in an apartment in the Rue Longeraie, taking care to remain inconspicuous as one among thousands of idle foreigners seeking rest and relaxation in Switzerland. His small circle of private friends in Lausanne never suspected that he was engaged in espionage, and years later, when Foote's memoirs were published, the *Gazette de Lausanne* ran a series of articles on him written by his former friends. One of these, *Madame* Colette Muraille, recalled that

> He was stout and placid, with small, porcelain-like eyes and thin blond hair. He once made an appearance in our group, and nobody gave him a second thought. He was the least mysterious fellow in the world! His face was so completely unexpressive that he never aroused curiosity on the part of his friends. Foote pretended to be in Switzerland for reasons of health. We made fun of his imaginary ills, which we suspected were a cover for his innate laziness. However, his paleness and slight cough, which he exhibited at the right moment, made these reasons plausible.
>
> He used to drink a lot, but never too much. He enjoyed eating immensely; he gave the impression that if the restaurant and the whole town collapsed over him he would not let himself be disturbed. He was a perfect listener. Every little story made him laugh heartily, but noiselessly; even when his pale eyes brightened during conversations on military matters, nobody became suspicious. Everybody liked him very much . . .[511]

Foote's transmitter was built into the cover of a typewriter which from the outside looked like a thousand others. It was Foote who made hiding places for the transmitters used by the Hamels and Margrit Bolli. The Hamels' set was hidden behind a wall board and 'Rosie''s was secreted in an ordinary-size gramophone.[512] On his own set it was Foote who, between March and July 1943, transmitted 'Lucy''s VYRDO-prefixed messages, the content of which was to destroy Hitler's last chance of regaining the initiative on the Eastern Front.

After the defeat at Stalingrad the German forces on the southern wing of the Russian Front were pushed back 250 miles, almost to their jumping-off positions at the start of the summer offensive. By the beginning of March 1943 the German front had stabilized and Hitler began searching for a way of regaining the initiative. His attention fixed on the dangerous situation in a huge protrusion in the front line (100 miles wide and 100 miles deep) jutting out westwards around the city of Kursk. In this salient the Russians had assembled several Tank Armies and forty per cent of their total Field Armies in preparation for a new offensive. This dangerous concentration of offensive strength offered Hitler a tempting prize, for if these huge forces could be encircled and annihilated the Red Army would dealt a mortal blow.

In his operational plan Hitler explained how this was to be achieved: 'The objective of the attack is to encircle the enemy forces by armies attacking from the areas of Belgorod and south of Orel and to annihilate the enemy by a concentric attack' – in other words a battle similar to that which the Russians had launched at Stalingrad. The northern 'jaw' of the pincers was to be formed by Colonel-General Model's 9th Army (seven infantry and eight panzer and panzer-grenadier divisions), whose task it was to strike in a south-easterly direction from an area south of Orel towards Kursk, where it was to link up with the spearhead of the southern strike on the high ground east of Kursk. The southern 'jaw' was to be formed by Colonel-General Hoth's 4th Panzer Army (seven infantry and eleven panzer divisions and three assault-gun brigades), which was to strike north-eastwards towards Kursk from north of Kharkov.

Planning for the offensive, which was code-named *'Zitadelle'* ('Citadel'), began early in March 1943; the original intention was to start the attack in mid-April but the date was postponed, partly because of delays in assembling the troops, partly because Model had doubts as to the adequacy of his resources and repeated requests for additional troops but mainly because Hitler decided to wait until sufficient numbers of the powerful new Tiger tanks and the very latest Panther tanks could be completed and assembled.

All of this was known to Moscow because, through Radó and Foote, 'Lucy' supplied nothing less than the day-to-day decisions made by the German High Command relating to *'Zitadelle'*. In mid-March, when the Germans began their strategic concentration for the offensive, ten divisions were transferred to the Orel area in a total of 320 railway transports. Colonel Hermann Teske, who was responsible for the transportation, complained:

> The Russians must have been informed about the German strategic concentration plans at a very early stage because both deployment lines were the targets of heavy bomber and fighter raids ever since the middle of March. Since the enemy invariably used the most effective forces for these operations, it must be assumed that their employment was controlled from the highest strategic command.[513]

Through 'Lucy' the Soviet High Command possessed such accurate, reliable and detailed information about the German preparatory deployment for *'Zitadelle'* that it was able to direct its counter-moves on a strategic scale. Only the exceptional gift for improvisation displayed by the German railway engineers prevented the deployment from becoming dangerously disorganized.[514]

On 15 April 1943 Hitler signed Operation Order No 6, which contained a succinct summary of the objective of *'Zitadelle'*:

> ... to encircle the enemy forces in the Kursk area by means of strongly concentrated, merciless and rapid thrusts by one offensive army each from the areas of Belgorod and south of Orel, and to annihilate them by concentric attack ... Army Group South will jump off with strongly concentrated forces from the Belgorod–Tomarovka line, break through across the Prilepy–Oboyan line and link up with the attacking army of Army Group Centre at and east of Kursk ... Army Group Centre, with its attacking army jumping off from the line Trosna–north of Maloarkhangelsk, after the strongest concentration of forces will break through across the Fatezh–Verey–Tenovo line, with the main effort on the eastern wing, and will link up with the attacking army of Army Group South at and east of Kursk.[515]

The entire text of Operation Order No 6, which laid down the earliest launch date as 3 May, was transmitted to the 'Centre' by Foote on following day (16 April). Four days later, on 20 April, Radó reported to the Director: 'Date of offensive against Kursk, originally envisaged for the first week of May, has been postponed.' On 29 April Radó added: 'New D-day for German offensive is 12 June.'[516]

This information, transmitted to 'Lucy' from his sources in Berlin, was entirely accurate. It betrayed one of the best guarded secrets of the German *Wehrmacht*, a secret known only to a dozen men – including General Erich Fellgiebel, one of the officers involved in the conspiracy to provide 'Lucy' with secret information. On 7 May 1943 the Director instructed 'Dora' (Radó) to 'Discover from Werther through Lucy all details about the plans and intentions of OKW and report to us urgently.' The reply came promptly on 9 May in a long signal of more than 1,120 five-figure enciphered groups, which gave a flood of information about the ideas held in the German High Command about *'Zitadelle'* and defensive operations along the rest of the Eastern Front. On 12 June, before a single German soldier had seen the very latest Panther tank, Radó relayed to Moscow the technical characteristics of the tank, the locations of the factories manufacturing it and the monthly output figures.[517]

Hitler's decision to postpone the offensive until sufficient numbers of his new 'miracle' tanks could be assembled amongst the attacking armies allowed the Russians time to prepare for the encounter. On the strength of 'Lucy''s information Stalin and his generals decided that, instead of spoiling the

German plan by mounting a pre-emptive strike, they would prepare to absorb the German blow and only after they had severely mauled the attacking German forces would they go over to the offensive, with the intention of smashing the southern wing of the German front and liberating the eastern Ukraine and the industrial region of the Donbas.[518] Defensive works inside the salient were constructed at a feverish pace, and 300,000 civilians in the area were pressed into service to assist the troops. The defence system consisted of a number of parallel lines of trenches and anti-tank ditches, reminiscent of those used on the Western Front during the First World War. The main forward defensive zone was up to three miles deep and consisted of sets of five lines of trenches one behind the other, all interconnected and provided with pits and shelters. A second defensive zone lay about seven miles behind and resembled the first, and a third zone lay a further twenty miles behind the second. The front reserve, assembled some forty miles in the rear from the forward defended localities, also dug miles of linear trenches. When they were completed the trenches ran for hundreds of miles, through the cornfields and villages and up the long gradual slopes of the steppe hills. The strength of the defences lay in their formidable anti-tank protection, the whole area being heavily mined and covered with anti-tank strongpoints: the mines were laid with a density of 2,400 anti-tank and 2,700 anti-personnel mines for every mile of frontage.[519] While all this was going on masses of reinforcements and over 20,000 artillery pieces, along with more than 6,000 anti-tank guns and 920 Katyusha rocket launchers, were moved into the salient.

Although 'Lucy' provided the Soviets with the most important information relating to 'Zitadelle', another source also furnished intelligence which the Russians were able to use to good effect. John Cairncross, the 'fifth man' of the 'Cambridge Spy Ring' (the other four were Kim Philby, Guy Burgess, Donald Maclean and Anthony Blunt), was transferred from the Foreign Office to the GC&CS at Bletchley Park in March 1942, where he was employed to analyse intercepted *Luftwaffe* Enigma signals. His Soviet controller, Anatoli Gorsky, gave Cairncross the money to buy and run a cheap car to bring copies of the 'Ultra' material he was dealing with to London on his day off, the contents of which were then transmitted to Moscow from the Soviet Embassy.[520] The Enigma intercepts passed on by Cairncross identified the dispositions of the *Luftwaffe* squadrons being assembled for 'Zitadelle'. This allowed Soviet bombers to make a number of pre-emptive strikes on seventeen German airfields selected with the help of Cairncross's intelligence. One thousand four hundred sorties were flown, resulting in the destruction of over 500 German aircraft caught on the ground by the Soviet planes.[521] Cairncross's activities provide further proof that Read and Fisher's hypothesis is completely erroneous. If 'Ultra' material had been passed to 'Lucy' there would have been no reason for

Cairncross to take the considerable risk of handing over copies of the Enigma decrypts to Anatoli Gorsky.

On 1 July 1943, at his headquarters in East Prussia, the *Führer* addressed a meeting of the senior commanders taking part in *'Zitadelle'* in which he harangued them about the need to demonstrate German superiority and the necessity to open the way to final victory; this was to be done at Kursk, where the offensive would open on the morning of the 4 July. Present at this conference was General Erich Fellgiebel, and as a result Stalin was in possession of the details of Hitler's conference by the following day. Forewarned, the Soviet troops in the salient were at once deployed in their defensive lines, ready to meet the German attack, which commenced with the strike by Hoth's 4th Panzer Army on the southern face of the salient at 0430 hours. The northern strike by Model's 9th Army commenced on the following morning. By 9 July the southern German advance had been stopped dead in its tracks after penetrating only twenty miles on a narrow front, while the northern thrust only managed to advance six miles before it was blocked by the Russian defences.

On 12 July the Soviets counter-attacked near Prokhorovka in the south, where the tanks of both sides massed and manoeuvred on a scale hitherto unseen in the history of warfare. Almost 4,000 Soviet tanks and nearly 3,000 German tanks and assault guns, and two million men, were drawn into the gigantic battle, which roared on hour after hour for seven days, leaving ever greater heaps of dead and dying, clumps of blazing and disabled tanks, shattered personnel carriers and lorries and thickening columns of smoke coiling over the steppe.[522]

By 19 July, by which time Hitler had decided to call off the offensive, the Germans' attack had been smashed beyond recovery. It had cost them 70,000 dead, 2,952 tanks and 195 assault guns, together with 844 field guns, 5,000 lorries and 1,392 aircraft. The infantry divisions had been torn to shreds, while the losses in individual panzer divisions were calamitous.[523] By 20 July all the German forces were in full retreat. The Soviets maintained their momentum, which developed into a general offensive on the central and southern areas of the Eastern Front which did not end until November 1943, having pushed the German line back some 200 miles. Before Kursk a German victory was still a possibility; after Kursk defeat was inevitable, for the failure of *'Zitadelle'* lost the Germans all hope of regaining the initiative on the Eastern Front. The war in the east had been irrevocably turned in the Russians' favour – thanks in the main to 'Lucy' and the Swiss *apparat*.

41. The Long Shadow of the *Gestapo*

While the *Gestapo* in Berlin set about trying to discover the identity of the mysterious 'Werther', moves were put afoot by the *Sonderkommando* in Paris to try and infiltrate the Swiss *apparat*. In the summer of 1943 *Kriminalrat* Heinz Pannwitz, the head of the *Sonderkommando*, working on information provided by 'Kent', dispatched an agent to Geneva with the intention of making contact with Radó and trying to discover the identity of 'Werther' from the Swiss end. This agent went under the name of Yves Rameau but he was in fact Ewald Zweig, a German Jew who had fled to France when the Nazis seized power and had worked for the French Intelligence service, the *Deuxième Bureau*. When the Germans conquered France, Zweig offered to work for them as a way of saving his skin.[524]

Armed with the name of a 'cut-out' provided by 'Kent', Zweig arrived in Geneva and presented himself as a member of the *Grand Chef*'s French *apparat* who had been sent by his chief to make personal contact with 'Dora' (Sándor Radó). At this time 'Kent' and the *Grand Chef* were assisting the *Sonderkommando* with the *Funkspiel* from the house in Neuilly. The 'cut-out' passed on the request to Radó, who smelt a rat and ordered him to break off all contact with the man calling himself Yves Rameau.[525]

A new threat presented itself in July 1943 when Radó received a message from the 'Centre' informing him that an agent in Italy called 'Paolo' urgently needed to renew his Swiss passport. As Radó had control of the courier lines into Italy he was instructed to arrange for the old passport to be brought to him so that it could be passed on to 'Max the Cobbler' (Max Habijanic, the police official in Basle who provided the *apparat* with blank passports). Accordingly, an Italian courier took the passport to a tailor's shop (which acted as a 'letter-box') in Como on the Swiss–Italian frontier, where it was collected by a Swiss courier, who carried the passport to Doctor Emilio Bianchi in Geneva (who was also acting as a 'letter-box' for the *apparat*). Radó then arranged for 'Rosie' to collect the passport from the doctor's surgery and pass it on to Allan Foote, who took a train to Basle and handed it over to Anna Müller, who in turn passed it on to 'Max the Cobbler'.

Four days later the renewed passport was returned along the same tortuous route, but when the Swiss courier reached the tailor's shop in Como he found it being watched by Italian security men. Slipping away, he reported the matter to Radó, who in due course managed to get the passport into Italy by another route through Tirano. But it quickly became evident that the whole thing had been set up by the Italian security service, who had arrested 'Paolo' in June, along with other members of his ring. The Italians had forced them to carry on a brief radio play-back game with the 'Centre' in which they had requested the new passport for 'Paolo'. The Italian courier, it transpired, had been a plant, and he had uncovered the line leading to 'Max the Cobbler' in Basle. This information was passed on to the *Gestapo* by the Italians, giving the Germans concrete evidence as to the size and complexity of the *apparat*.[526]

Following the failure of Ewald Zweig to penetrate the Swiss *apparat*, Pannwitz devised a plan to kidnap Allan Foote. 'Kent' had informed Pannwitz that Foote was responsible for the regular hand-over of funds to a courier, who passed the money on to the French Communist Party underground. By way of the *Funkspiel* that the *Sonderkommando* was playing with Moscow, 'Kent' sent a message to the 'Centre' informing them that the French Communists were desperately short of funds. The 'Centre' responded by ordering 'Kent' to dispatch a courier to Switzerland to collect money from Foote, who had been informed by Moscow of the date and place where he was to rendezvous with 'Kent''s emissary.[527] Foote recalled that

> The Director had ordered me to have no conversation with the courier but merely to hand over the cash and go away. However, when the 'courier' turned up at the entrance to the Botanical Gardens in Geneva as arranged, he handed over to me a large book wrapped in bright orange paper and told me that between two of the pages I would find three ciphered messages which must be sent off urgently by radio to the 'Centre'. He also said that he had valuable information which he wanted to pass on to Moscow and suggested a further meeting as soon as possible, naming a place near Geneva – which was also very near the German-controlled French frontier [where Pannwitz planned to kidnap Foote].
>
> All this made me very suspicious as such loquacity against strict orders was unusual in a Soviet agent. I began to suspect that perhaps the original courier had been arrested and his place taken by an *Abwehr* agent. The orange wrapping would serve as a convenient beacon light for anyone who was trailing me home, and the meeting place near the frontier would serve admirably for an abduction in the best *Gestapo* traditions. As for the cipher messages – if these were also phoney, then they would serve as admirable pointers towards identifying my transmitter. I had no doubt that the Germans had long been monitoring the network, and if on one of the broadcasts that they were listening to they suddenly found the three messages they had planted being transmitted, it would at once identify that transmitter as mine.
>
> I tried to dissemble my suspicions as much as I could and said that I could not attend a meeting that week as I had business elsewhere and so fixed on a meeting in a week's time. On leaving the rendezvous I hid the book as well as I could under my coat and returned home by a roundabout route, taking evasive action. In my next transmission I reported on this fully to the Director and he agreed that I should not attend the meeting. As regards the cipher messages, which were in the book as the courier had said, gummed between two pages and in a cipher that I did not know, the Director asked me to transmit them but to disguise them with dummy groups and by re-enciphering them in my own cipher, that they would neither be recognizable as the original messages to the radio monitors nor serve as a guide to our cipher to the German cryptographers.[528]

When the courier, who was a German agent, reported back to Pannwit and 'Kent' both men realized that Foote's suspicions had been aroused and that the *Funkspiel* was endangered. In an attempt to retrieve the situation 'Kent' immediately transmitted a message to the 'Centre' informing the Director that his courier had been captured by the Germans and replaced by one of their agents. The Director was obviously taken in by this, because a fortnight later the 'Centre' informed Foote that his suspicions had been correct and that the courier had been a German agent. Foote was also warned that, as he had been recognized by at least one *Abwehr* agent, he must regard himself as being in jeopardy and at least partially compromised.[529]

As the *Gestapo* in Berlin had made no headway in discovering the identity of 'Werther' and Pannwitz's machinations had proved abortive, the German decided to force the Swiss to take action against the Russian spies operating on their territory. Switzerland never joined in international coalitions. Her neutrality was no hypocritical term but a sincere principle in foreign relations. Tested and re-tested through centuries, Swiss neutrality had grown from a device to a doctrine, and from a doctrine to a tradition. There was little to spy on, therefore, in Swiss diplomatic and defence areas, nor was there an extensive war industry to arouse the curiosity of a foreign agent. If, however an agent was caught spying in Switzerland, not against Switzerland but against another power, he was usually expelled from the country. In only a few cases, mainly those involving Nazi spies, was sterner punishment meted out, this because the spies were paving the way for a projected (though postponed) German invasion of Switzerland.

After the annexation of the Saarland, Austria, the Sudetenland, Danzig and Silesia by Germany, the northern half of Switzerland was the last remaining independent area in Europe with a sizeable German-speaking population there was no question in Berlin but that sooner or later the 'Südmark' canton would be incorporated into Greater Germany. Stuttgart, the nearest large German city to Switzerland, was made the seat of various official and unofficial German agencies assigned to operate in the 'Südmark' to conduct propaganda, organize spying and carry out acts of sabotage. Some German nationals living in Switzerland were organized into a section of the Nazi Party while Swiss nationals with Nazi leanings were united into the National Front and other organizations, all of them controlled and financed by Berlin.

In December 1945 the Swiss Government published a factual report on German plans for clandestine operations in Switzerland during the Nazi era. The report conveys a picture of a huge German machine – in many ways similar to a Soviet *apparat* – penetrating, spying on and preparing to occupy the country. Members of the German Embassy in Berne as well as members of the German consulates had been assigned to espionage work to learn Swiss military

ecrets, radio and teletype machines had been installed and material for time
ombs and a quantity of explosives had been brought in from Germany.
According to the report, the total number of persons arrested in Switzerland
or espionage and sabotage (most of them working for Germany or Italy) was
9 in the year 1939, 310 in 1942 and 294 in 1944. In the seven years from
939 to 1945 a total of 1,389 arrests were made.

More than once Germany had been on the verge of attacking Switzerland,
nd the fate of the small country, whose population was only five million
ompared to Greater Germany's 74 million, hung perpetually in the balance.
Despite the fact that the Swiss Army was mobilized and supplied with new
veapons, there was no doubt about what the outcome would be if German
livisions crossed the frontier.

Of all the German-speaking countries and areas in Europe, Switzerland was
he least sympathetic towards Nazi Germany, and the majority of Germans living
n Switzerland were especially antagonistic toward Nazism. Efforts in the north
o build up in Switzerland an organization like the Henlein movement in the
udetenland were fruitless; pro-Nazi organizations in Switzerland remained small
nd were suppressed, when necessary, by the police.

The constant threat posed by her powerful neighbour made Switzerland
natural ally of Britain and France. There were no treaties of alliance between
hem, nor public pronouncements of co-operation, for Switzerland never
bandoned the principle of strict neutrality. Political reality, however, is
tronger than pacts and more eloquent than solemn declarations. Swiss public
pinion was almost unanimous in its support of the cause of the anti-German
oalition, and the Government, although outwardly taking no sides, was
aturally anti-Hitler. The Swiss General Staff, attentively watching and
larmed by the strength of German forces on the frontier, was ready to co-
perate with, and give aid to, anyone capable of putting a brake on the
xpected German move into the 'Südmark'.

After the German invasion of the USSR the Russians, though not officially
ecognized as such, became another natural ally of Switzerland; in fact, for
time the fate of the small nation hinged even more on Russian resistance
han on the successes or failures of the Western powers. A German victory
n Russia would undoubtedly lead to an early invasion of Switzerland;
Germany's difficulties on the Eastern Front and her growing losses meant
ecurity for the Swiss. Switzerland was interested in Russia's war, and that she
ould help Russia, if possible, was a matter of course, but the only aid
witzerland could give was by way of tolerating and thus facilitating the Soviet
RU apparat that they knew was operating in the country against Germany.[530]

However, beginning in March 1943, Walter Schellenberg, the head of the
D (Sicherheitsdienst, the counter-intelligence agency of the SS), paid a number

of visits to Roger Masson, the head of Swiss Military Intelligence. The meetings were held in the Hotel Bären, at Biglen, near Berne, and the Hotel Baur au Lac in Zürich. During these meetings Schellenberg presented Masson with evidence that a Russian espionage *apparat* was at work in Switzerland, and he demanded that the Swiss authorities take action against it. Masson, however, informed the German that he had no intention of taking action against the Russian agents because they were not operating against Switzerland or Swiss interests. A few days later, however, 'Lucy' passed a message to the Bureau Ha, via Xaver Schnieper, which warned that Hitler had ordered active preparations to be put in hand for the military occupation of Switzerland. The import was clear: if the Swiss did not move to suppress the Soviet *apparat* the Germans would invade. In fact the threat was a bluff engineered by Schellenberg, but it spelt doom to Radó's circuit.

42. Last Echoes in Switzerland

On 8 September 1943 Italy capitulated to the Allies and German forces moved in to occupy the country. Alarmed that Hitler would invade Switzerland to protect his southern flank and secure his supply lines through the alpine passes, the Swiss *Bundespolizei* (BUPO) set about silencing the three transmitters of *Die Rote Drei* in an attempt to placate the German dictator.

The action began when a Swiss Army short-range radio monitoring company, under the command of Lieutenant Maurice Treyer, began taking cross-bearings on the pianists operating in Geneva. The Hamels' transmissions were picked up during the night of 11/12 September 1943 and Treyer code-named this set 'LA'. The following night they monitored 'Rosie'' transmissions, which Treyer designated set 'LB'.[531]

It took a few weeks for Treyer's radio-direction finder vans to pin-point the actual locations from which the 'LA' and 'LB' transmissions were coming. In the latter stages of the hunt he did this by arranging to have the power supply to each house on the particular streets involved to be cut off for short periods, until a sudden break in the transmissions confirmed the precise houses in which the short-wave radios were operating. Having pin-pointed the locations, Treyer passed the matter over to Inspector Charles Knecht, head of the BUPO in the Geneva canton, who placed the two buildings under surveillance.[532]

This did not go unnoticed, because at the beginning of October Radó's wife Lène returned home after delivering a sheaf of messages to 'Rosie' with the news that the latter was in an agitated state and wanted to see Radó urgently. The next day Radó met the young woman in a café in the suburbs of Geneva nd she told him that she was sure that her flat was under surveillance. She had noticed strange men loitering outside her apartment block and vans had been driving slowly past at night. In addition a man had called saying he was from the electricity company and had come to check that her installation was in good order – though she had made no request for a service call: she had no doubt that he was a security man.[533]

It was obvious to Radó from what 'Rosie' told him that the BUPO were moving in on the *apparat*. He told her to cease transmitting, to destroy any incriminating papers and to leave Geneva and take a train to Basle to stay with her parents. He also instructed Edmond Hamel to collect 'Rosie''s transmitter, which was disguised in a portable gramophone, and to take it to his shop for storage: as a local radio mechanic Hamel would be able to do this without arousing suspicion.[534]

Unfortunately 'Rosie' was persuaded to stay in Geneva by her 37-year-old lover, Hans Peters, and instead of travelling to Basle as instructed she moved into Peters' apartment in Geneva. She fled her own apartment in such haste that she forgot to destroy a number of enciphered messages and her list of radio schedules, wavelengths and call-signs. The BUPO agents keeping her flat under surveillance discreetly followed her to Hans Peters' apartment. When Radó questioned the Hamels, they reported that they had not noticed anyone watching their villa at 92 Route de Florissant nor their radio repair shop at 26 Rue de Carouge, and although there was danger in the air they volunteered to carry on with their nightly transmissions. By so doing they played into the hands of the BUPO, who during the night of 13/14 October 1943 mounted a raid.

As Edmond slept and Olga tapped away on the Morse key of the transmitter in the attic of the villa on the Route de Florissant, Inspector Knecht and a squad of policemen crept silently into position outside. At thirty minutes past midnight a police expert picked the lock on the front door and Knecht and his men rushed inside. Swiftly they climbed the stairs to the attic and burst in on Olga as she was transmitting. As the police swarmed through the villa, Edmond Hamel appeared, dressed incongruously in an embroidered nightshirt, and in this attire he and Olga were spirited away to the Bois-Mermet prison. Alongside the transmitter the police discovered twenty-three pages of enciphered messages and a list of radio schedules, wavelengths and call-signs.[535]

After withdrawing from the Hamels' villa Inspector Knecht and his squad raided 'Rosie''s flat, where the police found incriminating evidence in the form of six pages of enciphered messages along with her transmitting schedules. After leaving 'Rosie''s flat Knecht and his men swooped on Hans Peters' flat, where they found the two lovers in bed. They were both arrested, but Peters was released from prison after a few days since he had no connection with the network apart from his affair with 'Rosie'. It had been a good night's work for

Knecht: he had silenced the two Geneva transmitters and a number of incriminating documents had been found.[536]

Radó did not become aware of the arrests until the following afternoon when, at about 4.00 p.m., he went to the Hamels' shop to deliver a batch of messages for transmission that night. He found the shop shuttered and closed, and there was no sign of the Hamels. From a telephone box he tried phoning them at their villa, but with no success. His suspicions that the worst had happened were confirmed when he read the evening edition of the *Tribune de Genève*. Sandwiched between a brief report of a drunken brawl in the Rue de Mont Blanc and crash involving two cyclists in the Place de Molard was a short report entitled 'Discovery of a Secret Communist Radio':

> For three days the *Sûreté* have been searching the canton for a radio which is transmitting tendentious information. The search began on Thursday morning around 4.00 a.m. when this Communist organization was discovered near Meinier. Several arrests have been made.[537]

There was no doubt in Radó's mind that those arrested were the Hamels, but to make sure he telephoned a contact he had in the local police, who confirmed his fears and also informed him that Margrit Bolli, who Radó believed had escaped to Basle, had also been caught in the police net.

One of the prison officers in the Bois-Mermet was a Communist sympathizer, and he carried written messages from the Hamels to Radó which warned him that 'Rosie' had broken down, confessed everything and identified him as the head of the *apparat*. Without a moment to lose, Radó and his family fled their apartment and took refuge with Doctor Emilio Bianchi in the university quarter of Geneva, who gave the Radós a room to themselves and kept their presence secret.

After a few days Radó emerged from hiding to meet Foote at a prearranged rendezvous in Geneva's Park des Eaux-Vives, where he instructed him to travel from Lausanne to Geneva twice a week to collect the messages that Radó was still receiving daily from 'Lucy' via 'Taylor', who delivered the piles of messages to Dr Bianchi's surgery. Foote made these journeys by train during evening so as to arrive during the hours of darkness. On his arrival in Geneva he would walk through the streets for a while before going into a café or restaurant to check that he was not being followed. Finally he would take a taxi, which he always stopped a few blocks away from Dr Bianchi's home, walking the last leg of the journey to make a final confirmation that no one was tailing him. It was a tiring, time-consuming but necessary procedure.[538]

Radó meanwhile came up with the idea of contacting the British SIS agents operating in Switzerland, who seemed to enjoy a privileged existence in the eyes of the Swiss Police. He asked Otto Pünter to contact the British legation hrough Léon Sousse (code-name 'Salter'), one of Pünter's agents who also provided information for the British and the Free French intelligence agencies n Switzerland, asking if the British would give him extra-territorial asylum n the British Legation in Geneva, which was protected by diplomatic mmunity. Radó was in fact suggesting that he be allowed to use the SIS ransmitter housed in the Legation to send his messages to the Soviet Embassy n London, from where they could be relayed to Moscow. In exchange he offered to make available the information he was receiving from 'Lucy', not 'ealizing that the SIS was already receiving this information via Hausamann's 3ureau Ha and Masson. What worried Radó most of all was the possibility hat, if he were arrested by the Swiss police, they might choose to expel him 'rom Switzerland rather than imprison him, in which case he would fall into he hands of the Germans who now controlled every country with which the 5wiss had a frontier.

A positive reply was returned via 'Salter', but before he could seek asylum n the British Legation Radó had to first obtain permission from the Director. On 26 October Foote transmitted Radó's request:

Director. Since general situation in regard to unhampered continuation of work is getting more and more unfavourable ['Centre' had already been informed of the arrest of the Hamels and 'Rosie'] and there is the danger of destruction through police action, I suggest, after serious consideration, getting in touch with the British and continuing work from these in a new camouflaged way . . . [Our] endangered people can only be saved by contact with the British . . . Organization seriously endangered . . . Swiss police obviously intend to destroy whole organization. Since matter urgent request immediate detailed instructions. Dora.[539]

The 'Centre''s reply, received by Foote during the night of 2/3 November 1943, was clear and uncompromising:

Dora.
1. Your suggestion to hide with the British and to work from there is absolutely unacceptable. In this case you and your organization would lose independence.
2. We are aware of your grave situation and are trying to help you. That is, we are trying to retain a prominent United States lawyer with good connections in Switzerland. This man will certainly be able to help the casualties [those arrested] and yourself. Inform us immediately whether you could somehow manage for two or three months, perhaps hide somewhere. Upon receipt of your answer we shall arrange the lawyer's trip.
3. Answer following questions: Who, besides you, is endangered in the organization? What is the situation of 'Sissy' and 'Pakbo'? Did the radio operators [the Hamels and 'Rosie'] receive the text of the indictment against them? At present we are more than ever in need of further co-operation with 'Lucy' and hope this will be possible as soon as your personal situation as well as that of 'Jim' [Foote] is cleared.
4. We ask you to be calm and to do everything necessary for your safety and to retain your ability to work. Director.[540]

This was not the first time that the Director had refused to consider sensible contact with an Allied intelligence network. Once, in 1942, Radó obtained certain documents and plans which would have been great value to the British as well as the Russians, but the material was so bulky that it was impossible for his pianists to pass it over the air. Radó therefore suggested that it be handed over to the Allies through a suitable and secure 'cut-out'. The 'Centre''s reaction was immediate: Radó received instructions to burn the information at once. From the Director's point of view there was little difference between information falling into German hands or into British hands. It was Russian information, and if it could not be passed to the 'Centre' then the right place for it was the wastepaper basket, however valuable might be to Russia's allies.[541] Despite the Director's order not to approach the British, Radó made further enquiries regarding asylum through 'Salter' and reported the positive response to Moscow. On 5 November the Director reacted with a violent reprimand:

Dora.
1. Your contact with Cartwright [the British Military Attaché], made without our authorization, is an unprecedented breach of discipline. Your step was unexpected. Our evaluation of the situation of your organization and the prospects of our continued work with 'Lucy' lead us to the conclusion that an official appeal to the British is not necessary. We repeat, it is impossible for us.
2. You must take immediate steps somehow to undo this unpleasant action and to hush it up. Simultaneously take care of 'Jim''s security so that information from 'Lucy' can continue to be dispatched through him. Send immediately an explanation of your incomprehensible actions and of your suggestions. Director.'[542]

Despite this reprimand, Radó renewed his appeal on 11 November:

Director. Do not see any other possibilities to continue to work usefully. 'Jim' is very much endangered, he can do little work and cannot meet 'Sissy' often. I myself am completely paralysed. Only from a building that enjoys diplomatic immunity could I continue work on the previous scale. I believed I was acting in your spirit when I turned to the British through 'Salter'.

I would arrange work with British Embassy in such a way that the independence of our organization would be preserved. Repeat: this is the only possibility to forward immediately very urgent and important information and to keep on sending it. We ought to make the best of 'Lucy' now in order not to lose him in the future.

Since there is no way to receive money from you for the time being, the organization is unable to continue work because of lack of funds. 'Sissy' states that 'Lucy' will not continue if payments stop. 'Lucy' says it is senseless to go on working if the information will not reach you. Working from the British Embassy would also solve the financial question, since you could send me money that way. Dora.[543]

The answer to this plea, received by Foote during the night of 14/15 November, is what David Dallin has described as 'a jewel of a message from

Moscow'. In effect, it said that Radó's reports about the dangerous situation in Switzerland were inspired by British intelligence and that Radó was nothing more than their tool:

Dora. After a thorough study of all your messages and a detailed investigation of your situation we are inclined to think that the whole story was built up – for reasons which we absolutely do not understand ≈ by a few members of the British intelligence service in Switzerland. They obviously do not realize the significance of the present events for the common cause of the United Nations. We think therefore that neither you yourself nor the others are seriously endangered at present. We know your extraordinary ability to quickly and correctly evaluate the political situation, and we are certain you will be able to find a way out of this serious and complicated situation and hold your own at the battle post in this historic moment of the last war days . . .

Work must be continued above all with 'Lucy'. You must arrange for immediate dispatch of the most important information from 'Lucy' through 'Jim'. Besides, new radio stations must be set up without delay. Director.[544]

Stung by the accusation, Radó replied on 17 November that

The only way you can help is by introducing me and 'Maria' [Lène Radó] to an Allied embassy before it is too late. So far no address for money available. We are without funds.

Your reproach of breach of discipline was a hard blow to me. Regardless of my grave situation I am concerned above all for the continuation of the work. The situation is such that I have to remain in hiding. Making following suggestion: further work at present possible only if you accept the risk of 'Jim's continuing his activity.[545]

Moscow's reply is unknown, but whatever it was the 'Centre' transmitted it into the void for there was no one to receive it. While Foote was busy sending and receiving the messages of Radó's wrangle with the Director, Lieutenant Treyer's radio direction-finder vans had closed in on the location of the third *Die Rote Drei* transmitter – Foote's flat at 2 Chemin de Longeraie in Lausanne.

During the night of 20/21 November 1943 Inspector Knecht and a squad of policemen battered down the door of Foote's flat while he was in the process of receiving a message from Moscow. When the pounding on the door commenced Foote calmly tore up the few sheets of enciphered messages he was to transmit, put them in a large ashtray and, dousing them with lighter fuel, set them on fire. Knecht entered the flat to be greeted with a broad smile from Foote, who made a welcoming gesture. 'Ah, gentlemen,' he said with a casual air. 'Dropped in for a drink? A whisky, perhaps?' Knecht smiled wryly and gave a Gallic shrug. 'Ah, Mr Foote, it's more serious than that.' After the police had made a thorough search of the flat, Foote was whisked away to the Bois-Mermet prison, where he was held on remand awaiting trial for ten months.[546]

On 19 April 1944, four months after Foote was apprehended, the police, acting on information obtained from the Hamels and 'Rosie', arrested Rachel Dubendorfer ('Sissy'). Documents found in her flat led the police to Christian

Schneider ('Taylor') and Rudolf Rössler ('Lucy'), who were both arrested May 1944. They were held in the Bois-Mermet prison until they were releas on bail, awaiting trial, in September 1944. 'Sissy', 'Rosie', and the Ham had all been released the previous July.[547] Allan Foote was released the sam day as Schneider and Rössler. He was told that if he made a full confessio he would be released on bail. Foote agreed, signing a statement in which I confessed to having worked as an agent 'for one of the United Nations in th struggle against Nazi Germany'.

By this time the Swiss considered themselves safe from attack by th Germans: France had been liberated, the Western Allies had reached th German frontier and were poised to invade the Reich and no power on ear was now capable of stopping the victorious Red Army as it advance relentlessly towards Berlin. After November 1943, when the three transmitte of *Die Rote Drei* were silenced, the Russians had fought without the aid of th day-to-day information concerning the Germans' planning and order of batt provided by 'Lucy'. But after Kursk the *Wehrmacht* on the Eastern Front w a spent force, capable only of conducting a continuous retreat.

Even when 'Lucy' was released on bail in September 1944 he was no long in a position to provide Moscow with high-grade intelligence because, apa from having no means of communicating with the 'Centre', his sources Berlin – including the all-important Lieutenant-General Fritz Thiele in th Communications Department of the Bendlerstrasse – had nearly all bee executed for their part in the abortive July 1944 'Bomb Plot' to kill Hitle Ironically, the *Gestapo* never realized that they had silenced the group German officers that collectively made up the mysterious 'Werther', and the investigations to unmask the culprits went on until the end of the war.

The magistrate who granted Foote bail released him from prison c condition that he stay within the canton of Vaud (in which Lausanne w situated) and live in a place chosen by the police until he was brought to tri Privately, however, the magistrate advised the Englishman to get out Switzerland as quickly as he could. Foote acted on this advice and on November 1944, with the aid of the Swiss Communist Party, he crossed th frontier into France near the Swiss town of Annemasse and made his way Paris. Without any means of support, Foote made his way to the recent reopened Soviet Embassy in the French capital, where he was received l Lieutenant-Colonel Novikov, leading the Russian Military Mission. There l was joined by Sándor Radó, who had escaped from Switzerland by hidir amongst the churns on a milk train, and none other than Leopold Trepp – the fugitive *Grand Chef*.

43. The Price of Freedom

was midday on Monday 13 September 1943 when Leopold Trepper entered
e Pharmacie Bailly on the Rue de Rome while his escort Willy Berg remained
the *Gestapo* car prostrate with a violent hangover. To effect his escape the *Grand*
ef simply walked through the pharmacy and left by the rear entrance on to the
ue de Rocher, on the west side of the Gare St-Lazare railway station. Hurrying
rough the crowds, he disappeared into a Metro station and caught a train to
nt de Neuilly in the north-western suburbs of Paris. From there he caught a bus
Saint Germain, some eight miles to the west, where he sought refuge in a
arding school. In his memoirs Trepper recalled:

I knew that, during the summer of 1942, Georgie de Winter had boarded out her
son Patrick [he was not Trepper's son: Georgie was already pregnant by another
man when she met the *Grand Chef*] in a boarding school in Saint Germain, run by
two sisters. I felt that by seeking refuge there I would be making the safest choice.
I could tell them I was a friend of Georgie's and ask for a place to stay, and also
find out where Georgie was staying. I decided to be completely open and explain
my situation to the two sisters. To my great astonishment they showed no emotion
at the story of my escape from the *Gestapo*. They told me that Patrick had left their
school and was living with a family in Suresnes. As for Georgie, she was still living
in Vésinet. My hostesses tried to telephone her all afternoon and offered to let me
stay with them in case I could not find her. Finally, that evening, they succeeded
in getting Georgie on the phone, and she rushed to join me.[548]

Leaving the boarding school, Trepper spent his first night of freedom in
eorgie's house at 22 Rue de la Borde in Vésinet, but he quickly decided that
was not an ideal hide-out: it was situated in a rather isolated spot, and he
ould soon be noticed by the locals.
In an attempt to throw Pannwitz off the scent, Trepper wrote him letter.
e told him that he had not escaped but had been forced to disappear. He
d entered the pharmacy only intending to get medicine for Berg, but he
d been approached by two NKVD counter-intelligence agents, who had
d him he was in grave danger of being arrested by the *Gestapo* and that they
d orders to take him to a safe place. He then explained that the two agents
d driven him out of Paris, and 100 kilometres outside the capital they had
ught a train for the Swiss border. He added that he had taken advantage
a moment of inattention on the part of his guards to mail the letter at the
ilway station in Besançon and that he would keep Pannwitz informed of the
urse of events. To give credence to the story, one of the two sisters at the
arding school in Saint Germain agreed to take a train to Besançon and post
epper's letter from there.[549]

After examining various possibilities regarding a more secure hide-ou Trepper and Georgie spent a few days with a couple called the Queyries i a small house in Suresnes who were looking after Georgie's son. Treppe recalled:

> I had a few days' head start on the *Sonderkommando*, yet prudence dictated that I should not nourish too many illusions. Pannwitz's men would certainly try to pick up my trail through Georgie. Sooner of later they would work their way from Saint Germain to Vésinet, and from Vésinet to Suresnes. A week later, in fact, they had identified the boarding school in Saint Germain, after having arrested and imprisoned numerous relatives of Georgie's, both near and distant. In Brussels her mother and several of her friends were harassed by the *Gestapo*. Probably this was the way they learned that Georgie's son had been in a boarding school in Saint Germain.
>
> The *Gestapo* were getting warm. I had not been at Suresnes three days when I received a telephone call from the two sisters who ran the boarding school, informing me that a man had come to the school claiming that he had something for *Madame* de Winter. From the description they gave I realized that the caller had been 'Kent', working on behalf of the *Sonderkommando*.[550]

A few days later the *Sonderkommando* arrested the two sisters, who ver courageously denied all knowledge of the *Grand Chef*'s whereabouts. Learnin that they had been arrested, Trepper decided that he would have to leave th Queyries' home in Suresnes in case the sisters broke down under interrogatio and revealed his hide-out.

Persuading *Madame* Queyrie to take Patrick to stay with her sister-in-la in Correze, beyond the reach of the *Gestapo*, Trepper and Georgie de Wint found a new refuge in the attic apartment of a friend of Georgie's calle Denise, whom she had met during her dancing classes. Denise lived on th Rue Chabanais, and the two fugitives moved in during the evening of 2 September. Trepper recalled:

> I agreed to this solution against my better judgment. Something told me that Denise was not very trustworthy and that we might be putting out heads into the lion's mouth. I spent a very restless night, unable to sleep, listening to every noise, expecting the *Gestapo* to appear at the door at any moment.[551]

Trusting his instinct, Trepper decided to quit Denise's apartment at daw the next day, and he and Georgie hurried through the streets of Paris to th home of Suzanne and Claude Spaak, on the Rue de Beaujolais. The Spaa were not Communists, but they were members of the French Resistance wh had been friends of Myra and Hersch Sokol. Trepper had met them whe he went to warn them that Myra and Hersch had been arrested in July 194 and they readily agreed to give refuge to him and Georgie.

Trepper's instinct proved to be correct, for Pannwitz had learned th Georgie had taken dancing lessons in the Place Clichy, and from the propri rs of the school he obtained a list of her friends, amongst them Denise. aving tracked down Denise's address, the *Sonderkommando* paid a night-time ll to her apartment, and, terrified, she told the *Gestapo* everything she knew. his did not include the fact that Trepper had sought refuge with the Spaaks, it she was able to divulge the whereabouts of *Madame* Queyrie, for Georgie id unwisely told her that she was looking after her son Patrick in Corrèze. Quickly tracking down *Madame* Queyrie's whereabouts in Corrèze, innwitz seized her and Patrick and placed them under guard in the Legion ' Honour building in Saint Germain, which had been requisitioned by the *'ehrmacht* as a convalescent home. By holding the child, Pannwitz believed at Georgie would give herself up, and that from her he would be able to tract, by one means or another, the whereabouts of the *Grand Chef.* owever, although beside herself with worry, Georgie did not play the *stapo*'s game. Despite having great faith in the Spaaks, Trepper quickly came realize that staying with them for any length of time was out of the question, r reasons he explained in his memoirs:

I knew that both the Spaaks belonged to the French Resistance, but I did not realize the degree to which Suzanne, in particular, was involved in a variety of underground activities. In 1942 she had devoted herself to rescuing Jewish children and had been a militant in the national movement against racism; but I did not realize that by September 1943, at the time she took me in, she was also working with several Gaullist and Communist organizations, and that she took part in the most perilous actions, without regard for the danger involved. Consequently she was very much exposed to the danger of arrest by the *Gestapo*, and Georgie and I decided it was wiser to part company with the Spaaks.[552]

With the help of Claude and Suzanne, Trepper found refuge in the Maison anche, a home for the retired in Bourg-la-Reine just outside Paris, owned and anaged by *Madame* Parrend – rather an incongruous establishment for a 39- ar-old, but the Spaaks considered it to be one of the best possible places to ide the *Gestapo*. Trepper recalled that

The first few days at the Maison Blanche were peaceful, but I noticed that several of the boarders seemed to be having as much trouble as I in playing the role of peaceful old men. Certain unmistakable signs betrayed both their real age and their real condition. I had the impression – and it worried me – that they too had been obliged to elude the curiosity of the Germans. The atmosphere was cordial, but everyone kept his distance, as if afraid of his neighbour's indiscretions, and we all took our meals in our rooms. It was a very peculiar retirement home![553]

Since it was out of the question for Georgie to seek refuge in the Maison anche, the Spaaks spirited her away to live with a farmer and his family in the lage of La Beauce, near Chartres. To keep in contact with Trepper, Georgie iployed the services of one of her acquaintances, a certain *Madame* May, the widow of a well-known French songwriter and a virulent anti-Nazi. Unfortunately *Madame* May was also friendly with Denise, who had given the *Sonderkommando* a list of all Georgie's friends and acquaintances. When the *Gestapo* finally got around to visiting *Madame* May they found a slip of paper in her apartment with Georgie's name and her address in La Beauce written on it. Acting on this information, Pannwitz and the *Sonderkommando* descended on La Beauce on Sunday 17 October 1943.

That afternoon Georgie had gone for a long walk along the lanes of La Beauce to kill time. She returned to the farmhouse where she was hiding out just in time for the evening meal. Pannwitz was lying in wait outside. His men, armed to the teeth, were hiding in the farmyard and waiting for his signal. The place was surrounded by the *Gestapo* and the Secret Field Police, numbering fifty men in all; Pannwitz believed that Trepper was also hiding in the farmhouse. When Pannwitz and Willy Berg burst into the farmhouse at the head of nine men, they were disappointed not to find Trepper but they bundled Georgie into a Citroën and drove her to the house in Neuilly where they held her hostage.

When he learned that Georgie had been arrested, Trepper immediately fled the Maison Blanche, in case the *Gestapo* managed to extract his address from Georgie, and headed back to Paris. After seeking temporary refuge in a brothel, he roamed around the city in search of a new hide-out. In his memoirs he recalled:

On 19 October I passed by the building that was the headquarters of the French Neo-Nazi Party. As I looked up at the building it came to me in a flash that *Madame* Lucie, a nurse who had once given me some injections, had an apartment in the same building. I conceived the somewhat mad idea that I – the fugitive, the man hunted by the *Gestapo* – would seek refuge in the same building that housed the *Rassemblement National Populaire*, the most fanatical advocates of collaboration in France. What was more, it was only a stone's throw from the Rue des Saussaies, where Pannwitz was running the manhunt. Quite a disreputable neighbourhood, in sum.

The idea smacked of mental derangement. But this was only appearance, I told myself, not reality: nobody in my circle knew *Madame* Lucie. Besides, the *Sonderkommando* would never think of looking for me so nearby, would never imagine I would hide two steps away from their lair. I noticed, however, that there were some guards on duty and decided to wait for them to leave. So I cooled my heels for a while, to make the best of my chances, and at ten o'clock that evening walked with a confident step towards the part of the building that was not occupied by the collaborators. I climbed to the fourth floor and rang the bell. *Madame* Lucie came to the door, stared at me and went as white as a sheet.

'What's the matter, *Monsieur* Gilbert?' the good woman exclaimed. 'Are you sick?' I ushered her gently through the doorway so we could continue our conversation inside. She added, 'You've changed terribly, you're scarcely the man I knew before.' The man she had known before had been a Belgian industrialist who spent a few days of the week in Paris.

'*Madame* Lucie,' I told her in one breath, 'I am a Jew. I am an escaped prisoner who's being hunted by the *Gestapo*: can you keep me in your apartment for a few days? Please just tell me yes or no. If it's impossible I won't hold it against you, and I will leave at once!'

Her eyes filled with tears, and she replied in a voice full of emotion, 'How could you think for a moment that I would refuse you?'[554]

Three days after Trepper moved in to *Madame* Lucie's apartment a notice appeared amongst the personal columns on page 2 of the newspaper *Paris-Soir*. Edgar! Why don't you call? – Georgie.' The meaning was immediately clear to Trepper. Edgar was one of the cover-names that Georgie used when communicating with him, and Pannwitz had obviously thought up this distress call as a way of urging the *Grand Chef* to emerge from the shadows to save his mistress. The following day's edition of *Paris-Soir* carried the same message, repeated three times in the personal columns.[555] But Pannwitz had underestimated Trepper's instinct for self-preservation, which was above concern for the suffering of others on his account: in short, he had no intention of giving himself up to save Georgie from the tender mercies of the *Gestapo*.

By the middle of November Pannwitz realized that his ploy had failed, and, having completely lost the scent, he caused a 'wanted' notice to be sent to every police station in France. It read:

Wanted. Jean Gilbert. Infiltrated police organizations on behalf of the Resistance. Fled with documents. Must be apprehended by any means.

A photograph, taken by the *Sonderkommando* shortly after Trepper's arrest the previous November, and a detailed description were included. At the same time, all sections of the *Gestapo* and the *Abwehr* and all German administrative, economic and military organizations in France, Belgium and the Netherlands received posters with Trepper's photograph topped with the inscription 'Escaped Spy – Very Dangerous'.[556]

By this time Trepper's appearance had changed considerably from that depicted by the photograph published by the *Gestapo*. He had lost a lot of weight, had grown a thick moustache and now wore glasses. However, the 'wanted' notices, which were also distributed to the offices of the *Rassemblement National Populaire* – whose head office was on the ground floor of the same building as *Madame* Lucie's apartment – made it extremely dangerous for Trepper to go on hiding there. As a result *Madame* Lucie managed to find him a new hide-out in an apartment in the Avenue du Maine which was owned by an employee of the Credit Lyonnais. Trepper recalled that

The story I invented [for my new landlord] suited my situation: I was a man alone in the world, I was sick and I had been mistreated by Fate. I had lost my whole family in an air raid. The neighbours I passed on the stairs, who had heard about my misfortunes [from the landlord] treated me with great sympathy. My landlord,

Monsieur Jean, a bachelor whose family name I have forgotten, was a calm and intelligent man with whom I got along very well. He had no idea whom he had under his roof, but my new refuge turned out to be so safe and so hospitable that I stayed there until the Allies liberated Paris in August 1944.[557]

Trepper had outwitted the *Sonderkommando*, but at a terrible cost to those who harboured him during the eleven months he was on the run. The two sisters who ran the boarding school in Saint Germain were both deported to concentration camps and only one survived. *Madame* Parrend, who ran the Maison Blanche home for the retired in Bourg-la-Reine, was also thrown into a concentration camp in Germany for harbouring Trepper, and although she survived to return home to France she died after only a few years as a result of illnesses contracted in the camp. *Madame* Queyrie and Georgie de Winter's son Patrick were released unharmed in May 1944, but *Monsieur* Queyrie spent eight months in Fresnes prison for granting the fugitive refuge. Suzanne Spaak was arrested in November 1943 and executed in Fresnes on 12 August 1944, although her husband Claude managed to escape the *Gestapo* net. Hillel Katz was brutally tortured by the *Sonderkommando* for refusing to disclose a list of hiding places that the *Grand Chef* might use – mainly, one suspects, to protect other members of the Red Orchestra still at large – and he was finally executed, probably in Fresnes in November 1944.

After her arrest at the farmhouse in La Beauce on 17 October 1943, Georgie de Winter was held in the house in Neuilly from where the *Sonderkommando* conducted the *Funkspiel* with Moscow. She was well treated until the Allies began advancing on Paris, when her loyalty to her lover paid a terrible dividend. Deported to Germany, she was first incarcerated in Karlsruhe prison, and from there she was transferred to the prison in Frankfurt-am-Main and then to a labour camp in Leipzig. There she was held in a small hut crowded with Russian women. They slept huddled together on the floor and woke up each morning amidst the excrement that had overflowed from the sanitary can. Her stay was brief because the Germans evacuated the camp, and she was amongst the wretched band of women who were marched to the railway station, enduring insults and stones thrown by German civilians. She was packed into a freight car and suffered a long and tortuous journey without food or water which ended at the Ravensbrück concentration camp. During her time in Ravensbrück she witnessed a German woman SS guard split a female prisoner's head open with a spade, but her outstanding memory amongst all the horrors, which was to haunt her for the rest of her life, was that of a gipsy woman standing in line outside the death-selection hut hugging in her arms her baby, hardly a fortnight old, both naked in the bitter cold.[558]

When Ravensbrück was evacuated, Georgie was sent to a labour camp near Berlin, where she worked in a synthetic-rubber factory making wires for field telephones. From there she was transferred to another camp outside Frankfurt-an-der-Oder, where she was put to work with thousands of other slave labourers digging anti-tank ditches to stem the advance of the Red Army. The ground was so frozen that the pick she used bounced off the solid earth. With the approach of the Red Army the wretched prisoners were forced on a 'death march', during which thousands of bewildered, starving women were kept plodding around in the ever-narrowing gap between the Eastern and Western Fronts, driven along by the cudgels of the SS whose hatred was exacerbated by fear. Stragglers were shot on the spot. On many occasions women would deliberately step out of the long column and passively wait for a bullet in the nape of the neck to put an end to their sufferings. The only food they had was a ration of watery soup which they gulped down by the roadside.

One evening there was some jostling in the line at the field kitchen. The woman in front of Georgie stumbled against the soup pot. Georgie recalled that

> The SS man supervising the distribution pulled out his pistol as one pulls out a handkerchief and shot her, without the slightest expression, as though it was the most ordinary thing to do. I was so hungry that I stepped forward and held out my mess tin while she, poor thing, was dying at my feet, clawing at the earth with fingers that moved slower and slower.[559]

They slept in barns which were too small to take all of them, and the women fought savagely for a place inside; those who were unsuccessful usually froze to death during the night. They were kept moving and given less and less to eat. The death toll mounted, and Georgie realized that she was not going to survive unless she tried to escape. The most opportune moment was during the hours of darkness, when the starving column stumbled on blindly to the rattle of mess tins and spoons dangling from their tattered clothing. Late one evening, as they approached a village, Georgie and another woman saw an open gate which led into a garden. They rushed through it and hid behind a wall. A dog started to bark, but the SS guards took no notice and the two trembling women listened to the tinny sound of the column becoming fainter and fainter until it was out of hearing. Heading back east, they were finally rescued by a Russian unit which fed and sheltered them.[560] Emaciated, sick and exhausted, Georgie was repatriated to France on 15 May 1945. There she was reunited with Patrick, who had been cared for by *Madame* Queyrie at her home in Suresnes.

By this time Trepper was suffering his own martyrdom in Moscow, and he was not alone. Pannwitz and the *Sonderkommando* moved out of Paris in the middle of August 1944 as lead elements of General Jacques Leclerc's Free French 2nd Armoured Division began advancing into the southern suburbs of the city. With them the *Sonderkommando* took 'Kent' and Margarete Barcza, who had given birth to a son the previous April. Paris was in a state of insurrection when the convoy of cars bearing the *Sonderkommando* moved off from the Rue des Saussaies, and they had to make several detours because of street barricades, but eventually they reached the eastern suburbs and joined the stream of German Army units hurriedly retreating toward the Rhine.

The *Sonderkommando* retreated to Hornberg in the Black Forest, from where they dispatched Margarete and her son to a requisitioned guest house in Friedrichroda, where the *Gestapo* had already interned other harmless notabilities. During February 1945, as the Western Allies advanced into the Reich, the *Sonderkommando* fled to an isolated chalet at Bludenz, about eight miles from the Swiss frontier. To reach this southern corner of Germany Pannwitz and his entourage had to travel 200 miles, threading their way through a mass of retreating German units and past road blocks manned by police and the SS, who were quick to shoot anyone who they believed was attempting to desert.[561]

Not long after the *Sonderkommando* reached Bludenz the town was overrun by a unit of the French First Army, and at the end of May 1945, nine months after they had fled from Paris, Pannwitz and 'Kent' were escorted back to the French capital, where they were handed over to Lieutenant-Colonel Novikov of the Soviet military mission. A week later they were flown to Moscow, where, after enduring a lengthy period of interrogation in the notorious Lubianka prison, 'Kent' was executed for collaborating with the Germans. Pannwitz was sent to the Vorkuta labour camp in Siberia, near the Kara Sea, where he remained for ten years. He was repatriated to West Germany at the end of 1945, eventually becoming the manager of a bank in Ludwigsburg.[562]

Friedrichroda, where Margarete Barcza and her son were interned, was captured by the Americans but then handed over to the Red Army as the town was in the Russian Occupation Zone. She was finally repatriated to France in September 1945, where the French authorities interned her in a camp with hundreds of other people suspected of collaborating with the Germans during the occupation. She was released on 18 May 1946, to face a life dogged by illness, poverty and bitter memories.

Two other members of the Red Orchestra who had opted to collaborate with the Germans also faced a bleak future. Shortly before the Allies liberated Paris, Abraham Raichmann, 'The Cobbler', and his mistress Malvina Gruber, were sent back to Brussels by the *Sonderkommando*, where the local *Gestapo*, who had no use for the pair, threw them into the Saint Gilles prison. When Brussels was liberated by the Allies the Belgian authorities did not release Raichmann and his mistress but held them on remand awaiting trial on two counts, working for Soviet Intelligence against Belgian interests prior to May 1940 and collaborating with the Germans between July 1942 and August 1944. They were both found guilty at a trial held shortly after the end of the war, Raichmann receiving a sentence of twelve years' imprisonment and Malvina four years. In 1948, while they were both serving their terms, United States counter-intelligence agents in West Germany arrested Malvina's son, Eugene Gruber, on a charge of forging passports for the use of Soviet intelligence agents. Eugene had obviously decided to follow in the family tradition![563]

In 1946 the Belgian military authorities arrested Captain Harry Piepe of the *Abwehr*, but after a series of lengthy interrogations conducted by André Moyen of the Belgian *Sûreté*, he was cleared of committing war crimes and released. After the war Piepe returned to the legal profession and became a member of the administrative board of the Hamburg Rotary Club. He died in Hamburg in 1972, aged seventy-nine.[564]

44. The Rewards

On 5 January 1945 a Soviet aircraft took off from Paris bound for Moscow. On board were twelve passengers, including Leopold Trepper, Sándor Radó and Allan Foote. As the war was still raging in the heart of Europe, the aircraft had to make a long detour. From Paris it headed south, making refuelling stops at Marseilles, Castel Benito, Cairo, Teheran and Baku, before finally putting down at a small airfield near Moscow during the afternoon of 14 January 1945.

Six years had passed since Trepper left Russia to take up his post as *Grand Chef* of the Western GRU *apparats*. He was not welcomed back as a hero. His decision to collaborate with the *Sonderkommando* in the *Funkspiel* with the 'Centre' from the time of his arrest in November 1942 until his escape in September 1943 earned him nine years and seven months in the Lubianka and Lefortovo prisons. When he was released in May 1954 Trepper was reunited with his wife Luba and his two sons after a separation that had lasted for fifteen years. He found them eking out an existence in a hovel in the village of Babuchkin on the outskirts of Moscow. The last time he had seen his two children they had been nine and four years old respectively; now he was confronted by a man of twenty-three and a youth of eighteen.

In April 1957 Trepper obtained permission from the Soviet authorities to return to Poland, his native country. He and his family settled in Warsaw, where Trepper, having abandoned Communism, devoted himself entirely to the preservation of Jewish social and cultural life and the welfare of his fellow Jews in Poland. He also set up a small publishing house which dealt exclusively with Jewish classical literature. In 1967, twenty-two years after the end of the war, in the country where the Jews has suffered more than anywhere else from Nazi barbarity (3 million Polish Jews were exterminated) the monster of anti-semitism rose its ugly head again when the Polish Communist Party became openly hostile towards the Jewish community. Finding himself treated as a mistrusted stranger in his native land, Trepper decided to leave the country and emigrate to Israel, but he was refused permission to leave by the Polish authorities until November 1973. After spending a short time in the West he finally arrived in the Promised Land in the summer of 1974. He died in Jerusalem in 1983, at the age of seventy-seven.

Sándor Radó received the same reward as Trepper when he arrived in Moscow. His overtures to British Intelligence during October and November 1943, and the fact that he had misappropriated GRU funds during the war years to fund a comfortable life-style in Geneva, earned him ten years in the Lubianka and other Soviet prisons. On his release in 1955 he returned to his native Hungary, whence he had fled in 1919, where he was reunited with his wife Lène, who had lived in France through the long years of her husband's incarceration. She died in September 1958. Politically 'rehabilitated' by the Hungarian Communist Party, Radó spent the rest of his life living and working in Budapest as a cartographer for the Hungarian Government. He died in the early 1980s.

Allan Foote was better received in Moscow but he paid a different kind of penalty for the stress and strain of espionage work during the war. In November 1945 he fell seriously ill with a duodenal ulcer. After an operation in the Central Military Hospital in the Russian capital he spent a considerable period of time convalescing at a sanatorium at Bolshava. When his health had improved he was dispatched to Berlin by the 'Centre' in the summer of 1947, under the cover-name of Albert Müller, posing as a repatriated German prisoner of war who had been captured at Stalingrad. After residing quietly for three months in the Soviet sector of Berlin, patiently building up his cover, he crossed into the British sector of the occupied German capital on 2 August 1947 and surrendered to the British security authorities. The treatment afforded Sándor Radó by the GRU and the stark realities of life under the Soviet system which he had witnessed in Moscow had caused him to abandon Communism.

On his arrival in London in October 1947 Foote was placed under house arrest in a flat in Hammersmith for two and a half months while he was debriefed by MI5. In 1949 he published a book, *Handbook for Spies*, which was in fact 'ghosted' by MI5 officers who set out to discredit and embarrass Soviet Intelligence with a work full of subtle disinformation. Eventually Foote found work as an executive officer in the Ministry of Agriculture and Fisheries. He died in August 1956 at the age of fifty-one, in the University College Hospital, London, of acute peritonitis due to a perforated duodenal ulcer.

The post-war years were equally unkind to Rudolf Rössler – agent 'Lucy'. On 22 October 1945 the Swiss brought him to trial, on the charge of having been associated with an illegal intelligence service operated by a foreign power. Christian Schneider ('Taylor') and Rachel Dübendorfer ('Sissy') were also arraigned, but only Schneider turned up to stand in the dock with Rössler because 'Sissy' had fled to Leipzig in the Russian Zone of Germany. Both Rössler and Schneider were found guilty, but on the discretion of the judge Rössler was set free because the court found that he had acted in the best interests of the Swiss state. Strangely, although Schneider was also found to have acted in the same spirit, he was sentenced to thirty days' imprisonment.

Eight days later, on 30 October, Edmond and Olga Hamel and Margrit Bolli ('Rosie') also stood trial. They were charged with having worked for an illegal intelligence service operated by a foreign power and having passed Swiss military secrets to the Soviet Union (the BUPO had found incriminating documents of this nature when they raided their flats). Edmond received a sentence of one year's imprisonment, less three months of the time he had spent in detention after his arrest, and a fine of 1,000 francs. Olga was sentenced to seven months' imprisonment, less three months already served in detention. Margrit Bolli was sentenced to ten months in prison, minus the 272 days she had spent in detention after her arrest.

After the war Rössler was beset by business worries. His publishing house, Vita Nova, began to fail, and to obtain funds he began working for Czech Intelligence, having been introduced to agents of that service by his old friend Xaver Schnieper, who had become the president of the Lucerne branch of the Swiss Communist Party. Both men were discovered and arrested by the BUPO in March 1953. They were charged with operating from Swiss territory an espionage ring dedicated to the service of a foreign power, namely Czechoslovakia, and against the interests of other foreign powers, namely West Germany, the USA, Great Britain, France and Denmark. At their trial, held in Lucerne in November 1953, Rössler was sentenced to one year's imprisonment, less the 242 days he had already spent on remand; while Schnieper received a nine-month sentence, less the 242 days he had spent on remand. After his release Rössler continued to work in Lucerne, just managing to keep his publishing house alive, but his health started to decline and he suffered from chronic asthma, dying of the disease in October 1958 at the age of 61.

Those who survived the war may not have had particularly happy experiences, but it was preferable to the fate of the 217 agents and informers of the Red Orchestra who were arrested by the *Gestapo* in France, Belgium, Holland and Germany. A total of 143 of these were executed or murdered during 'intensified interrogations', died in concentration camps or committed suicide. The price in individual suffering had been terrible, but the 74 survivors from amongst those who had been subjected to the tender mercies of the *Gestapo*, along with the members of the Swiss *apparat*, had the satisfaction of knowing that the suffering had not been in vain, for the Red Orchestra had played a vital part in the destruction of the vile scourge of Nazism.

APPENDIX

Code-Names and Cover-Names

Adash	Abraham Raichmann	Brussels *apparat*
Alamo (Carlos)	Mikael Makarov	Brussels *apparat*
Alta	Ilse Stöbe	Berlin *apparat*
Arier	Rudolf von Scheliha	Berlin *apparat*
Arwid	Arvid Harnack	Berlin *apparat*
Bauer	Adam Kuckhoff	Berlin *apparat*
Bordo	Konstantin Yefremov	Brussels *apparat*
Camille	David Kamy	Brussels *apparat*
Choro	Harro Schulze-Boysen	Berlin *apparat*
Cobbler, The	Abraham Raichmann	Brussels *apparat*
Danilov (Anton)	David Kamy	Brussels *apparat*
Desmets (Albert)	David Kamy	Brussels *apparat*
Dora	Sándor Radó	Swiss *apparat*
Edward	Edmond Hamel	Swiss *apparat*
Gilbert (Jean)	Leopold Trepper	Resident Director in the West
Grand Chef	Leopold Trepper	
Harry	Henry Robinson	French *apparat*
Hermann	Johann Wenzel	Brussels *apparat*
Hoscho	Anna-Margaret Hoffmann	French *apparat*
Hilda		Dutch *Apparat*
Jernstroem (Eric)	Konstantin Yefremov	Brussels *apparat*
Jim	Allan Foote	Swiss *apparat*
Juzefa	Sophie Poznanska	Brussels *apparat*
Kent	Victor Sukulov-Gurevich	Brussels *apparat*
Lucy	Rudolf Rössler	Swiss *apparat*
Lunette	Hermann Isbutsky	Dutch *apparat*
Maria	Hélène Radó	Swiss *apparat*
Maude	Olga Hamel	Swiss *apparat*
Mikler (Adam)	Leopold Trepper	
Pakbo	Otto Pünter	Swiss *apparat*
Petit Chef	Victor Sukulov-Gurevich	Brussels *apparat*
Phantomas	Isaiah Bir	French *apparat*
Professeur, Le	Johann Wenzel	Brussels *apparat*
Rosie	Margrit Bolli	Swiss *apparat*
Salter	Léon Sousse	Swiss *apparat*
Schmetterling	Germaine Schneider	Brussels *apparat*
Sierra (Vincent)	Victor Sukulov-Gurevich	Brussels *apparat*

Sissy	Rachel Dübendorfer	Swiss *apparat*
Sonia	Ruth Kuczynski	Swiss *apparat*
Strahlmann	Hans Coppi	Berlin *apparat*
Taylor	Christian Schneider	Swiss *apparat*
Tino	Anton Winterinck	Dutch *apparat*
Verlinden (Anna)	Sophie Poznanska	Brussels *apparat*
Wassermann	Maurice Peper	Dutch *apparat*
Wolf	Arvid Harnack	Berlin *apparat*

Glossary

Abwehr	German Military Intelligence
Apparat	Spy network
Brigadeführer	An SS rank equivalent to Major-General
BUPO	*Bundespolizei* (Swiss Federal Police)
Bureau Ha	A private Swiss intelligence bureau created by Hans Hausamann
'Centre'	The GRU headquarters in Moscow
Comintern	The Communist International, formed in 1919
Funkabwehr	Radio counter-espionage or Signals Security
GC&CS	Government Codes & Cipher School (the British Cryptanalytic Section – the predecessor of the present-day GCHQ)
Generaloberstabsrichter *Generalrichter* *Generalstabsrichter*	Ranks in order of seniority in the German Military Legal Service
Gestapo	*Geheime Staatspolizei* (the German Secret State Police)
GRU	*Glavno Razvedyvatelno Upravlenie* (Soviet Military Intelligence)
Gruppenführer	SS rank equivalent to Lieutenant-General
Hauptsturmführer	SS rank equivalent to Captain
ILO	International Labour Office
KPD	*Kommunistische Partei Deutschlands* (German Communist Party)
Kriminaldirektor *Kriminalrat* *Kriminalinspektor* *Kriminalkommissar* *Kriminalobersekretär* *Kriminalsekretär* *Kriminaloberassistent*	Ranks in the *Gestapo* in order of seniority
NKVD	*Narodny Kommissariat Vnutrennich Dyel* (People's Commissariat for Internal Affairs)
Oberführer	SS rank equivalent to Brigadier
Obergruppenführer	SS rank equivalent to General
Oberregierungsrat	Rank in the German Civil Service equivalent to Lieutenant-Colonel
OKH	*Oberkommando der Heeres* (High Command of the German Army)
OKL	*Oberkommando der Luftwaffe* (High Command of the German Air Force)
OKW	*Oberkommando der Wehrmacht* (High Command of the German Armed Forces)

Ordnungspolizei	The regular uniformed police in Germany
OT	*Organisation Todt* (a semi-military German government agency established in 1933 for the construction of strategic highways and military installations)
Regierungsrat	German Government Counsellor (the most junior rank in the Higher Civil Service)
Reichsführer	Himmler's title as head of the SS
Reichskriminaldirektor	Heinrich Müller's title as head of the *Gestapo*
RKG	*Reichskriegsgericht* (Reich Court Martial – the most senior military court in Germany)
SD	*Sicherheitsdienst* (Security Service of the SS)
Standartenführer	SS rank equivalent to Colonel
Sturmbannführer	SS rank equivalent to Major
Untersturmführer	SS rank equivalent to Second Lieutenant

Source Notes

Chapter 1
1. Flicke, *Spionagegruppe Rote Kapelle*, p.8.
2. *Ibid.*, p.12.
3. 'Das Geheimnis der Roten Rapelle', an article in the *Norddeutsche Rundschau*, 31 January 1951.

Chapter 2
4. Reile, *Geheime Westfront*, p.482.
5. Perrault, *L'Orchestre Rouge*, p.60.
6. Höhne, *Codeword Direktor*, p.77.
7. 'Final Report of the Rote Kapelle Case' (United States Armed Forces Security Agency translation of the captured German Security Police and Security Service report 'Abschlussbericht über den Fall *Rote Kapelle*' dated 22 December 1942), National Archives, Washington, RG 457 SRH-380.

Chapter 3
8. For details of the German invasion of the USSR up to December 1941 see Tarrant, *Stalingrad: Anatomy of an Agony*, pp.18–23.

Chapter 4
9. Höhne, p.79.
10. Perrault, p.83.
11. *Ibid.*, p.87.
12. *Ibid.*
13. Piepe's deposition on the *Rote Kapelle* case made during a series of interrogations conducted by André Moyen of the Belgian security authorities in 1946.
14. Dallin, *Soviet Espionage*, p.153.

Chapter 5
15. Piepe's deposition.
16. Trepper, *Le Grand Jeu*, p.153.
17. *Ibid.*
18. *Rote Kapelle* Final Report.

Chapter 6
19. For example, Perrault, p.188.
20. Best, *Die Deutsche Abwehrpolizei bis 1945*, p.19.
21. Höhne, p.84.
22. Perrault, p.118.
23. *Rote Kapelle* Final Report.
24. Trepper, p.147.
25. *Rote Kapelle* Final Report.
26. Höhne pp.41–3, 47, 80, 85, 221.
27. Perrault, p.87.
28. Trepper, pp.230–1.

Chapter 7
29. Perrault, p.127.
30. 'Capitaine Freddy', 'La Verité sur la Rote Kapelle', *Europe-Amérique*, 2 October 1947, pp.14–15. 'Capitaine Freddy' was the pseudonym of André Moyen, a Belgian intelligence officer.
31. *Ibid.*
32. Dallin, pp.86–8.
33. Trepper, p.106.
34. Piepe's deposition.
35. *Ibid.*
36. *Ibid.*
37. 'La Verité sur la Rote Kapelle', p.15.

Chapter 8
38. Perrault, p.134.
39. *Ibid.*

40. *Ibid.*
41. Piepe's deposition.
42. *Ibid.*
43. *Ibid.*
44. Perrault, p.138.

Chapter 9
45. Thälmann was arrested by the *Gestapo* in March 1933 and suffered eleven years of hell in concentration camps which finally ended with his execution in Buchenwald in August 1944.
46. Perrault, pp.145–6.
47. *Rote Kapelle* Final Report.
48. Trepper, p.196.
49. *Ibid.*
50. *Ibid.*
51. *Ibid.*
52. *Rote Kapelle* Final Report.
53. Statement by *Kriminalkommissar* Johann Strübing, 18 January 1950, in the files of the Public Prosecutor of the Lüneburg Provincial Court in the case against *Dr* Manfred Roeder, Vol. VIII, f.131.
54. *Ibid.*, Vol. X, ff.220 *et seq.*
55. *Ibid.*
56. Perrault, p.313.

Chapter 10
57. Dallin, p.162.
58. *Ibid.*
59. Trepper, p.163.
60. Betty Depelsenaire, *Symphonie Fraternelle*, p.28.
61. *Ibid.*

Chapter 11
62. Piepe, 'Harburger jagte Agenten', *Harburger Anzeiger und Nachrichten*, 11 October 1967.
63. *Ibid.*
64. *Ibid.*
65. *Rote Kapelle* Final Report.
66. *Ibid.*
67. Dallin, p.155.
68. Trepper, p.157.
69. Dallin, p.155.
70. Perrault, p.146.

71. *Ibid.*
72. *Rote Kapelle* Final Report.
73. Piepe, 'Harburger jagte Agenten'.

Chapter 12
74. *Rote Kapelle* Final Report.
75. Trepper, pp.233–4.
76. Piepe, 'Harburger jagte Agenten'.
77. *Rote Kapelle* Final Report.
78. Dallin, p.156.
79. Piepe, 'Harburger jagte Agenten'.
80. Piepe's deposition.
81. *Rote Kapelle* Final Report.

Chapter 13
82. Piepe, 'Harburger jagte Agenten'.
83. Höhne, p.211.
84. *Ibid.*
85. *Ibid.*, p.212.
86. *Ibid.*
87. Perrault, p.159.
88. Höhne, p.212.
89. Perrault, p.157.

Chapter 14
90. For the planning and course of the 'Case Blue' offensive, see Tarrant, *Stalingrad: Anatomy of an Agony*, pp.25–38.
91. Erickson, *The Road to Stalingrad*, p.484.
92. Allen Dulles, *The Craft of Intelligence*.
93. Accoce and Quet, *La Guerre a été en Suisse*, p.162.
94. Seaton, *The Russo-German War 1941–1945*, p.262; and Erickson, *The Road to Stalingrad*, pp.337–8, 340, 342, 354–5.
95. Hinsley, *British Intelligence in the Second World War*, p.97n.
96. For a full account of the Battle of Stalingrad and its effect on the course of the war, see Tarrant, *Stalingrad: Anatomy of an Agony*.
97. Trepper, p.130.
98. Höhne, p.242.
99. A number of the messages captured in the Atrébates raid which were subsequently deciphered by the *Funkabwehr* are in the papers of the late W. F. Flicke.

100. Trepper, p.133.
101. Höhne, p.89.

Chapter 15
102. Dallin, p.153.
103. Pünter, *Der Anschluss fand nicht Statt*, pp.141–7.
104. Kahn, *The Codebreakers*, pp.370–1.

Chapter 16
105. *Rote Kapelle* Final Report.
106. Schellenberg, *Memoiren*, p.251 (German edn).
107. Horst Kopkow was born in Ortelsburg, East Prussia, on 29 November 1910. He matriculated in 1928 and was apprenticed to a chemist, working in the 'Rathaus' drug store in Allenstein until 1934. He joined the Nazi Party in 1931 and the SS a year later. His *Gestapo* career began in Allenstein in September 1934 and he was seconded to *Gestapo* headquarters in Berlin in 1938, becoming head of the 'counter-sabotage' desk. He was promoted *Kriminalrat* in 1941 and *Kriminaldirektor* in 1944.
108. Johann Strübing was born in Berlin on 24 February 1907. From 1927 to 1937 he served in the Berlin *Schutzpolizei* (Metropolitan Police). He transferred to the *Gestapo* on 1 February 1937 and was promoted *Kriminalkommissar* shortly thereafter. He joined the SS in 1937 and the Nazi Party in 1940. He was promoted *SS-Obersturmführer* on 1 September 1942.
109. Höhne p.96.
110. *Rote Kapelle* Final Report.
111. Vauck's statement relating to this telephone conversation is in *Rote Kapelle* Final Report.
112. Höhne p.141.
113. Hildebrandt, *Wir Sind die Letzten*, p.141.
114. *Rote Kapelle* Final Report.
115. Höhne p.153.
116. Elsa Boysen, *Harro Schulze-Boysen*, p.23.
117. Lüneburg Trial, Vol. VIII, f.114.

Chapter 17
118. Egmont Zechlin, *Arvid und Mildred Harnack zum Gedachtnis*, p.2.
119. Friedrich Panzinger was born in Munich on 1 February 1903. He joined the police in 1919 and worked alongside Heinrich Müller as a medium-level official from 1927 to 1929, in the Munich police headquarters. He was promoted to the higher ranks of the police in 1934, joining the *Gestapo* in 1937.
120. Statement by Johann Strübing, 18 January 1950: Lüneberg Trial, Vol. X, f.202.
121. Perrault, p.206.
122. Dulles, *Germany's Underground*, p.100.
123. Karl Paetel, *Versuchung oder Chance?*, p.192.
124. Höhne, p.105.
125. Marie-Louise Schulze, *Warum Ich im Jahre 1933 Parteigenossin Geworden bin*, p.3.
126. Von Salomon, *Der Fragebogen*, p.477.
127. Perrault, p.215.
128. Von Salomon, p.477.
129. *Rote Kapelle* Final Report.
130. *Ibid.*
131. Weisenborn, *Der Lautlose Aufstand*, pp.206–7.
132. Höhne, p.113.
133. Buschmann, 'De la Résistance au Défaitisme', *Les Temps Modernes*, p.264.

Chapter 18
134. Costello and Tsarev, *Deadly Illusions*, pp.78≈9 .
135. Dallin, p.234.
136. Axel von Harnack, 'Arvid und Mildred Harnack', *Die Gegenwart*, Nos 26 and 27, January 1947.
137. Dallin, p.236.
138. Costello and Tsarev, p.73.
139. Zechlin, *Arvid und Mildred Harnack zum Gedächtnis*, p.4; and Costello and Tsarev, pp.73–4.
140. Boveri, *Treason in the Twentieth Century*, p.256.
141. Von Harnack, *op. cit.*
142. Costello and Tsarev, p.74.

143. Dallin, p.235.
144. *Ibid.*, p.236.
145. Costello and Tsarev, pp.77–8.
146. Russian Intelligence Service Archives, file no 34118, quoted in Costello and Tsarev, p.76.
147. Statement by Greta Kuckhoff, Lüneburg Trial, Vol. VIII, f.131.
148. Russian Intelligence Service Archives, file no 34118, quoted in Costello and Tsarev, p.71.
149. Statement by Greta Kuckhoff, Lüneburg Trial, Vol. VIII, f.131.
150. Costello and Tsarev, p.84.
151. Statement by Greta Kuckhoff, Lüneburg Trial, Vol. VIII, f.131.
152. *Ibid.*
153. *Ibid.*
154. Russian Intelligence Service Archives, file no 34118, quoted in Costello and Tsarev, pp.83–5.

Chapter 19
155. Statement by Greta Kuckhoff, Lüneburg Trial, Vol. VIII, f.131.
156. Buschmann, p.274.
157. Statement by *Dr* Werner Krauss, Lüneburg Trial, Vol. X, f.159.
158. Statement by *Dr* Alexander Kraell, Lüneburg Trial, Vol. XII, f.104.
159. Statement by *Dr* Werner Krauss, Lüneburg Trial, Vol. X, f.159.
160. *Ibid.*
161. *Rote Kapelle* Final Report.
162. Buschmann, p.274.
163. Perrault, p.272.
164. Von Salomon, *The Answers of Ernst von Salomon*, pp.301–2.
165. Statement by Coppi's mother, Frieda Coppi, 14 November 1949, Lüneburg Trial, Vol. X, f.45.
166. This message and all subsequent messages in this section are from Russian Intelligence Service Archives file no 34118, quoted in Costello and Tsarev, p.484.
167. Statement by Greta Kuckhoff, Lüneburg Trial, Vol. VIII, f.131.

Chapter 20
168. *Rote Kapelle* Final Report.
169. Höhne, p.146.
170. Perrault, pp.73–4.
171. Wilhelm Flick papers. The full text of this message is given in Chapter 15.
172. Wilhelm Flick papers.
173. Collective report on the Red Orchestra, Lüneburg Trial, Vol. VIII, f.107.
174. Dallin, p.124.
175. *Rote Kapelle* Final Report.
176. Statement by Johann Strübing, 18 January 1950, Lüneburg Trial, Vol. X, f.196.
177. *Rote Kapelle* Final Report.
178. Statement by Johann Strübing, Lüneburg Trial, Vol. X, f.196.
179. Report by Alexander Kraell, 30 July 1946, Lüneburg Trial, Vol. III, f.371
180. Perrault, p.208.
181. *Ibid.*
182. *Rote Kapelle* Final Report.
183. Statement by Johann Strübing, 18 January 1950, Lüneburg Trial, Vol. X, f.197.
184. *Rote Kapelle* Final Report.
185. Statement by Karl Schmauser, 9 September 1950, Lüneburg Trial, Vol. XII, f.188.
186. Report by Alexander Kraell, 6 August 1948, Lüneburg Trial, Vol. III, f.384.
187. *Ibid.*
188. *Rote Kapelle* Final Report.
189. Russian Intelligence Service Archives, file no 34118, quoted in Costello and Tsarev, p.399.
190. *Ibid.*
191. Collection of intercepted Soviet radio messages in the papers of Wilhelm Flicke.
192. *Ibid.*
193. Höhne, p.146.

Chapter 21
194. Statement by Johann Strübing, 18 January 1950, Lüneburg Trial, Vol. X, f.202.

195. Statement by Reinhold Ortmann, 16 February 1950, Lüneburg Trial, Vol. XII, f.65.
196. Statement by Greta Kuckhoff, Lüneburg Trial, Vol. VIII, f.152.
197. Höhne, p.160.
198. *Ibid.*
199. *Ibid.*
200. Quoted in Höhne, p.161.
201. Poelchau, *Die Letzten Stunden.*
202. Statement by Greta Kuckhoff, Lüneburg Trial, Vol. VIII, f.152.
203. Höhne, p.169.
204. Report by Werner Krauss, Lüneburg Trial, Vol. X, f.161.
205. Quoted in Höhne, p.168.
206. Perrault, p.277.
207. *Ibid.*
208. Statement by Manfred Roeder, 30 June 1949, Lüneburg Trial, Vol. VIII, f.12 *et seq.*
209. Dallin, p.167.
210. Höhne, p.170.
211. Statement by Johann Strübing, 18 January 1950, Lüneburg Trial, Vol. X, f.202 *et seq.*
212. Statement by Greta Kuckhoff, Lüneburg Trial, Vol. VIII, f.132.
213. *Ibid.*
214. Quoted in Höhne, p.161.
215. Boehm, *We Survived.*
216. Perrault, p.285.
217. This account was published in the June 1951 edition of the German weekly *Der Stern* as part of the series 'Rote Agenten Mitten Unter Uns'.
218. Statement by Erich Edgar Schulze, 5 December 1948, Lüneburg Trial, Vol. VI, f.783 *et seq.*
219. *Ibid.*
220. Statement by Johann Strübing, 2 February 1950, Lüneburg Trial, Vol. XII, f.3.

Chapter 22
221. *Rote Kapelle* Final Report.
222. *Ibid.*
223. W. Kudryavzev and R. Raspevin, 'She was called "Alta"', *Pravda*, 5 July 1967.
224. Statement by Johann Strübing, 18 January 1950, Lüneburg Trial, Vol. X, f.200.
225. *Rote Kapelle* Final Report.
226. Statement by Johann Strübing, 18 January 1950, Lüneburg Trial, Vol. X, f.202.
227. Statement by Rudolf Lehmann, 28 September 1948, Lüneburg Trial, Vol. IV, f.525.
228. *Rote Kapelle* Final Report.
229. Costello and Tsarev, p.405.

Chapter 23
230. Statement by Admiral (Retd) Karl Jesko von Puttkamer, 30 September 1948, Lüneburg Trial, Vol. IV, f.537.
231. Günther Weisenborn, *Der Lautlose Aufstand.*
232. Ulrich von Hassell, *D'une Autre Allemagne*, p.263.
233. Perrault, p.279.
234. Joachim von Ribbentrop, *De Londres à Moscau*, p.41.
235. Report by *Dr* Finck, the Public Prosecutor in the trial of *Dr* Manfred Roeder in the Lüneburg Court, 1951. Manfred Roeder was born in Kiel on 20 August 1900, the son of a county court clerk. He attended preparatory school in Recklinghausen and high school in Berlin. In late 1917 he volunteered for service as a cadet in a field artillery regiment. In 1919 he served with the Guards Cavalry Rifle Division and in 1920 with the West Russia Volunteer Army in the Baltic States. Shortly thereafter he left the Army with the rank of Lieutenant. During the 1920s he began studying law, passing the preliminary law examination in 1931 and the state finals in 1934. On 1 April 1935 he joined the *Luftwaffe* Legal Service. In late 1935 he was appointed Judge Advocate of Air Region I, and in 1937 Senior Judge Advocate of Air Region III. He was promoted Judge Advocate

General (*Oberstkriegsgerichtsrat*) in 1941.

236. Statement by *Dr* Eugen Schmitt, 22 September 1948, Lüneburg Trial, Vol. III, f.510.

237. Statement by Manfred Roeder, 30 June 1949, Lüneburg Trial, Vol. VIII, f.13.

238. *Ibid.*, Vol. VIII, f.396.

239. Costello and Tsarev, p.404.

240. Statement by Jan Tonnies, 10 March 1950, Lüneburg Trial, Vol. XII, f.143.

241. Statement by Heinz Bergmann, 20 February 1951, Lüneburg Trial, Vol. XII, f.228.

242. Perrault, p.291.

243. *Ibid.*

244. Statement by Heinz Bergmann, 20 February 1951, Lüneburg Trial, Vol. XII, f.228.

245. Statement by Rudolf Behse, 20 February 1950, Lüneburg Trial, Vol. XII, f.68.

246. *Ibid.*, Vol. XII, f.69.

247. Statement by Alexander Kraell, 14 March 1950, Lüneburg Trial, Vol. XII, f.95.

248. Statement by Gerhard Ranft, 7 March 1950, Lüneburg Trial, Vol. XII, f.87.

249. Statement by Alexander Kraell, 6 August 1948, Lüneburg Trial, Vol. III, f.389.

250. Perrault, p.291.

251. Statement by Karl Schmauser, 9 September 1950, Lüneburg Trial, Vol. XII, f.186.

252. *Ibid.*

253. Statement by Alexander Kraell in the Provincial Court of Stade, 12 February 1958 (in Bontjes van Beek papers).

Chapter 24

254. Lehmann, *Widerstandsgruppe Schulze-Boysen/Harnack*, p.30.

255. Perrault, p.295.

256. Lehmann p.32.

257. Zu Eulenburg, *Erinnerungen an Libertas*, p.30.

258. Poelchau, *Die Letzten Stunden.*

259. Lehmann, p.35.

260. Perrault, p.296.

261. Trepper, p.412.

262. Poelchau.

263. *Ibid.*

264. Höhne, p.202.

265. Poelchau.

266. Lehmann, p.36.

267. Quoted in Weisenborn, *Der Lautlose Aufstand.*

268. *Ibid.*

269. Memorandum drawn up by *Kriminalkommissar* Schwarz on persons of the Schulze-Boysen/Harnack group known to have been executed (in *Der Spiegel* archives).

270. Trepper, p.412.

271. Statement by August Ohm, 28 March 1950, Lüneburg Trial, Vol. XII, f.151.

272. Lehmann, p.43.

273. Schwarz memorandum.

274. Lehmann, p.54.

275. *Ibid.*

276. Bontjes van Beek papers.

277. Lehmann, p.54.

278. *Ibid.*

Chapter 25

279. Perrault, p.221.

280. *Ibid.*, p.225.

281. Piepe's deposition.

282. *Ibid.*

283. *Ibid.*

284. *Ibid.*

285. *Ibid.*

286. *Ibid.*

287. Perrault, p.229.

288. Dallin, p.153.

289. Piepe's deposition.

290. Perrault, p.232.

291. *Ibid.*, p.233.

Chapter 26

292. Piepe's deposition.

293. Perrault, p.236.

294. *Ibid.*, p.237.

295. *Rote Kapelle* Final Report.
296. Perrault, p.238.
297. *Ibid.*, p.267.
298. Dallin, p.140–1.
299. *Ibid.*
300. Perrault, p.37.
301. Höhne, p.54.
302. *Ibid.*, p.55.
303. *Rote Kapelle* Final Report.
304. *Ibid.*
305. Trepper, p.156.
306. *Ibid.*
307. Perrault, p.98–9.
308. *Ibid.*, p.194.

Chapter 27
309. Höhne, p.216.
310. John Nemo, *Das Rote Netz*, p.13.
311. *Ibid.*
312. Perrault, p.244.
313. *Ibid.*, pp.246–7.
314. *Ibid.*, p.242.
315. *Ibid.*, p.249.
316. Nemo, p.13.
317. Perrault, pp.249–50.
318. *Ibid.*, p.251.
319. Dallin, pp.165–6.
320. *Ibid.*
321. Perrault, p.255.
322. *Ibid.*, p.256.
323. *Ibid.*
324. *Ibid.*

Chapter 28
325. Trepper, p.5.
326. *Ibid.*, p.11.
327. *Ibid.*
328. Perrault, p.17.
329. Trepper, p.15.
330. *Ibid.*, p.16.
331. *Ibid.*, p.17.
332. *Ibid.*, p.19.
333. Höhne, p.44; and Trepper, pp.20–1.
334. Trepper, p.21.
335. *Ibid.*
336. *Ibid.*, p.24.
337. *Ibid.*, pp.29–31.
338. Höhne, pp.44–5.

339. *Ibid.*, p.45.
340. Trepper, pp.36–7.
341. *Ibid.*, p.38.
342. *Ibid.*, p.40.
343. Höhne, p.46.
344. Perrault, p.21.
345. *Ibid.*
346. Trepper, p.87.
347. Höhne, p.46.
348. *Ibid.*, p.47.
349. *Ibid.*
350. Trepper, p.97.

Chapter 29
351. Höhne, p.40; and Trepper, p.96.
352. Höhne, p.40.
353. Trepper, p.96.
354. Trepper, pp.96–7.
355. Perrault, p.23.
356. Trepper, p.97.
357. *Rote Kapelle* Final Report.
358. *Ibid.*
359. *Ibid.*
360. Trepper, p.106.
361. Höhne, pp.49–50.
362. *Ibid.*, p.50.
363. Trepper, pp.107–8.
364. *Ibid.*, p.108.
365. *Ibid.*, pp.111–12.
366. *Rote Kapelle* Final Report.

Chapter 30
367. Perrault, p.20.
368. *Ibid.*, pp.96–7.
369. *Ibid.*, pp.40–1.
370. Trepper, p.114.
371. Perrault, pp.168–9.
372. Trepper, p.115.
373. *Ibid.*, p.116.
374. Wilhelm von Schramm, *Verrat im Zweiten Weltkrieg*, p.369.
375. Dallin, p.145.
376. Schramm, p.369.
377. Dallin, p.161.
378. Schramm, pp.369–70.
379. *Ibid.*
380. Perrault, p.178.
381. Trepper, p.118.

382. Perrault, p.266.
383. Trepper, p.118.
384. *Ibid.*
385. Trepper, p.126.
386. *Ibid.*
387. *Ibid.*
388. Höhne, p.58.
389. Trepper, p.135.
390. *Ibid.*, pp.149–50.
391. *Ibid.*, p.167.

Chapter 31
392. Perrault, p.258.
393. *Ibid.*, p.311.
394. *Ibid.*
395. Dallin, p.168.
396. Höhne, p.223.
397. Nemo, p.3.
398. Perrault, p.264.
399. *Ibid.*, p.314.
400. *Ibid.*, pp.265–6.
401. Höhne, p.218.
402. Nemo, p.16.
403. *Ibid.*
404. Perrault, p.314.
405. *Ibid.*, pp.314–15.

Chapter 32
406. Höhne, p.221.
407. Trepper, pp.415–23.
408. *Ibid.*
409. Perrault, p.331.
410. *Ibid.*
411. *Ibid.*, p.332.
412. Trepper, pp.407–8.

Chapter 33
413. Perrault, pp.317–18.
414. Höhne, p.220.
415. *Ibid.*, p.221.
416. *Abwehr* files on the *Funkspiel*, in the German Federal Archives.
417. *Ibid.*
418. *Abwehr* files.
419. *Ibid.*
420. *Ibid.*
421. *Ibid.*
422. *Ibid.*

423. *Ibid.*
424. *Ibid.*
425. *Ibid.*
426. *Ibid.*
427. *Ibid.*
428. Höhne, p.229.
429. *Ibid.*
430. Dallin, p.176.
431. Trepper, pp.269, 420.
432. *Ibid.*, pp.319–20.
433. Dallin, p.180.
434. *Ibid.*
435. *Ibid.*, p.181.
436. *Abwehr* files.
437. *Ibid.*
438. *Ibid.*
439. Trepper, p.244.
440. *Ibid.*

Chapter 34
441. Radó, *Sous le Pseudonym Dora.*
442. *Ibid.*
443. Read and Fisher, *Operation Lucy*, p.43.
444. Radó.
445. *Ibid.*
446. *Ibid.*
447. Read and Fisher, pp.44–5.
448. *Ibid.*, p.46.
449. Radó.
450. Read and Fisher, pp.48–9.
451. *Ibid.*, p.49.

Chapter 35
452. Radó.
453. *Ibid.*
454. Pünter, *Guerre Secrète en Pays Neutre.*
455. *Ibid.*
456. *Ibid.*
457. *Ibid.*
458. *Ibid.*

Chapter 36
459. Knightley, *The Second Oldest Profession*, p.204.
460. Werner, *Sonjas Rapport.*
461. *Ibid.*
462. *Ibid.*
463. Accoce and Quet, p.108.

Chapter 37
464. Radó.
465. *Ibid.*
466. Accoce and Quet, pp.58–9.
467. *Ibid.*, p.61.
468. Read and Fisher, p.81.
469. Accoce and Quet, p.70.
470. *Ibid.*
471. *Ibid.*, pp.73–4.
472. Hans Rudolf Kurz, *Nachrichten-Zentrum Schweiz.*
473. *Ibid.*
474. Read and Fisher, p.87.

Chapter 38
475. Radó.
476. Read and Fisher, p.90.
477. Dallin, pp.195–6.
478. Read and Fisher, p.89.
479. Bullock, *Hitler and Stalin: Parallel Lives*, p.792.
480. *Ibid.*, p.793.
481. *Ibid.*
482. *Ibid.*
483. Accoce and Quet, p.119.
484. Radó.
485. Accoce and Quet, p.119.
486. *Ibid.*
487. Dallin, p.196.
488. Foote, *Handbook for Spies*, pp.92–5.
489. Pünter.
490. Accoce and Quet, pp.162–3.
491. Dallin, p.210.
492. *Ibid.*, p.211.
493. *Ibid.*
494. Read and Fisher, p.129.
495. Dallin, p.212.
496. Read and Fisher, p.143.

Chapter 39
497. Accoce and Quet, p.72.
498. Hinsley, *British Intelligence in the Second World War*, Vol. 2, p.60.
499. Knightley, p.203.
500. *Ibid.*
501. *Ibid.*
502. Hinsley, Vol. 2, p.59.
503. *Ibid.*

504. *Ibid.*, p.60.
505. *Ibid.*, pp.60–1.
506. *Ibid.*, p.61.
507. CIA study, *The Rote Kapelle*, pp.165, 193.

Chapter 40
508. Dallin, p.198.
509. *Ibid.*, p.199.
510. Dallin, p.199; and Read and Fisher, p.32.
511. Quoted in Dallin, p.200.
512. Dallin, p.201.
513. Carell, *Scorched Earth*, p.102.
514. *Ibid.*
515. Operation Order No 6 (*Zitadelle*), dated 15.4.1943, quoted in Carell, p.515.
516. Carell, p.102.
517. *Ibid.*
518. Erickson, *The Road to Berlin*, p.65.
519. Seaton, *The Russo-German War*, p.360.
520. Andrew and Gordievsky, *KGB: The Inside Story of its Foreign Operations from Lenin to Gorbachev*, p.242.
521. *Ibid.*
522. Erickson, *The Road to Berlin*, p.101.
523. *Ibid.*

Chapter 41
524. Schramm, p.288.
525. *Ibid.*
526. Read and Fisher, pp.135–6.
527. Dallin, p.178.
528. Quoted in Dallin, pp.178–9.
529. Dallin, p.179.
530. *Ibid.*, pp.191–3.

Chapter 42
531. Read and Fisher, p.171.
532. *Ibid.*
533. *Ibid.*, p.174.
534. *Ibid.*
535. *Ibid.*, pp.175–6.
536. *Ibid.*, p.176.
537. *Ibid.*, p.177.
538. Foote.
539. Dallin, p.217.
540. *Ibid.*, pp.217–18.

541. Foote.
542. Dallin, p.218.
543. *Ibid.*, pp.218–19.
544. *Ibid.*, p.219.
545. *Ibid.*, p.220.
546. Foote.
547. *Ibid.*

Chapter 43
548. Trepper, p.276.
549. *Ibid.*, p.278.
550. *Ibid.*, p.280.
551. *Ibid.*, p.283.

552. *Ibid.*, p.285.
553. *Ibid.*, p.286.
554. *Ibid.*, p.301.
555. *Ibid.*, p.310.
556. Perrault, p.394.
557. Trepper, p.311.
558. Perrault, pp.422–3.
559. *Ibid.*, p.423.
560. *Ibid.*, pp.423–4.
561. Perrault, p.432.
562. Trepper, p.424.
563. Perrault, p.467.
564. Trepper, p.424.

Bibliography

Accoce, P., and Quet, P., *La Guerre a été Gagnée en Suisse*, Librairie Academique Perrin (1966)

Andrew, C., *Codebreaking and Signals Intelligence*, Frank Cass (London, 1986)

Andrew, C., and Gordievsky, O., *KGB: The Inside Story of its Foreign Operations from Lenin to Gorbachev*, Hodder & Stoughton (London, 1990)

Bartz, K., *The Downfall of the German Secret Service*, William Kimber (London 1956)

Bohm, E. H., *We Survived*, Yale University Press (New Haven, 1949)

Boveri, M., *Treason in the Twentieth Century*, Putnam (New York, 1963)

Boysen, Elsa, *Harro Schulze-Boysen*, Komet Verlag (Düsseldorf, 1947)

Buchheim, H., *SS und Polizei im NS-Staat*, Selbstveriag der Studiengesellschaft für Zeitprobleme (Bonn 1964)

Buchheit, G., *Der Deutsche Geheimdienst: Geschichte Militärischen Abwehr*, List (Munich, 1966)

———, *Spionage im Zwei Weltkriegen*, Politisches Archiv (Landshut, 1975)

Bullock, A., *Hitler and Stalin: Parallel Lives*, Harper Collins (London 1991)

Buranelli, V. and N., *Spy/Counter Spy: An Encyclopedia of Espionage*, McGraw-Hill (New York, 1982)

Buschmann, H. 'De la Résistance au Défaitisme', *Les Temps Modernes*, Nos 46 and 47, 1949

Carell, P., *Scorched Earth*, Harrap (London, 1970)

Central Intelligence Agency, *The Rote Kapelle: The CIA's History of Soviet Intelligence and Espionage Networks in Western Europe, 1936–1945*, University Publications of America (Washington, DC, 1984)

Cline, M. W., Christiansen, C. E., and Fontaine, J. M. (eds.), *Scholar's Guide to Intelligence Literature*, University Publications of America (Baltimore, 1983)

Cookridge, E. H. *Soviet Spy Net*, Frederick Muller (London, 1955)

Costello, J., and Tsarev, O., *Deadly Illusions*, Century Publishing (London, 1993)

Dallin, D., *Soviet Espionage*, Oxford University Press (1955)

Deakin, F. W., and Storry, G. R., *The Case of Richard Sorge*, Harper & Row (New York, 1964)

Depelsenaire, B., *Symphonie Fraternelle*, Éditions Lumen, (Brussels, n.d.)

Deutsch, H. C., *The Conspiracy against Hitler in the Twilight War*, Oxford University Press (1968)

Drago, A., *Genève Appelle Moscou*, Laffont (Paris, 1969)

Dulles, A. W., *Germany's Underground*, Macmillan (New York, 1947)

———, *The Craft of Intelligence*, Weidenfeld & Nicolson (London, 1963)

Erickson, J., *The Road to Stalingrad*, Weidenfeld & Nicolson (London, 1975)

———, *The Road to Berlin*, Weidenfeld & Nicolson (London, 1983)

Eulenburg, Thora zu, *Erinnerungen an Libertas* (n.d.)

Fischer, R., *Stalin und der Deutsche Kommunismus*, Verlag Frankfurter Hefte (Frankfurt, 1948)

Flicke, W. S., *Agenten Funken nach Moskau*, Neptun Verlag (Munich-Wels, 1954)

———, *Spionagegruppe Rote Kapelle*, Neptun Verlag (Kreuzlingen, 1954)

———, *War Secrets in the Ether* (2 vols), Aegean Park Press (California, 1977)

Foote, A., *Handbook for Spies*, Museum Press (London, 1964)

Hagen, W., *Die Geheime Front*, Nibelungen Verlag (Linz and Vienna, 1950)

Harnack, Axel von, 'Arvid und Mildred Harnack', *Die Gegenwart*, Nos 26 and 27, January 1947

Heilbrunn, O., *The Soviet Secret Service*, Allen & Unwin (London, 1956)

Hinsley, F. H., *et al.*, *British Intelligence in the Second World War*, 3 vols in 4 parts, HMSO (London, 1979–1988).

Höhne, H., *Codeword: Direktor* (Frankfurt, 1970)

———, *Canaris: Patriot im Zwielicht* (Munich, 1976)

Jukes, G., 'The Soviets and Ultra', *Intelligence and National Security*, Vol. III No 2, 1988

Kahn, D., *The Codebreakers*, Macmillan (New York, 1967)

———, *Hitler's Spies: German Military Intelligence in World War II*, Hodder & Stoughton (London, 1978)

Kater, M., *The Nazi Party: A Social Profile of Members and Leaders 1919–1945*, Blackwell (Oxford, 1983)

Knightley, P., *The Second Oldest Profession*, Andre Deutsch (London, 1986)

Lehmann, K., *Widerstandsgruppe Schulze-Boysen/Harnack*, VVN Verlag (East Berlin, 1948)

Leverkuhn, P., *German Military Intelligence*, Weidenfeld & Nicolson (London, 1954)

Mulligan, T. P., 'Spies, Ciphers and "Zitadelle": Intelligence and the Battle of Kursk', *Journal of Contemporary History*, Vol. XXII No 2, 1987

Palii, A., 'Radio-Electronic Combat in the Course of the War', *Voyenno Istorichesky Zhurnal*, No 4, 1977

Perrault, G., *L'Orchestre Rouge*, Libraire Artheme Fayard (Paris, 1967)

Piepe, Harry, 'Harburger jagte Agenten', *Harburger Anzeiger und Nachrichten*, 30 September–31 October 1967

Piepe, Harry, 'Ich Jagte Rote Agenten', *Der Mittag*, 11 February–15 March 1953

Polchau, H., *Die Letzten Stunden* (Magdeburg 1949)

Pünter, O., *Guerre Secrète en Pays Neutre* (Lausanne, 1967)

Radó, S., *Sous le Pseudonym Dora* (Paris, 1972)

Read, A., and Fisher, D., *Operation Lucy*, Hodder & Stoughton (London, 1980)

Reile, O., *Geheime Westfront: Die Abwehr 1935–1945*, Welsermühl (Munich-Wels 1963)

Rothfels, H., *Die Deutsche Opposition gegen Hitler*, Sherpe Verlag (Krefeld, 1949)

Salomon, E. von, *The Answers of Ernst von Salomon*, Putnam (New York, 1954)

Seaton, A., *The Russo-German War 1941–45*, Arthur Barker (London, 1971)

Scheel, H., 'Wesen und Wollen der Widerstandsorganisation Schulze-Boysen/ Harnack', *Neues Deutschland*, 29 June 1968

Schellenberg, W., *Memoirs*, Andre Deutsch (London, 1956)

Suvorov, V., *Soviet Military Intelligence*, Hamish Hamilton (London, 1984)

Tarrant, V. E., *Stalingrad: Anatomy of an Agony*, Leo Cooper (London, 1992)

Trepper, L., *Le Grand Jeu*, Albin Michel (Paris, 1975)

Weisenborn, G., *Der Lautlose Aufstand* (Hamburg, 1953

Werner, Ruth, (pseudonym for Ruth Kuczynski), *Sonjas Rapport*, Verlag Neues Leben (East Berlin, 1977)

Wollenberg, E., *Der Apparat* (Essen, 1950)

Index

Abetz, Otto, 130
Abwehr (German Military Intelligence), 12,
  14–15, 20–5, 29–34, 41–2, 47, 59, 67, 84,
  92, 96–7, 103, 107, 113, 117, 125, 131,
  133, 136–7, 142, 146, 172, 180, 193, 197
Ackermann, Vera, 39
Adash, 22, 29; *see also* Raichmann,
  Abraham
Adolf Circuit, 14, 18, 33
Afrika Korps, 51
Alamo, Carlos, 21–2, 25–7, 123–4, 126; *see
  also* Makarov, Mikael
Ampletzer, *Kriminalkommissar* Thomas, 35,
  91, 141–2
*Arbeitsgemeinschaft zum Studium der
  Sowjetrussischen (Arplan)*, 70
Arnould, Rita, 21–4, 29, 47, 53, 124, 126,
  132, 138

Barcza, Margarete, 47, 109–13, 138, 140,
  195–6
Bastian, Admiral Max, 95, 98
Bastlein, Bernhard, 37
Baum, Herbert, 74
Beek, Cato Bontjes van, 74, 87–9, 98, 105
Beek, Jan Bontjes van, 87
Behrens, Karl, 99, 104
Behse, *Dr* Rudolf, 95, 97
Bentivegni, Major-General von, 34, 59
Berg, *Kriminalobersekretär* Wilhelm, 27, 46,
  106, 147, 189
Berger, Joseph, 118
Bergmann, *Dr* Heinz, 95
Berkowitz, Liane, 98, 105
Bessonov, Sergei, 70
Beublet, Maurice, 138
Bianchi, Dr Emilio, 178, 184
Bir, Isaiah, 119–21

Blunt, Anthony, 176
BMM (British Military Mission to
  Moscow), 171
Bödiker, Lieutenant, 29–30, 41
Boetzel, Colonel Fritz, 172
Boeumelburg, *Kriminalrat*, 38, 110
Bokelberg, Colonel, 62
Bolli, Margrit ('Rosie'), 168, 173, 178,
  182–4, 187–8, 199
Bourgain, Louis, 25
Boveri, Margaret, 70
Braun, Eva, 132
Breendonk, *SS-Auffanglager*, 28–9, 35, 39–40,
  43–6, 139
Breiter, Gertrüd, 86–7, 92
Brewer, Len, 154
Brockdorff, Countess Erika von 81, 87,
  96–8, 104
Brussels *Bourse*, 22, 24–5, 107
Buch, Eva-Maria, 37, 105
Bühnenvolksbund, 157–8
BUPO (Swiss *Bundespolizei*), 152–3, 182–3
Bureau Ha, 160–1, 164, 182, 185
Burgess, Guy, 176
Buschmann, *Dr* Hugo, 68, 73–4, 87

Cairncross, John, 176–7
Canaris, Admiral Wilhelm, 14, 34
Carlos, Emil, 25
Cavell, Edith, 40
Christen, Robert, 138–9
Churchill, Winston, 169, 171
Clais, Josephine, 138
Clais, Renée, 138
Cointe, Suzanne, 115, 138
Coppi, Hans, ('Strahlmann'), 76, 79–81,
  85, 87–8, 96–7, 99, 102, 132
Coppi, Hilde, 99, 102, 105

Mann, Thomas, 157
Marivet, Marguerite, 138
Marquardt, Helmut, 79
Marx, Karl, 148
Masson, Roger, 160–1, 164, 182, 185
Mathieu, Inspector, 29–30, 41, 43, 45–6
Mauthausen (concentration camp), 139–40
Maximovich, Anna Pavlovna, 129, 136, 138
Maximovich, Baron Vassily Pavlovich, 129, 136, 138
Menzies, Stewart, 171
Midnon, Emmanuel, 127
Mikler, Adam, 121–2; *see also* Trepper, Leopold
Model, Colonel-General Walter, 174, 177
Moyen, André, 197
Müller, Anna, 154, 178
Müller, *Gruppenführer* Heinrich, 26, 59, 93, 144
Muraille, Colette, 172

Nemitz, Klara, 37
Neutert, Eugen, 105
Nicole, Léon, 154, 168
Nikolai, *Hauptsturmführer* Wilhelm, 108, 114
Novikov, Lieutenant-Colonel, 188, 196

Ohm, August, 104
Ordnungspolizei, 38
Ortmann, *Kriminalobersekretär* Reinhold, 86
Oster, Major-General Hans, 172
Ozols, Waldemar, ('Solja'), 145–6

Pacciardi, Randolfo, 152
Pannwitz, *Kriminalrat* Heinz, 144–6, 178–80, 189–96
Panzinger, *Oberregierungsrat* Friedrich, 62, 87–92
Pass-Apparat, 29–30
Passelecq, Jean, 138
Paul, *Dr* Elfriede, 67
Paulus, General Wilhelm Ernst, 49–51
Pauriol, Fernand, 134, 144–5
Pauriol, Hélène, 145
Pellepoix, Darquier de, 129
Peper, Maurice, ('Wassermann'), 44–5, 138
Peresypkin, General Ivan Terenchevich, 35, 80

Peters, Hans, 183
Petit Chef, 22, 24, 42, 46, 57–8, 80, 109–11, 126, 154; *see also* 'Kent' *and* Sierra, Vincent
'Phantomas', 119–21
Phelter, Simone, 105, 124, 136, 138
Philby, Kim, 176
Piatniysky, Osip, 70
Piepe, Captain Harry, 14–26, 29–34, 41–7, 106–17 *passim*, 135–7, 197
Podsialdo, Giuseppe, 136, 138
Poelchau, Pastor Harald, 87, 100–3
Poellnitz, Gisla von, 67–8, 72
Poznanska, Sophie, 28, 52–3, 55, 118, 124, 126, 132; *see also* Verlinden, Anna
Pressgéographie (agency), 150
Pünter, Otto, ('Pakbo'), 54–5, 152–3, 165, 167–8, 184–5
Puttkamer, Admiral Karl von, 98

Rabcor (industrial informer network), 119–20
Radó, Hélène, ('Lèna'), 150, 167, 182
Radó, Sándor, ('Dora'), 148–57 *passim*, 162–70 *passim*, 175, 178, 182–8 *passim*, 197–8
Raichmann, Abraham, ('Adash'), 29–31, 41–3, 45–7, 106–7, 109–10, 114, 124–5, 127, 142, 148, 196
Rameau, Yves, 178
Ranft, *Dr* Gerhard, 95, 98
Rauch, Henry, 138
Ravensbrück (concentration camp), 140, 194
Rehmer, Fritz, 98, 104
Reichel, Major, 49–50
Reichhart, Johann, 102
Reiser, *Kriminalkommissar* Heinrich, 38–9
Rempka, Ella, 106
Ribbentrop, Reich Foreign Minister Joachim, 94
Richter, Rolf, 105
Riepert Imports and Exports, 15
Rillboling, Hendrika, 45
Rillboling, Jakob, 45
Rittmeister, *Dr* John, 76, 98–9, 104
Robinson, Henry, 129, 136–8, 148, 152
Roeder, *Dr* Manfred, 94–9 *passim*, 137–8
Rohleder, Colonel Joachim, 14, 18–19, 23, 25, 34